Kinds of Being

Aristotelian Society Series

Volume 1
COLIN MCGINN
Wittgenstein on Meaning:
An Interpretation and Evaluation

Volume 2
BARRY TAYLOR
Modes of Occurrence:
Verbs, Adverbs and Events

Volume 3
KIT FINE
Reasoning with Arbitrary Objects

Volume 4
CHRISTOPHER PEACOCKE
Thoughts:
An Essay on Content

Volume 5
DAVID E. COOPER
Metaphor

Volume 6
DAVID WIGGINS
Needs, Values, Truth:
Essays in the Philosophy of Value

Volume 7
JONATHAN WESTPHAL
Colour:
Some Philosophical Problems from Wittgenstein

Volume 8
ANTHONY SAVILE
Aesthetic Reconstructions:
The Seminal Writings of Lessing, Kant and Schiller

Volume 9
GRAEME FORBES
Languages of Possibility:
An Essay in Philosophical Logic

Aristotelian Society Monographs Committee:
Martin Davies (Monographs Editor)
Thomas Baldwin
Jennifer Hornsby
Mark Sainsbury
Anthony Savile

E.J. Lowe

Kinds of Being
A Study of Individuation, Identity and the Logic of Sortal Terms

Aristotelian Society Series

Volume 10

Basil Blackwell

Copyright © E.J. Lowe 1989

First published 1989

Basil Blackwell Ltd
108 Cowley Road, Oxford, OX4, 1JF, UK

Basil Blackwell Inc.
432 Park Avenue South, Suite 1503
New York, NY 10016, USA

All rights reserved. Except for the quotation of short passages for the purposes of criticism and review, no part of this publication may be reproduced, stored in a retrieval system, or transmitted, in any form or by any means, electronic, mechanical, photocopying, recording or otherwise, without the prior permission of the publisher.

Except in the United States of America, this book is sold subject to the condition that it shall not, by way of trade or otherwise, be lent, re-sold, hired out, or otherwise circulated without the publisher's prior consent in any form of binding or cover other than that in which it is published and without a similar condition including this condition being imposed on the subsequent purchaser.

British Library Cataloguing in Publication Data

A CIP catalogue record for this book is available from the British Library.

Library of Congress Cataloging in Publication Data

Lowe, E. J. (E. Jonathan)
   Kinds of being: a study of individuation, identity and the logic of sortal terms / E. J. Lowe.
      p. cm. — (Aristotelian Society series; v. 10)
   Includes index.
   ISBN 0–631–16703–X: $50.00
   1. Identity. 2. Individuation. 3. Mind and body. 4. Logic.
5. Languages—Philosophy. I. Title. II. Series.
BC199.I4L69   1989
126—dc19   88–39255
                                                                   CIP

Typeset in 11 on 13 pt Times by
Vera-Reyes, Inc.
Printed and bound in Great Britain at
The Camelot Press plc, Southampton

CONTENTS

Acknowledgements		vi
1	Introduction	1
	1.1 The Varieties of 'is'	3
	1.2 Individuals, Kinds and Realism	4
	1.3 Semantics, Metaphysics and Necessity	6
2	Sortal Terms and Criteria of Identity	9
3	Individuals, Sorts and Instantiation	28
4	The Absoluteness of Identity: A Defence	43
	Appendix: Some Formal Principles and Arguments	63
5	Identity and Constitution	67
6	Parts and Wholes	84
7	Persons and their Bodies	97
	7.1 Matter and Organisms	97
	7.2 Organisms and Persons	108
	7.3 Is There a Criterion of Personal Identity?	121
8	Sortal Terms and Natural Laws	138
9	Laws, Dispositions and Sortal Logic	164
	Appendix: An Axiomatic System of Sortal Logic	181
10	Complex Sortal Terms and the Differentiation of Sorts	185
Index		205

Acknowledgements

In the course of this study I have drawn on material contained in the following previously published articles of mine, and I am grateful to the editors and publishers of the journals and book in which they appeared for permission (where necessary) for re-using this material. Chapter 2 draws in part on my chapter on 'Substance' in *An Encyclopaedia of Philosophy* ed. G.H.R. Parkinson (London: Routledge, 1988). Chapters 3, 4 and 5 are based largely on 'Instantiation, Identity and Constitution', *Philosophical Studies* 44 (1983), pp. 45–59, published by D. Reidel Publishing Company, and on 'Sortal Terms and Absolute Identity', *Australasian Journal of Philosophy* 64 (1986), pp. 64–71. Parts of Chapter 5 are drawn from 'The Paradox of the 1,001 Cats', *Analysis* 42 (1982), pp. 27–30, 'Reply to Geach', *Analysis* 42 (1982), p. 31, and 'On Being a Cat', *Analysis* 42 (1982), pp. 174–7. Chapter 8 is based on 'Sortal Terms and Natural Laws', *American Philosophical Quarterly* 17 (1980), pp. 253–60, and Chapter 9 on 'Laws, Dispositions and Sortal Logic', *American Philosophical Quarterly* 19 (1982), pp. 41–50.

I should also like to express my gratitude to all those who read the manuscript at various stages of its composition and revision, and whose comments and criticisms have contributed greatly to the book's improvement. In this regard, special thanks are owed to Jennifer Hornsby.

1

Introduction

My aim in this study is to examine a cluster of interrelated issues in metaphysics, logic and the philosophy of language, a common factor being the importance I attach to *sortal* concepts in my treatment of these issues. A sortal concept is a concept of a distinct *sort* or *kind* of individuals. Individuals may be either *concrete* (like chairs and people) or *abstract* (like numbers and sets), but my concern will be almost exclusively with concrete individuals and the kinds to which they belong. Where concrete individuals are concerned, kinds may be *natural* (horses, trees, stars, electrons, . . .) or they may be *artefactual* (tables, books, computers, cities, . . .), though in the present study I place much more emphasis on the former class. This stress on the concrete and the natural is motivated by the conviction that entities in this class must enjoy some sort of ontological priority over both abstract and artefactual objects; though the defence of this conviction is not something I undertake in the ensuing pages.

Sortal concepts are characteristically governed by *criteria of individuation and identity* – semantic principles which determine what are to count as individual instances of the sorts or kinds in question and the conditions for their identity or diversity at a time and (where this is applicable) over time. Criteria of identity may be the same for many closely related sortal concepts (e.g., for the concepts of various different kinds of animals) but differ radically for sortal concepts relating to different categories (e.g., for inorganic as opposed to biological sortal concepts). Where two sortal concepts are governed by different criteria of identity, it makes no sense to identify an individual falling under one of these concepts with an individual falling under the other. This is one of the principal claims that I advance in the present study, and I defend it in depth against a rival position advocated by adherents of the relativist conception of identity (notably P.T. Geach). The implications of the claim for metaphysics are profound, especially insofar as it provides a means to block various reductivist strategies, and I devote a substantial part of the study to illustrating this in connection with the issues of personal identity and the mind/body problem. I argue that *persons* constitute a distinct sort or kind of entity and are not to be identified with the biological entities in which they are embodied. The position which I defend is not, however, to be confused with any version of Cartesian dualism.

In the final third of the book I examine in detail the semantics and logic of sortal terms in natural language, though inextricably intertwined with this discussion is an account of the place of sortal concepts in the formulation and empirical confirmation of scientific laws and theories. Amongst other things I maintain that the most satisfactory approach to the semantics of sortal terms (or, at least, of natural kind terms) is to accord them a truly referential or name-like role, regarding their referents (i.e., sorts or kinds) as universals conceived after the manner of Aristotelian realism. I also urge that scientific laws are best interpreted precisely as propositions purporting to concern such 'real' sorts or kinds, and predicating of them properties and relations which only attach derivatively to their individual exemplars or instances. The approach that I recommend in the study is shown to have considerable advantages over more orthodox nominalist/inductivist accounts of scientific laws and method. Finally, I argue that when it comes to the question of precisely what sorts of things exist, our inquiries must be guided by a judicious mixture of *a priori* metaphysical principle and *a posteriori* scientific theory-construction. Such an approach, I maintain, will entitle us to claim to be 'carving nature at the joints' without pretending to an unwarrantable infallibility in such matters.

In what remains of this Introduction I shall focus on certain important topics which crop up repeatedly throughout the course of the study, and which accordingly find no concentrated and exhaustive treatment in any one place. Two of these topics are associated with alternative readings of the deliberately ambiguous title of the book, *Kinds of Being*. On one reading of that phrase, it is intended to convey my wish to defend the thesis that the verb 'to be' has a variety of uses, or may play a variety of different logical roles. On the other reading, it is intended to highlight two other pivotal contentions of the study: first, that particular objects are only individuable and identifiable as particulars of this or that *sort* or *kind* (there are no 'bare' particulars), and secondly that the notions of 'individual' and 'kind' are mutually dependent, with neither being in any sense more fundamental than the other (a corollary of which I take to be that individuals and kinds are ontologically on an equal footing, even though their modes of existence may obviously differ).

1.1 The Varieties of 'is'

I distinguish between the following four uses of 'is' as a copula: the 'is' of *attribution* ('Socrates *is* wise', 'Grass *is* green'), the 'is' of *identity* ('Napoleon *is* Buonaparte', 'Water *is* H_2O'), the 'is' of *instantiation* ('Mars *is* a planet', 'A horse *is* a mammal'), and the 'is' of *constitution* ('This ring *is* gold', 'A human body *is* a collection of cells'). I do not, however, claim that all of these uses of 'is' are equally fundamental from a logical point of view. I regard the 'is' of attribution as logically redundant, a superficial feature of the grammar of the English language. As for the 'is' of constitution, I suspect that it, too, is not logically irreducible (though I offer no explicit reductive analysis of constitution statements in this study). But the other two uses of 'is' so far mentioned I do consider to be logically primitive, even if for some purposes the 'is' of identity may effectively be definable in terms of the 'is' of instantiation. Now this still leaves one other important use of 'is' to which I have not yet alluded: the 'is' of *existence* ('There *is* a horse in that field', 'The Dodo *is* no more'). I take this use of 'is' also to be logically primitive, and follow current orthodoxy in identifying its role with that played in symbolic logic by the existential quantifier, '∃'. (I do not, then, treat 'is', in the sense of 'exists', as a first-level predicate, though nothing especially important hinges on my stance regarding this matter). One thing which I should particularly stress in this connection, however, is that I most emphatically do *not* wish the title of this study to convey the impression that I postulate different *kinds of existence*, as opposed merely to different *kinds of thing that exist*. 'Exist' is univocal. (This is not inconsistent with my acceptance, a few moments ago, that individuals and kinds may enjoy different *modes* of existence, for this was not intended to imply any ambiguity in the term 'existence'. Rather, what I intended to acknowledge was such relatively uncontroversial facts as that (concrete) individuals exist at specific times and places whereas kinds, being universals, are not spatiotemporally localized in their existence.)

1.2 Individuals, Kinds and Realism

As I have just said, I hold that there are no 'bare' particulars, only individual instances or exemplars of certain sorts or kinds (tokens of certain types, in another terminology). No doubt lip service is customarily paid to this thesis by many if not most modern philosophers, but I do not think that its far-reaching implications are even yet sufficiently appreciated by more than a few. I also hold, as a corollary of this thesis, that the notions of an 'individual' and of a 'sort' or 'kind' are opposite sides of a single conceptual coin: each is only understandable in terms of the other. Individuals are necessarily individuals *of a kind*, and kinds are necessarily kinds *of individuals*. In consequence I maintain that realism with regard to particulars or individuals – the belief, in my opinion correct, that they may exist independently of the human or indeed any other mind – implies realism with regard to sorts or kinds. I cannot, then, accept Locke's famous contentions that 'All Things, that exist, [are] Particulars'[1] and that *'General and Universal*, belong not to the real existence of Things; but *are the Inventions and Creatures of the Understanding.'*[2] Realism with regard to sorts need not, however, be unqualified: perhaps only *natural* kinds need to be accorded a wholly mind-independent status – though this of course raises the thorny problem of *how* we are to draw any objective distinction between natural and non-natural kinds.[3] My own view is that the crucial distinguishing feature of natural kinds is that they are subject to *natural law*. Laws of nature, I contend, are propositions concerning sorts or kinds, though derivatively they also concern particulars inasmuch as the latter instantiate this or that sort or kind; and the kinds that they concern are, precisely in virtue of that concern, *natural* kinds. Thus *gold*

---

[1] John Locke, *An Essay Concerning Human Understanding*, ed. P.H. Nidditch (Oxford: Clarendon Press, 1979), Book III, ch. III, § 1.
[2] Ibid. § 11.
[3] Observe that, even granting the general connection between individual and sortal realism, to deny the reality of non-natural kinds (such as artefactual kinds) does not entail denying the reality of individuals instantiating those kinds, so long as the individuals in question can be regarded as also instantiating some real, natural kind. Thus even if *tables* do not constitute a real kind, an individual table might still be acknowledged to be a real particular if it could be identified as, say, a tabular-shaped collection of pieces of wood. My own view is that such an identification would be incorrect, however. If this means that my kitchen table does not really exist, then so be it! Perhaps indeed it is a sort of fiction. But whether artefactual kinds are in fact unreal is, I should stress, an issue on which I remain agnostic in this study.

qualifies as a natural kind because there are laws governing its form and behaviour – such as that it is weighty, ductile, malleable, soluble in aqua regia, and so forth. Similarly, *mammals* comprise a natural kind, in virtue of there being such distinctively mammalian laws as that mammals are warm-blooded and that they suckle their young. (From these examples it will be seen that I perceive a close connection between laws and dispositional properties, a connection which is extensively explored in chapters 8 and 9). By contrast with the case of these natural kinds, there are no natural laws about tables or books or other such artefactual kinds.

1.3 Semantics, Metaphysics and Necessity

At many points in this study I make claims to the effect that certain propositions variously constitute *semantic* truths, *conceptual* truths, *metaphysical* truths, *necessary* truths, and *a priori* truths, and something needs to be said about how I understand the status of and relationships between these ways of characterizing propositions. The fact is that I have at present no fully worked-out theory of such matters, though I do have views concerning some of the implications that any such theory should possess. My realist predilections in metaphysics persuade me to regard metaphysical truths as revealing fundamental, and often necessary, features of a mind-independent reality. At the same time, I am uneasy with, because a little mystified by, the idea of metaphysical necessities that are not ultimately *a priori* and conceptual in character, despite the fact that at some places in this study I go along with the currently popular notion of *a posteriori* metaphysical necessity.[4] (Natural or physical necessity is

---

[4] The modern notion of *a posteriori* metaphysical necessity is, of course, due in large measure to the work of Saul A. Kripke: see his *Naming and Necessity* (Oxford: Basil Blackwell, 1980). I discuss some of the issues connected with it in my 'On the Alleged Necessity of True Identity Statements', *Mind* 91 (1982), pp. 579–84 and my 'Reply to Baldwin on *De Re* Modalities', *Mind* 94 (1985), pp. 101–3. See also the end of my chapter on 'Substance' in *An Encyclopaedia of Philosophy*, ed. G.H.R. Parkinson (London: Routledge, 1988).

another matter, and I am content to explicate this in terms of *a posteriori* natural law.) Such a position inevitably raises profound questions concerning the very possibility of metaphysical knowledge, and its relationship with empirical scientific inquiry and theory-construction: questions which I do not directly tackle in the chapters that follow. It also raises questions concerning concept-formation and the connection between metaphysics and the semantics of natural language. With regard to these latter questions, one thing that I would wish to emphasize is that conceptual truths, and their embodiment in the semantic structures of our native tongues, are not just for us to make up as we will. They are not for the most part the expression of more or less arbitrary stipulative definitions or culture-based conventions. How we should and do conceptualize the world is substantially constrained by the way the world is quite independently of our values and interests. And hence to the extent that metaphysics deals in conceptual truths it may at once claim to be addressing the nature of reality and profitably utilize the method of linguistic analysis (though I by no means subscribe to the view that the analysis of 'ordinary language' exhausts the business of philosophical investigation).

However, we must surely also concede that if our conceptual scheme is moulded by the way the world is, this can ultimately only be because it reflects our experience of the world – and this brings us again to the question of the relationship between metaphysics and empirical science. Here I should say that I see the proper relationship between scientific and metaphysical thinking as one of complementarity and cooperation rather than as one of opposition and rivalry. Both have as their ultimate aim a closer coincidence between the way we think of the world and the way the world is: in short, both are concerned with the pursuit of objective truth. But, as I see it, metaphysics and empirical science differ crucially in their attitudes to the content of experience. For the scientist, experience is a source of evidential support for speculative explanatory hypotheses, and as such its content is accepted relatively uncritically (even if partially interpreted in the light of prevailing theory). For the metaphysician, by contrast, the content of experience – and in particular the categories and relations which serve to structure that content – is itself the target of critical inquiry and systematic explication. In taking this stance I align myself quite self-consciously with what I take to be a broadly Kantian view of the aim and scope of metaphysical thinking, even though in the upshot many of the metaphysical theses advanced in the following chapters are more Aristotelian than Kantian in their sympathies. To conclude, then: because of their quite different attitudes to the content of experience, metaphysics can both help to underwrite some of the theories of empirical science and yet also to curb the wilder speculations of scientists and the ambitions of some of them to claim a monopoly of truth and understanding. Metaphysicians cannot afford to ignore developments in scientific theory, but they only promise to render themselves foolish in the eyes of posterity by slavishly accepting current scientific orthodoxy.

2

Sortal Terms and Criteria of Identity

It is a plausible contention – though one I shall seek to qualify shortly – that for any given *sort* of individuals there is a *criterion of identity* for individuals of that sort.[1] Linguistically, the point is reflected in a distinction emphasized by P.T. Geach between those general terms that are and those that are not 'substantival'. For Geach the mark of a substantival general term is precisely that it has associated with its use – as indeed a component of its very sense – a criterion of identity for instances falling under it; where by such a criterion Geach means 'that in accordance with which we judge whether identity holds' in assessing the truth or falsehood of an identity statement concerning individuals.[2] So,

---

[1] P.F. Strawson has recently put some pressure both on this assumption and on the very notion of a criterion of identity: see his 'Entity and Identity', in H.D. Lewis (ed.), *Contemporary British Philosophy, Fourth Series* (London: George Allen and Unwin, 1976). While I think Strawson is perhaps unduly severe in some of his criticisms, his paper certainly makes salutary reading for anyone inclined to think that the issues are straightforward or uncontentious ones.

[2] See P.T. Geach, *Reference and Generality*, 3rd edn (Ithaca: Cornell University Press, 1980), pp. 63f. Geach (who cites Aquinas as his model) calls those general terms that are not substantival 'adjectival'. In similar vein, P.F. Strawson distinguishes between what he calls *sortal* and *characterizing* universals, remarking that 'A sortal universal supplies a principle for distinguishing and counting individual particulars which it collects': see his *Individuals: An Essay in Descriptive Metaphysics* (London: Methuen, 1959), p. 168. In modern times, the first sustained examination of the notion of a criterion of identity seems to have been by Gottlob

for instance, 'man' and 'gold' are by this account substantival general terms – or, as I prefer to call them in deference to Locke, *sortal* terms – because it seems there are, at least in principle, ways of determining whether, if x and y are men or portions of gold, they are the *same* man or the *same* gold. But a general term like 'red thing' is not for Geach substantival precisely because it has no such criterion of identity associated with its use.

A sufficient, but not necessary, condition for a general term's being a sortal is that there should exist some principle for *counting* or *enumerating* individual instances falling under it. Thus there are ways of counting the number of *men* or *tables* or *books* in a given room, but no way of counting the number of *red things* there are: and this is not because there *is* such a number but one beyond our powers of determining (as in the case of the number of *atoms* in the room), but because it apparently does not even make sense to speak of such a number until the *sort(s)* of red thing one is to count have been specified. Suppose, for example, that the room contained a red table: then that, it might be urged, is clearly *one* red thing. But what about its red top and its red legs, or the red knob on one of its red drawers? Are *these* to be counted as different 'red things' in the room *in addition to* the red table itself? And what about, say, the red paint covering one of the table's legs: is *that* also to count as a distinct 'red thing' in its own right? It rapidly becomes apparent that there is no principled way of deciding these matters, until we are told what *sorts* of red thing we are supposed to be counting.[3]

Frege in his *Die Grundlagen der Arithmetik* (1884), translated by J.L. Austin as *The Foundations of Arithmetic* (Oxford: Blackwell, 1953), §§ 62ff. For further discussion of both Frege's and Geach's positions, see Michael Dummett, *Frege: Philosophy of Language* (London: Duckworth, 1973), ch. 16. I examine both Frege's view and Dummett's, and also expand on my own position as developed in this chapter, in my 'What is a Criterion of Identity?', *The Philosophical Quarterly* 39 (1989), pp. 1–21.

[3] Suppose we were instructed to count *every* sort of red thing in the room: would *that* in principle lead us to a determinate maximal number of red things in the room

For the foregoing reason, general terms like 'man', 'table' and 'book' (but *not* 'thing') have the logical (not just grammatical) status of *count nouns*, and they form, as I say, a subset of sortal terms. But, to repeat, the countability of instances falling under it is not a necessary condition for a general term's being a sortal, since so-called *mass nouns* like 'gold' and 'water' apparently have criteria of identity associated with their use despite the fact that it makes no sense to ask *how many* instances of gold or water exist in a certain place. (Significantly, though, it *does* make sense to ask *how much* gold or water exists in a given place.)

The general tenor of my remarks is not without venerable historical precedent. If we were to ask what it is that sortal terms denote, a plausible answer would seem to be that they denote what Aristotle in the *Categories* called *secondary substances* – that is, species and genera: in other words, *sorts* or *kinds*. Correspondingly, what Aristotle called *primary substances* we may refer to as the *individuals* or *particulars* instantiating such sorts or kinds. But an important point to appreciate here is that the notions of *individual* (or particular) and *sort* (or kind) are, very arguably, interdependent and mutually irreducible. Individuals are only recognizable as *individuals of a sort*, while sorts are only intelligible as *sorts of individuals*.

When I say that individuals are only recognizable as individuals *of a sort*, I am challenging a notion that has wreaked much havoc in the history of philosophy: the notion of a 'bare particular'. This is the bogus notion of something

---

(perhaps indeed an *infinite* number, but still determinate)? One problem which arises here is that of providing criteria for the identity and diversity of *sorts*; another is that of providing criteria for determining when two distinct sorts are *disjoint*, since one must avoid counting the same individual twice because, say, it is both a red ϕ and a red ψ. A still more fundamental problem arises, however, once we acknowledge quantities or portions of red *stuffs* (such as portions of red ink) to qualify as red things in the room, as I believe we should: for there is clearly *no* principled way of determining how many such portions there are in a given place, in view of the indeterminate extent to which any such portion is divisible into further portions. For further discussion of some of the issues, see Dummett, *Frege*, pp. 565ff.

that is individual or particular *tout court*, quite independently of its falling under any specifiable sortal distinction. In short, it is the purported idea of a mere individual 'thing'. The reason why this is a bogus notion is implicit in some of the observations I have already made. The point, to put it briefly, is that the noun 'thing' – though superficially a count noun in that it admits of a plural form, 'things' – has no criterion of identity associated with it, is not a genuine sortal, and consequently cannot be used unambiguously to pick out some identifiable individual either as an object of knowledge or as an object of reference. Thus, if I point my finger in the direction of my desk and say, with referential intent, 'That *thing* is brown', I shall by no means have expressed a proposition with determinate meaning (even though my intended audience may well be able to *gather* what I meant), and this is because my words have left it quite indeterminate what *sort* of thing I am supposedly referring to – a desk, a portion of wood, a surface, or what not (all of which sorts of things carry different criteria of identity).[4] Locke, as I implied in the Introduction, was one philosopher who was evidently beguiled by the notion of bare particulars. But again I would urge that realism with regard to individuals simply is not compatible with a conventionalism as apparently extreme as his with regard to sorts or kinds: we cannot, with Locke, simply suppose that the mind somehow constructs certain 'abstract general ideas' from its experience of concrete particulars, and then proceeds to classify all particulars by reference to such ideas alone – for particulars

---

[4] It might be objected that this fails to accommodate the fact that the question 'What is that large brown *thing* over there in the room?', which apparently precisely exhibits ignorance of the *sort* of thing being referred to, nonetheless has perfectly determinate sense. My own view is that in such a question determinate reference is *not* made, and that while the question does have determinate *sense* this is only because it effectively means something like: 'There is something large and brown over there in the room – what is it?' – in which the 'it' plays the role of a variable rather than a genuinely referential role. Support for my view may be extracted from Dummett, *Frege*, p. 577 and his *The Interpretation of Frege's Philosophy* (London: Duckworth, 1981), p. 217, where he argues that not all uses of demonstratives serve to perform acts of singular reference to particular objects. (But see further my 'What is a Criterion of Identity?')

cannot be so much as *experienced* at all save as particulars *of some sort* (a fact which argues for the innateness of at least some of our sortal distinctions).

The other side of the coin is that sorts, equally, are not intelligible in abstraction from the individuals which instantiate them. A doctrine of Platonic 'Forms' as the referents of sortal terms is untenable for reasons which Aristotle himself made plain long ago. To go further into this issue would involve us too deeply for present purposes in the so-called Problem of Universals, but I shall return to the matter in a later chapter.

Now, as I have already implied, *different* sorts of things very often have different criteria of identity (though often, too, they do not – for instance, lions and tigers do not, surprising though this may be *prima facie*.) But the *general* form that a criterion of identity will take is just this:

If x and y are ϕs, then x is identical with y if and only if x and y satisfy condition C_ϕ

where, for the reason just stated, the relevant criterial condition C_ϕ may be different for different sorts ϕ. Clearly, the criterion which determines whether or not a certain *body or quantity of water* encountered on one occasion is *the same* as a body or quantity of water encountered on a previous occasion is different from the criterion which determines whether or not a certain *river* encountered on one occasion is *the same* as a river encountered on a previous occasion. As the water in a river flows down to the sea it is replaced by more and different water, but the river remains the same. Hence – or so I shall argue in due course, since the point is by no means uncontroversial – a river is by no means to be *identified* with the water which, at any given time, 'constitutes' it. (Locke was perhaps the first philosopher to recognize explicitly the sortal-relativity of criteria of identity, exploiting it extensively in his discussion of personal identity in the *Essay*, where he makes much of the fact that the sortal terms 'man' and 'person' apparently carry different criteria of identity. I shall myself be examining some of the issues this raises in a subsequent chapter.)

One thing that emerges from the example of the water and the river just mentioned is that different sorts of things may have different *persistence-conditions*, which are determined precisely by their criteria of identity. (Thus a body or quantity of water ceases to exist if all or part of it undergoes molecular dissociation into its constituent oxygen and hydrogen; but a river may arguably continue to exist even if it has temporarily run dry.) An individual x of a sort ϕ, existing at a time t_1, *still exists* at a later time t_2 just in case there exists at t_2 a unique individual y of a sort ψ such that, according to the common criterion of identity governing the sorts ϕ and ψ, x may be identified with y. Or so, at least, I wish to maintain. Observe that I am prepared to allow that an individual may be able to change from being an individual of a sort ϕ to being one of a different sort ψ – otherwise indeed I would be unable to accommodate the phenomenon of *metamorphosis* (though we shall in due course see that transformations most commonly described in these terms, such as that of a caterpillar into a butterfly, are doubtfully genuine instances of the phenomenon). However, a logical restraint that I would wish to place on any such transformation is that the relevant sorts ϕ and ψ should share *the same criterion of identity*: and that is why, for instance, I believe that Lot's wife in the biblical story cannot literally have 'become' a pillar of salt, if by this it is suggested that she *continued to exist* under this new form.[5] These considerations, of course, lend support to the Aristotelian distinction between 'qualitative' and 'substantial' change, and consequently also to the correlative Aristotelian distinction between 'essence' and 'accident'.

While on the subject of *persistence*, I should mention that not all modern philosophers would wholeheartedly endorse

---

[5] Cf. David Wiggins, *Sameness and Substance* (Oxford: Blackwell, 1980), pp. 60f.

the neo-Aristotelian picture that I have just been sketching. There is in particular a school of thought – of which W.V. Quine is perhaps the foremost exponent – according to which all our common-sense talk of persistent objects (or 'continuants') undergoing qualitative change without loss of identity would be replaced in a more 'scientific' description of reality by talk in terms of uninterrupted temporal sequences of instantaneous or momentary objects.[6] On this view, for instance, what we call a *river* is in fact a *process in time*, a four-dimensional 'spacetime worm' whose temporal parts are the momentary three-dimensional 'time-slices' of that 'worm' – a view of reality which obviously derives its inspiration from the work of twentieth-century physicists like Einstein and Minkowski. I must confess that I have grave doubts about the ultimate coherence of this view of things, suspecting that what superficial intelligibility it possesses is parasitic upon our prior grasp of the very neo-Aristotelian or 'common-sense' conception which it seeks to challenge. Some of my doubts on this score stem from what I take to be the implications of the work of P.F. Strawson, in particular his arguments to the effect that material objects (conceived as what I have just termed 'continuants') necessarily constitute 'basic' particulars in our conceptual scheme.[7] However, these and related matters will receive a more extensive airing in later chapters, so I shall dwell on them no further at present.

Let me turn now to some more general considerations concerning identity and criteria of identity. One thing I should emphasize is that a 'criterion of identity', as *I* am now using the expression, is not to be conceived of as a *heuristic* or *evidential* or in any other sense purely *epistemic* principle, but rather as a *semantic* rule (though, obviously, questions

---

[6] See, e.g., W.V. Quine, 'Identity, Ostension and Hypostasis', in his *From a Logical Point of View*, 2nd edn (Cambridge, Mass.: Harvard University Press, 1961).
[7] See Strawson, *Individuals*, passim.

of knowledge and meaning cannot be wholly separated).[8] That is to say, it is not a requirement of a criterion of identity in my sense that it should necessarily provide us with an effective means of coming to *know* whether or not a given identity statement, 'x is identical with y', is true: rather it should tell us, so to speak, *what it takes* for x and y to be the same or different or, in terminology drawn from Locke, 'wherein their identity or diversity consists'.[9] In other words, it should specify – in an informative way, be it added – the *truth*-conditions of the statement 'x is identical with y', rather than, say, its *assertibility*-conditions. (Obviously, 'anti-realists' in matters of semantic theory will want to question this distinction, but being no anti-realist myself I shall here simply take it for granted.) I shall try to indicate, shortly, what I mean by stipulating that such a criterion should specify truth-conditions 'in an informative way'. Meanwhile, as a further *caveat*, I should perhaps just mention that my use of the term 'criterion' has rather little connection with the way that this term is typically used in works of Wittgensteinian exegesis.

Perhaps a very straightforward example of a criterion of identity will be useful at this point. This and the next example I shall invoke are, it is true, ones which involve *abstract* individuals rather than the *concrete* individuals that are the primary concern of this study; but this is partly why the examples are relatively simple ones and thus useful for purposes of illustration. Consider then the criterion of identity for *sets*. A set is a collection of things, each of which 'belongs to' or 'is a member of' that set; examples would be the set of the first three odd numbers, {one, three, five}, and the set of intra-Jovian planets of the sun, {Mercury, Venus, Earth, Mars}. And the criterion of identity for sets, based

---

[8] Cf. Anil Gupta, *The Logic of Common Nouns* (New Haven: Yale University Press, 1980), pp. 2, 22; Gupta uses the expression 'principle of identity' to mean more or less what I mean by 'criterion of identity'.

[9] John Locke, *An Essay Concerning Human Understanding*, ed. P.H. Nidditch (Oxford: Clarendon Press, 1979), Book II, ch. XXVII, § 9.

on the Axiom of Extensionality of set theory, is quite simply as follows:

> If x and y are *sets*, then x is identical with y if and only if x and y *have the same members*.

Thus the sets {one, three, five} and {three, five, one} are by this criterion the *same*. It is, however, instructive here to compare the criterion of identity for sets with the criterion of identity for *ordered sets*, namely:

> If x and y are *ordered sets*, then x is identical with y if and only if x and y *have the same members in the same order*.

For this makes it clear that while the sets {one, three, five} and {three, five, one} are the same *set*, the ordered sets ⟨one, three, five⟩ and ⟨three, five, one⟩ are *not* the same *ordered set*, even though the same three numbers are involved in each case.

Now, a question which arises here, and which will arise again later in other forms, is this: granted that the ordered sets ⟨one, three, five⟩ and ⟨three, five, one⟩ are not the same *ordered set*, may it nonetheless be said that they are the same *set*, and thus that they are both identical with the set {one, three, five}, the set of the first three odd numbers? The obvious answer, which I would urge is also the right answer, is 'No'. For, in the first place, ordered sets are not *sets* at all, in the sense in which this term was understood when the criterion of identity for sets was given (and in due course we shall see that the criterion of identity for any given sort of things, ϕ, is partly constitutive of the *meaning* of the sortal term 'ϕ'). No ordered set can be *identical* with any 'mere' or 'plain' set (as we might call it), since ordered sets and 'plain' sets are quite *different sorts* of things. (I realize that this remark will strike many set theorists as overlooking the work of Wiener, Kuratowski and others in 'reducing' ordered pairs to sets, but leave its clarification and defence to a footnote.[10]) Strictly, of course, just because x belongs to a sort ϕ and y belongs to a different sort ψ, we cannot automatically infer that x and y are not identical – though if they *are* identical each must obviously belong to *both* sorts. However, where such an identity does obtain – so I shall argue – the sorts in question must have the *same* criterion of identity, which will in particular be the case if ϕ and ψ are related as *species* to *genus*, e.g. as *horse* to *mammal*. But *ordered set* and *set* are *not* so related, despite what might be suggested by the *grammatical* relations of these sortal terms.

What *can* be said, of course, is that an ordered set and a 'plain' set may *have the same members*: but *that* does not make them the same set (or the same anything) – certainly not by the criterion of identity for sets, since that only has implications for *sets*. That criterion explicitly states that *if x and y are sets*, then x is identical with y if and only if x and y have the same members, not (say) that x is the same set as y if and only if x and y have the same members (which *would* make the ordered set ⟨one, three, five⟩ and the ordered set ⟨three, five, one⟩ the same set). Of course, this latter point

---

[10] On Kuratowski's definition, the ordered pair $<x,y>$ is 'defined' as the set $\{\{x\}, \{x,y\}\}$: see, e.g., Patrick Suppes, *Axiomatic Set Theory* (New York: Dover, 1972), p. 32. However, in the first place, it is not apparent to me how this can strictly and literally be understood as a *definition* – because, for instance, the ordered pair $<x,y>$ contains x and y as members, but the set $\{\{x\}, \{x,y\}\}$ does not. Rather, what the 'definition' effectively does is to identify, for any ordered pair, a unique set which can, for certain logico-mathematical purposes, be regarded as its surrogate or representative. But furthermore, it is in any case clear that this sort of 'reduction' provides no prospect of legitimizing the suggestion that different *ordered sets* might be the same *set*: for if, say, the different ordered pairs $<x,y>$ and $<y,x>$ are defined as proposed, they will of course turn out to be *different* sets by virtue of having *different members*; though again I would urge that for this very reason the 'definition' cannot be taken as such seriously, since these ordered pairs surely *do* in fact have the same members, at least on any natural understanding of what it is for something to be a member of an ordered pair. It is hardly plausible to suggest that on this natural understanding x is a 'member' of $<x,y>$ by virtue of its unit set being a member of $\{\{x\}, \{x,y\}\}$ and hence that 'membership' is quite naturally understood in a special way as applied to ordered pairs. In short, I would contend that we have a primitive conception of ordered pairs certain features of which simply are not retained by the proposed reduction. At the same time, it must be stressed that I have only invoked this example for illustrative purposes, so that nothing crucial to my general position turns on this debate.

is not decisive in itself, since it is perhaps open to an opponent to challenge my presumptions about the form that a criterion of identity should take.

Another reason, however, for denying that the ordered sets ⟨one, three, five⟩ and ⟨three, five, one⟩ can be the same set but different ordered sets is that this seemingly flies in the face of the laws of identity, in particular the law that things that are identical with a third thing are identical with each other. The only way of evading this would be to attempt to *relativize* the notion of identity, admitting only *sortally relativized* identity relations (like *being the same set as* and *being the same ordered set as*) and not classical 'absolute' identity (just *being the same as*). This strategy, which is more or less followed by Geach, is a subject to which I shall return in due course.[11] The point, however, is that, on the classical view, if x and y are the same set, then they are identical *tout court*, while if they are different ordered sets they are non-identical *tout court*. Our alternatives to contradiction are thus *either* to abandon classical absolute identity *or* (as I would urge) to insist that no individual can instantiate *both* of two sorts φ and ψ if φ and ψ have *different* criteria of identity associated with them: that, for instance, nothing can be *both* a 'plain' set *and* an ordered set. Later I shall argue that we are bound on pain of absurdity to insist on the latter point and consequently that there can be no reason for abandoning classical absolute identity.

Notice this about the criteria of identity cited so far: they do not avoid use of the notion of *identity* itself in stating the condition for the identity of things of a given sort – and this, I suspect, is no merely parochial feature of the examples selected. Thus the criterion of identity for sets speaks of *same members* and that for ordered sets speaks of *same*

---

[11] Geach develops this view in his *Reference and Generality*, 3rd edn. Other recent developments of relativism may be found in Nicholas Griffin, *Relative Identity* (Oxford: Clarendon Press, 1977) and Harold W. Noonan, *Objects and Identity* (The Hague: Martinus Nijhoff, 1980).

members and *same order*. From this it should first of all be clear that a criterion of identity is not to be thought of as a *definition* of identity – not even as a definition of identity for a given sort of things, since identity is univocal, as I shall stress below. (It cannot be a definition of *identity*, simply because a definition should not contain the *definiendum* in the *definiens*.) Another point that emerges here, however, is that where a criterion of identity for a given sort φ *does* make use of the notion of identity itself, it can apparently only do so *informatively* by alluding to the identity of things of *another* sort or sorts – thus the criterion of identity for *sets* is stated in terms of the identity of their *members*. And, while it is true that sets may *themselves* be members of sets, it is crucial to the viability of the criterion of identity for sets just stated that by means of it any question concerning set-identity can in principle ultimately be settled (if need be through repeated applications of the criterion) by reference to the identity of set-members which are *not* themselves sets.[12] (Obviously enough, though, there is no *one* criterion of identity applicable to all set-members: 'set-member' is not, that is to say, a genuine sortal term. What criterion of identity is applicable to any given set-member will simply depend on what *sort* of thing that set-member is, e.g. *planet*, *number* or indeed *set*.)

Now if it is a fact, as I suspect it may be, that a criterion of identity for things of a given sort φ can only be informatively stated in terms which presuppose the identity of things of another sort or sorts, the implication would appear to be that there must, on pain of an infinite regress, be *some* 'basic' sorts for which we can give *no* informative criterion of identity.[13] (Obviously, if there *are* 'basic' sorts, it cannot after all be a *necessary* condition for a general term's being a

---

[12] This effectively applies even in the case of set theory of the Zermelo-Fraenkel type, in which the empty set is the only set not having a set as member: for there the criterion serves to guarantee that there is just one empty set by reference to which questions concerning the identity of all other sets may ultimately be settled.

[13] Cf. Strawson, 'Entity and Identity', p. 200.

sortal that it should have a criterion of identity associated with it.[14]) Whether this is so, and if so what such 'basic' sorts might be, and what the truth of identity statements concerning individuals of these sorts could be grounded in, are deep and difficult questions which I cannot undertake to answer at present, though I may as well declare forthwith a leaning towards the view that *person* constitutes a 'basic' sort. For the time being, however, I want only to emphasize the requirement that has emerged regarding the *informativeness* of a criterion of identity, as an amplification of my earlier stipulation that criteria of identity should specify truth-conditions for identity statements 'in an informative way'; the crucial point being that in an informative criterion of identity for φs, an appeal to φ-identity will not itself figure, either explicitly or implicitly, in the statement of the relevant criterial condition C_ϕ. A *non*-informative way of specifying such truth-conditions, in the case of sets, would of course simply be to say 'If x and y are *sets*, then x is identical with y if and only if x and y *include exactly the same sets*.' The latter is true (recall that every set includes itself and that mutually inclusive sets are identical[15]) but quite vacuous as a criterion of identity for sets: not, however, because it makes use of the very notion of *identity* in stating the truth-conditions for an identity statement concerning sets – for, as we have seen, the accepted criterion cited earlier equally does this – nor even because it makes use of the very notion of a *set*, but rather because it presupposes an account of the *identity-conditions* of sets.[16]

---

[14] We might still however hold that it is necessary for a general term's being a sortal *either* that it should have a criterion of identity associated with it *or else* that it should belong to that select company of general terms supplying concepts which require to be appealed to in stating the criteria of identity associated with those sortals that do have such criteria associated with them, i.e. that it should denote a 'basic' sort.

[15] See, e.g., Suppes, *Axiomatic Set Theory*, p. 22. The set-*inclusion* relation should not of course be confused with the set-*membership* relation.

[16] I have no objection, then, to the fact that in the accepted criterion of identity for sets the variables 'x' and 'y' take *sets* as values: I develop this point at much greater length in my 'What is a Criterion of Identity?' But this is quite a different

As I indicated a moment ago, a criterion of identity, in telling us 'wherein identity and diversity consists' for a given sort of things, should *not* be thought of as telling us the *meaning* of the word 'identity', as applied to things of that sort. For 'identity' does *not* mean anything different when applied to one sort of things as opposed to another, though some philosophers misleadingly speak as if it did.[17] When I say that nine is *identical* with the sum of four and five, I do not mean anything different by 'identical' from what I mean by it when I say that Queen Elizabeth II is *identical* with the eldest daughter of King George VI, or that Phosphorus is *identical* with Hesperus, or that this chair is *identical* with the chair that I sat in at this time last week. Identity is *univocal*. There are not different *kinds* of identity for different kinds of thing (any more than there are different kinds of existence) – only different *criteria* of identity. (In insisting that identity is univocal I mean also, incidentally, to dismiss as misconceived any suggestion that such distinctions, legitimate in themselves, as those between 'numerical' and 'qualitative' identity and between 'synchronic' and 'diachronic' identity should be seen as distinctions between *kinds of identity*, as opposed to distinctions concerning the ontological status or temporal circumstances of items being identified.)

What, then, *is* identity, if it is not defined by any criterion of identity? Well, it is, of course, that unique relation which, of necessity, each thing bears to itself and to no other thing. But, obviously, this will not do as a *definition* of identity, since it makes use of the word 'other' and 'other than' just means 'diverse from', i.e. 'not identical with'. Again, one might point out, correctly, that the meaning of the English

---

matter from the question of whether a criterion of set-identity makes illicit appeal to considerations turning on the *identity* of sets.

[17] Joseph Butler provides an early example of this error: see *The Analogy of Religion* (1736), Dissertation I, 'Of Personal Identity': 'The word *same*, when applied to [vegetables] and to persons, is not only applied to different subjects, but it is also used in different senses' (reprinted in John Perry (ed.), *Personal Identity* (Berkeley: University of California Press, 1975), p. 100).

word 'identical' is such that the sentence '*x* is identical with *y*' has the following truth-condition: it is true if and only if the names '*x*' and '*y*' denote the same object. This is the sort of account of the meaning of the identity sign '=' one typically finds in recursive truth-conditional semantics for formalized languages, in which context, no doubt, it may be quite unexceptionable. But construed as an attempt to provide any sort of (philosophically illuminating) *definition* of identity this is even more transparently circular, since the very word 'same' is being used. Identity cannot, perhaps, be *defined* at all – not even in terms of the principle of the *identity of indiscernibles* (granting for the sake of argument the validity of that principle). The trouble with that principle, conceived as a definition of identity, is that 'indiscernible' just means 'having the *same* properties', so that the notion of identity is presupposed even here: understanding the principle requires at least an understanding of what it is to identify and distinguish *properties*, with a view to saying whether or not *x* has some property that is *different* from, i.e. not *identical* with, any property of *y*.

It might, I suppose, be wondered whether this last objection can really be sound in view of the fact that the principle of the identity of indiscernibles can be expressed formally without explicit use of identity expressions on *both* sides of the main biconditional connective, namely, by means of the formula:

$$x = y \longleftrightarrow (\forall F)(Fx \longleftrightarrow Fy)$$

(Strictly speaking, this formula combines the principle of the identity of indiscernibles proper (right-to-left) with the principle of the indiscernibility of identicals (left-to-right); but the latter I am for the moment assuming to be an uncontroversial logical truth. Of course, a *biconditional* is needed for a definition.) The answer to this query, however, is that a correct interpretation of the right-hand side of this biconditional formula presupposes the convention that where a symbol (in this case 'F') is repeated in a formula it is to be assigned the *same* interpretation at each of its occurrences: so the notion of identity is still presupposed, albeit implicitly rather than explicitly.

So perhaps, then we should just accept that identity is conceptually primitive – indefinable – and thus that it is pointless to expect an informative answer to the question 'What do we *mean* by *identity*?' Identity may simply be one of those conceptual primitives (like perhaps existence) of which it is true to say that if, *per impossibile*, one did not grasp what it is, one could not have it explained to one.

Given, however, that identity is a logically primitive concept, and that criteria of identity are not to be understood as *definitions* of identity, the question arises: what semantic information *do* such criteria convey – for they can presumably tell us nothing about the meaning of 'identity' that we do not already implicitly know. Yet such criteria are *semantic* rules, and so *are* concerned with *meaning*, albeit not with the meaning of the word 'identity'. The answer, of course, is that they tell us something about the meaning of whatever *sortal term* it is that they are associated with.[18] To give the criterion of identity for ɸs is (at least partially) to explain what sort of things ɸs *are*. Thus when I tell you that a 'set' is something whose identity 'consists in' its having the same members, I inform you about the meaning of the sortal term 'set'. And by contrasting the criteria of identity for 'plain' and ordered sets, I help to distinguish the meanings of these two sortal terms. This, incidentally, helps to explain why the principle of the identity of indiscernibles, apart from not providing a *definition* of identity, cannot even qualify as a *criterion* of identity in my sense. The reason is that the principle is not relativized to any specific *sort* of things, but affects to be a quite general law, holding of anything whatever. Accordingly it is not a *semantic rule* connected with the

---

[18] In taking this stance I am declaring my direct opposition to the views advanced by Baruch A. Brody in his *Identity and Essence* (Princeton: Princeton University Press, 1980), passim.

meaning of any particular sortal term, in the way that every genuine criterion of identity is. To put the point another way: the only *apparently* sortal terms that could be used in expressing the principle, in a sufficiently generalized form, are terms like 'thing' and 'object', which however are not genuine but only so-called 'dummy' sortals (a status that is revealed by the point made earlier that, although 'thing' is *grammatically* a count noun, one cannot intelligibly undertake to count how many *things* there are in a given room, in the way that one can attempt to count how many *books* or *chairs* or *persons* there are).

I conclude, then, that one only *fully* grasps the nature of a given sort or kind of thing, and hence the meaning of sortal terms designating it, when one grasps the criterion of identity associated therewith (assuming, of course, that there *is* one, i.e. that the sort in question is not 'basic'). And so, for example, grasping the respective criteria of identity for, say, *lumps of matter*, *living organisms* and (perhaps) *persons* will be partially constitutive of an adequate understanding of what it is for something to *be* a lump of matter, living organism or person. One would expect, then, that developing a grasp of such criteria comprises one of the major learning tasks of human infants, although indeed it may be that a grasp of at least *some* criteria of identity may have to be innate in human beings, perhaps playing a vital role in enabling the infant to pick out certain perceptual invariants amidst the continual flux of sensory stimulation.[19] Of course, manifesting a *practical* grasp of a particular criterion of identity in displaying an ability to re-identify an object of a certain sort correctly as 'the same one again' does not entail

---

[19] Some of the work of the developmental psychologist Tom Bower on early infant perception and related motor activity certainly seems to support the view that, even from the earliest months, human infants can perceptually individuate discrete objects in their immediate environment: see, e.g., Tom Bower, *The Perceptual World of the Child* (London: Fontana, 1977). For an illuminating discussion of some of the philosophical issues, see Eli Hirsch, *The Concept of Identity* (Oxford: Oxford University Press, 1982), chs. 8 and 9. For further elaboration of my own views on these matters, see my 'What is a Criterion of Identity?'.

possessing a capacity to *articulate* or *excogitate* such a criterion, so that attributing such a grasp to infants is not necessarily over-intellectualizing their cognitive abilities. Moreover, we need not, and indeed probably should not, suppose that the criteria manifested in the identity judgements of infants are in fact the fully fledged versions employed by adults, not least because at first infants only learn to re-identify objects over comparatively short periods of time or in otherwise restricted sets of circumstances. Thus an infant may grasp that losing its leaves is not inimical to the identity of a tree, while not yet grasping that a mature oak and a young sapling might be one and the same living organism encountered at different times. (It should be emphasized, too, that it is not to be supposed that infants have to grasp a distinct new criterion of identity for each new sortal term they learn, since species falling under the same genera share the same criterion of identity: there is not a different criterion for oaks and elms, say, both of which conform to the criterion of identity for living organisms in general.)

I should perhaps just add, finally, a word about my own conception of the distinctive role of *philosophical* theorizing about criteria of identity. It is not part of that conception that philosophers should see themselves as being merely in the business of revealing what criteria of identity the 'plain man' implicitly and perhaps unreflectively employs in making identity judgements concerning things of this or that familiar sort. Of course philosophical analysis must *start* with ordinary linguistic usage, but it need not, and will not if it is to be of much interest and profit, always *stay* with it. For ordinary linguistic usage is sometimes vague, confused and unduly limited in its range of application. At times, the task of philosophical analysis is not so much to tell us what we *do* mean, for at times our meaning may be far from clear. Rather, its task may be to offer a coherent and reasoned account of what we *should* mean: to improve our concepts, not just to report on them. And since I regard criteria of identity as semantic principles, I cannot regard them as entirely resistant to improvement of this sort. It should also be said, however, that the distinctively philosophical task of articulating and attempting to improve upon the concepts implicit in ordinary linguistic usage should not be confused with (though it may profitably draw upon the results of) the empirical psychological task of examining the cognitive processes underlying an individual's engagement in the linguistic practices which characterize that usage. Philosophers employed in conceptual analysis must constantly guard against the temptation to indulge in psychological speculation. But it would be equally mistaken of psychologists to suppose that this leaves philosophers without a subject.[20]

---

[20] See further my remarks on semantics, metaphysics and necessity in the Introduction.

3

Individuals, Sorts and Instantiation

Two kinds of 'is' that are commonly conflated by philosophers and logicians are the 'is' of *attribution*, figuring in a sentence like 'This pen *is* yellow', and what I call the 'is' of *instantiation*, figuring in sentences like 'Dobbin *is* a horse' and 'A horse *is* a mammal', that is, sentences of the form 'Such-and-such is (a) φ', where 'φ' is a sortal term and where 'such-and-such' may either be a particular or *individual* term (like the proper name 'Dobbin') or else again a sortal term. Sentences of this form I shall call *instantiation sentences*. Before saying more about the 'is' of instantiation, however, something further must be said about the terms, sortal and individual, that may figure in sentences featuring it.

As we saw in the previous chapter, an important feature of sortal terms from a *semantic* point of view is that they typically have associated with them a *criterion of identity* (unless, perhaps, they designate 'basic' sorts, if such sorts there be). But I would urge, with Geach,[1] that individual terms like proper names also typically have, as an essential semantic feature, criteria of identity associated with their application. This, of course, runs somewhat counter to the

---

[1] See P.T. Geach, *Reference and Generality*, 3rd edn (Ithaca: Cornell University Press, 1980), pp. 67–8.

currently popular view that proper names have no Fregean 'sense' and are purely denotative or referential: but not necessarily wholly counter to it.[2] I do not want to suggest that the sense of a proper name is the same as that of some identifying description, e.g. that 'Aristotle' might have the sense of 'the teacher of Alexander the Great' (say), nor even that the sense of a proper name is a function of the senses of such descriptions, as Searle seems to contend.[3] What I do hold is that, by whatever means a person has been introduced to a certain proper name, he has not grasped its correct use unless he has grasped whatever criterion of identity there may be associated with it. Thus, for example, if someone has picked up the name 'Aristotle' from overhearing a conversation amongst philosophers, but does not grasp that it has associated with it the criterion of identity for a *man* (say, because he thinks that these philosophers are referring to a *book*), then I should say that he fails to refer to Aristotle in his subsequent use of that name – indeed, he fails to refer to *anything*.

This thesis concerning the semantics of proper names is, of course, intimately connected with my contention that individuals must always be thought of as individuals *of some sort*. The criterion of identity associated with a proper name will just be that associated with whatever *sortal terms* there may be that designate the sort(s) or kind(s) which any individual capable of being referred to by that name must instantiate. Thus 'Aristotle', conceived as a name for a *man*, must have associated with it the criterion of identity which is also associated with the sortal term 'man'. So I do not (or need not) insist that the sense of a proper name should determine which *individual* it refers to, but only what *sort* of individual its referent is (for it is this that determines what criterion of identity is associated with the name).

From these remarks concerning the *semantics* of individ-

---

[2] I am thinking, of course, of the view developed by Saul Kripke in his *Naming and Necessity* (Oxford: Blackwell, 1980).
[3] See John R. Searle, 'Proper Names', *Mind* 67 (1958), pp. 166–73.

ual and sortal terms, I pass on now to a fuller characterization of their *syntax*. Typical *individual* terms, apart from *proper names* like 'Dobbin' and 'Scamander', are *demonstrative phrases* like 'that horse' and 'this river', and *definite descriptions* like 'the horse in Farmer Brown's field' and 'the river in which I stepped yesterday'. (It will be observed that such phrases and descriptions, though individual terms, involve sortal terms in their construction. Whether or not such phrases and descriptions are to be regarded as genuine *semantic* units in their own right is not an issue I shall address at present.) Typical *sortal* terms are *count nouns* like 'horse' and 'river' and *mass nouns* like 'water' and 'gold'. These, however, are *simple* sortal terms; there are also *complex* ones in which the nouns are qualified by adjectives or adjectival phrases, e.g. 'wild horse', 'boiling water', and 'tree which sheds its leaves in winter'. The semantics of complex sortal terms raise special problems which I shall discuss in a later chapter; for the time being I shall concentrate on simple sortal terms.

Observe, however, that for semantic purposes the simple/complex distinction for sortal terms cannot be drawn purely syntactically: for instance, 'ice', though syntactically simple, arguably (I do not say indisputably) has the same meaning as the syntactically (and semantically) complex sortal term 'frozen water'; but 'heavy water', though syntactically complex, is arguably *not* best seen as semantically determined by the meanings of its syntactic components, 'heavy' and 'water'. (Clearly, at least, 'heavy water' does not just mean 'water which is heavy', in the way that 'frozen water' means 'water which is frozen'.) To say that a sortal term is *semantically* simple is just to say that it is not semantically *analysable*, i.e. that its meaning is not a function of the meanings of certain other expressions, such as the meanings of its syntactic components (if it has any), or the meanings of the syntactic components of some syntactically complex sortal term which is synonymous with it. I would further venture to say – though detailed argument in favour of this view will have to wait until later – that a semantically simple sortal term is one which, superficial syntax notwithstanding, has no other semantic function than simply to designate a *distinct sort* of things or stuff. (The question of the criteria of sortal distinctness is one that I cannot yet address, however.) Thus one reason why I am persuaded to regard 'heavy water' as semantically simple is that heavy water (D_2O) is genuinely a distinct kind of substance in its own right – in fact, it is a kind of water; whereas, by contrast, 'frozen water' does not, I should say, denote a *kind* of water at all. It should be borne in mind, then, that when I say that I shall for the present concentrate on *simple* sortal terms, I have in view *semantically* simple ones, even though I am not yet in a position to explain fully what motivates an ascription of such semantic simplicity to a sortal term. Fortunately, we can for the time being rely on the (surely non-accidental) fact that natural language is not unduly misleading in its syntax: that cases like that of 'ice' are the exception rather than the norm, and that for the most part syntactic and semantic simplicity or complexity go hand in hand.

A further point about the syntax of sortal terms that I ought to mention is this. The question arises, in the case of a sortal term involving a count noun, of whether we should sometimes include the indefinite article or a plural suffix as part of that term. Consider, for example, the instantiation sentences cited at the outset of this chapter, 'Dobbin is a horse' and 'A horse is a mammal'. According to what I have so far said, 'horse' and 'mammal' are the two (simple) sortal terms figuring in these sentences. But it will often be convenient to speak rather of the indefinite noun-phrases 'a horse' and 'a mammal' as sortal terms. Again, when we consider that the sentence 'A horse is a mammal' may be paraphrased by the sentence 'Horses are mammals', we shall see that it will often be equally convenient to regard the plural nouns 'horses' and 'mammals' as sortal terms. The convenience I allude to is convenience in respect of *formalization*, or representation by means of symbols. The point is that I want to represent sentences like 'Dobbin is a horse' and 'A horse is a mammal' (or its equivalent, 'Horses are mammals') as being sentences of the forms, respectively, 'x is ϕ' and 'ϕ is ψ', where the 'is', of course, is the 'is' of instantiation. In thus absorbing the indefinite article or a plural suffix into a sortal term, I do not think I can be accused of ignoring any *logically significant* feature of English grammar, for I agree with what I take to be Geach's position, that these particles and suffixes are for the most part superficial peculiarities of English syntax not encountered in all natural languages. (Geach makes the point that the Latin translation of 'I met a man' has no word for 'a'.[4] This is not, of course, an instantiation sentence, but we could similarly point out that the Latin translation of the instantiation sentence 'Caesar is a man' is *Caesar est homo*, while 'A man is an animal' is similarly translated as *Homo est animal*; interestingly enough, indeed, English itself allows the indefinite article to be dropped in the latter case – 'Man is an animal' – though curiously this is not permissible with other count nouns like 'horse'.) I do not deny, I hasten to add, that the indefinite article or a plural suffix may have logical significance in *some* sentences, only that they have any such significance in *instantiation* sentences. In some English sentences these grammatical appendages may play a *quantificational* role, conveying distinctions of *number*: thus there is a clear difference in sense between the sentences 'There is *a* horse in that field' and 'There are horse*s* in that field' (by contrast with the already noted synonymy between 'A horse is a mammal' and 'Horses are mammals').

The foregoing considerations only apply, of course, to *count* nouns, as opposed to *mass* nouns like 'water' and 'gold'. But some may question my very lumping together of count and mass nouns within the single category of sortal terms. They might be willing to admit as sortal terms such complex count-noun-phrases as 'drop of water' or 'lump of gold', but not the simple mass nouns 'water' and 'gold' themselves. My own view, which I hope will be seen to be

---

[4] See Geach, *Reference and Generality*, 3rd edn, p. 8.

vindicated in the course of this study, is that analogies between the logical behaviour of mass nouns like 'gold' standing alone and those undisputed sortal terms involving count nouns, such as 'a horse' or 'horses', are sufficiently pervasive to warrant the assimilation I make. For example, there is the obvious analogy between 'Horses are mammals' or 'A horse is a mammal' and 'Gold is (a) metal'; and already in the previous chapter we have noticed that we may speak of 'the same gold' just as we may speak of 'the same man'. (Indeed, it is worth remarking that the very *grammar* of mass nouns is in some ways quite similar to that of *plural* count nouns, particularly in constructions involving expressions of quantity – for instance, we speak of 'a lot of horses' in very much the same way that we speak of 'a lot of wood'.) I shall return to this issue in due course. Meanwhile, I should just remark that I do not want to *deny* the status of *sortal term* to such complex count-noun-phrases as 'drop of water', only to extend that status to simple mass nouns like 'water' itself.

I return now to the distinction between the 'is' of attribution and the 'is' of instantiation. Traditionally, of course, these two varieties of 'is' have been conflated. But this, in my view, is certainly a mistake. First of all, we should observe that the 'is' of attribution is, from a logical point of view, really just redundant, while the 'is' of instantiation is not. For instance, it is merely a relatively parochial feature of English that instead of saying something like 'This pen *is yellow*' we don't say something like 'This pen *yellows*', utilizing a single verb instead of a copula plus an adjective. (In fact, Russian and Arabic do, I believe, employ precisely this sort of construction for ascriptions of colour.[5]) This is just to say that a predicate like '— is yellow' is, from a logical point of view, a simple semantic unit (i.e. semantically unanalysable), in a way that predicates like '— is a horse'

[5] See N.R. Hanson, *Patterns of Discovery* (Cambridge: Cambridge University Press, 1958), pp. 32–3.

and '— is water' are very arguably not. (I speak of *predicates* here in a broad sense in which they are just expressions completable by noun-phrases to form sentences.) The reason why the 'is' of instantiation is not redundant, and hence must be distinguished from the 'is' of attribution, is intimately connected with the fact that sortal terms can figure in sentences in the role of *grammatical subject*, from which role they cannot always be eliminated by paraphrase (except perhaps by paraphrases involving the use of *sortal variables* – or their natural language counterparts – in subject position).

This is in fact closely analogous with the reason why the 'is' of *identity* must also be distinguished from the 'is' of attribution, and so it may be of some help to expand on the latter point. Suppose that this last distinction were denied and that the 'is' in 'Cicero is Tully' were alleged to be the same as the 'is' in 'Cicero is wise'. This would make '— is Tully' a simple semantic unit like '— is wise'. But there would then threaten to be a quite intolerable *systematic ambiguity* between the use of 'Tully' as a grammatical subject, as in 'Tully is wise', and its appearance in its allegedly attributive role in 'Cicero is Tully'. Now of course the immediate difficulty here might be circumvented by arguing that 'Tully' can always be removed by paraphrase from subject position, so that it need only ever appear in the context '— is Tully'. Just such a programme of systematic removal has indeed notoriously been canvassed by Quine, in the context of a defence of a 'descriptive' theory of proper names.[6] (I am not, I should stress, an adherent of such a theory.) However, it is evident that even a descriptive theorist is not in virtue of this strategy relieved of the need for a distinctive 'is' of identity, so long as he retains at least the use of *individual variables* (or their natural language counterparts) in subject position: for such a theorist will still need to allow such variables to flank *both* sides of an 'is',

---

[6] See W.V. Quine, 'On What There Is', in his *From a Logical Point of View*, 2nd edn (Cambridge, Mass.: Harvard University Press, 1961), p. 8, where he uses the example of the name 'Pegasus'.

which in such an occurrence will still therefore have to be recognized as making an independent semantic contribution to the meaning of a sentence (unlike the 'is' of attribution).[7] The issue, thus, is not narrowly tied to a particular theory of proper names, but turns rather on ontological considerations connected with the use of quantifiers with individual variables.

Now, analogously, the need to recognize a distinctive 'is' of *instantiation* is connected with the fact that, just as in the case of individual terms, *sortal* terms too can often figure as grammatical subjects in sentences which cannot be paraphrased by other sentences in which sortal terms, or at least sortal *variables*, no longer appear in subject position.[8] One very important category of such sentences are those expressive of *natural laws*, or *nomological generalizations*, such as 'Water is translucent'. The sortal term 'water' appears here in subject position, and this sentence cannot (I contend) be paraphrased satisfactorily by any other in which 'water' only appears in the context '— is water', where the blank is occupied by an *individual* term or variable. Thus, for instance, 'For all x, if x is water, then x is translucent' will certainly *not* do as a paraphrase, as I shall argue in detail in a later chapter. Once more the crucial point is that in order to cope with the logic of such nomological sentences we shall

---

[7] Thus if, following Quine, 'Tully is wise' is first paraphrased as 'The thing which is Tully is wise' and the definite description is then eliminated in Russell's way to give 'For some x, x is Tully and for all y, if y is Tully then y is x, and x is wise', an 'is' of identity appears in the expression 'y is x'.

[8] Here it might be objected that colour terms like 'yellow', with which I am presently contrasting sortal terms, can also figure as grammatical subjects, as in sentences like 'Yellow is the colour of this pen' and 'Yellow is a colour'. However, in both cases an eliminative paraphrase *is* available, namely, 'This pen is yellow' and 'Everything that is yellow is coloured'. If colour terms *cannot* always be paraphrased out of subject position in this way (which I very much doubt), then for that very reason I shall be willing to countenance them (or at least certain occurrences of them) as sortal terms after all, perhaps taking up a suggestion of Quine's that they be regarded as *mass* terms: see W.V. Quine, *Word and Object* (Cambridge, Mass.: M.I.T. Press, 1960), pp. 91ff. Clearly, however, there is no prospect at all of regarding adjectives like 'long' or 'heavy' or 'wise' in this way, and this suffices to show that the contrast I am drawing is a genuine one even if there may be some disagreement about where precisely the boundary lies.

have to allow an 'is' to be flanked on *both* sides at least by sortal *variables*, and hence to concede that in such an occurrence the 'is' makes an independent semantic contribution – a contribution which, moreover, cannot always be identified with that of the 'is' of *identity*, since in at least some contexts it will prove not to involve a symmetrical relation. At root, then, the issue is again an ontological one connected with quantification: we need, that is, to recognize a distinctive 'is' of instantiation ultimately because we have to admit variables which range over *sorts* or *kinds*. (This is also something I shall discuss in detail later.)

I have of course been assuming that, just as it would be undesirable to be forced to recognize a systematic ambiguity in uses of a proper name like 'Tully', so it would with regard to uses of a sortal term like 'water'. Now Geach, it may be remarked, *is* prepared to allow just such a systematic ambiguity.[9] This is because he recognizes a sense in which sortal terms – or substantival general terms, as he calls them – occur in *semantically simple* (unanalysable) identity predicates of the form '— is the same φ as . . .', as well as a sense in which they occur as grammatical subjects. The supposed semantic simplicity of these predicates on Geach's view is connected, of course, with his relativist position on the nature of identity, which I shall examine more fully in the next chapter. Here I shall only remark that, in my view, a commitment to systematic ambiguity of the sort described is something to be avoided if at all possible; in the next chapter I shall try to show that Geach, at least, provides no good reason for thinking such avoidance to be *im*possible.

As I understand it, a sentence of the form 'Such-and-such is (a) φ' standardly affirms that such-and-such is an *instance of the kind or sort* φ. (I say 'standardly' because I acknowledge that sentences involving a distinctive 'is' of *constitution* may also take this form, though I believe that they may always be paraphrased so as to eliminate the ambiguity. I

---

[9] See Geach, *Reference and Generality*, 3rd edn, p. 172.

shall say more about the 'is' of constitution in the next chapter.) Thus 'Dobbin is a horse' affirms that Dobbin is an individual instance of the kind *horse*, and 'This piece of metal is gold' affirms that this piece of metal is an individual instance or sample of the kind *gold*. 'A horse is an animal' and 'Gold is (a) metal' are analogous, in that they affirm one sort or kind to be a *species* of another, and I take the species–genus relation to be the same as that between an individual and a sort or kind which it instantiates. Thus any *dis*analogy between 'Dobbin is a horse' and 'A horse is an animal' seems to me to reside not in the sense of the 'is' figuring in each, which I regard as univocal, but only in the fact that 'Dobbin' denotes an *individual* while '(a) horse' denotes a *sort* or *kind*. (I shall not undertake a detailed defence of this opinion at present; but on grounds of economy alone it seems a reasonable assumption, in the absence of countervailing evidence.)

Returning for a moment to the issue of whether mass nouns may be regarded as sortal terms – as I think may – I should say that it seems to me that individual bodies of water stand in the same relationship to the sort or kind *water* as individual horses do to the sort or kind *horse*, namely, as individual *instances*, *samples* or *exemplars*. I would certainly resist any tendency to see a mass noun like 'water' as denoting a 'scattered' *individual*, the mereological sum of all the various individual bodies of water in the world.[10] 'Water' is in *no* sense an individual term, like 'Dobbin'; for one thing, there are *kinds* of water (e.g. so-called heavy water), but no *kinds* of Dobbin. (It is no use, I believe, saying that 'heavy water' just denotes a *part* of the world's sum total of water, namely, that part of it whose molecules contain deuterium instead of ordinary hydrogen.) But given that 'water' is a sortal term, there is little alternative but to regard as its referent's individual instances all the various individual bodies of water, such as the body of water filling a

---

[10] See, e.g., Quine, *Word and Object*, pp. 97ff.

certain glass, or the body of water filling the river Scamander's bed on a certain day. (Actually, one alternative would be to regard *quatities* of water in this light, in Cartwright's technical sense of 'quantity'.[11] But for present purposes I do not really need to adjudicate between these two alternatives, since no vital thesis of mine hinges on which is chosen.)

Given, however, that both individuals and sorts may stand in the instantiation relation to sorts, the question arises: what, then, *is* an 'individual', and how is it to be distinguished from a 'sort'? I do not think that spatiotemporal considerations are of much use in elucidating the distinction, firstly because I suspect that spatiotemporal relationships already presuppose an ontology of identifiable particulars or individuals, and secondly because the notion of an individual which is not spatiotemporally located certainly does not appear to be incoherent. (I have already discussed, in the previous chapter, *abstract* individuals like sets, which certainly do not appear to be in any sense spatiotemporally locatable. But even if we limit ourselves to *concrete* individuals, there is the *prima facie* coherent hypothesis of Cartesian minds or egos, which are presumably to be conceived of as at least not being *spatially* locatable. I hasten to add that I do not want to suggest that I endorse this hypothesis, only that it seems coherent.)

My own answer (though only a tentative one) would be roughly along the following lines. X is an *individual* if and only if X is an instance of something Y (other than itself) and X itself has no instances (other than itself). X is a *sort* if and only if there is something Y such that Y is an instance of X and Y is distinct from X. More formally, the proposal is to adopt the following definitional equivalences, where '/' is used to signify instantiation:

$$X \text{ is an individual} =_{df} (\exists Y)(X/Y \ \& \ Y \neq X) \ \& \ \sim (\exists Y)(Y/X \ \& \ Y \neq X)$$

---

[11] See Helen M. Cartwright, 'Quantities', *The Philosophical Review* 79 (1970), pp. 25–42.

X is a sort $=_{df} (\exists Y)(Y/X \ \& \ Y \neq X)$

In this way the distinction between individuals and sorts is defined by means of the instantiation relation itself. Notice that I do not insist that sorts always instantiate 'higher' sorts: there may be 'highest' sorts of which this is not true. Individuals, by contrast, must instantiate sorts, for reasons already alluded to (there are no 'bare' particulars). Hence the asymmetry between the two definitions. Notice too that in the proposed definitions the variables 'X' and 'Y' must not, of course, be regarded as either individual or sortal variables but as quite 'neutral'. (I propose to call them simply 'objectual' variables.) The distinction between individual and sortal variables has to be introduced subsequently, precisely on the basis of the suggested definitions (if they are accepted). I myself follow the practice of using the lower case Roman letters 'x', 'y', etc. as individual variables and the lower case Greek letters 'ϕ', 'ψ', etc. as sortal variables.

It will be observed that the definitions just proposed make use not only of the 'is' of instantiation but also of the 'is' of identity. A further economy might be achieved by defining the latter 'is' *as used here* in terms of the former – specifically, by defining identity here as *mutual instantiation*, i.e. by adopting additionally the definitional equivalence:[12]

$X = Y =_{df} X/Y \ \& \ Y/X$

Such a definition would certainly preserve the logical charac-

---

[12] Note that this definition would still only define identity for 'objects' (i.e. individuals and sorts), and not identity quite generally. But if as I believe identity is *univocal* (see chapter 2), such a restricted 'definition' must be questionable – implying as it seemingly does that 'identity' has a special meaning as applied to objects (as opposed, say, to properties or states of affairs or what not). (Analogously, it would be questionable to think of *defining* identity for *sets* in terms of their mutual inclusion, even though mutual inclusion is a logically necessary and sufficient condition for set-identity. The analogy is however imperfect inasmuch as this condition for set-identity is simply derivable from the criterion of identity for sets together with the definition of set-inclusion, whereas no analogous derivation is available in the case under examination.)

ter of identity as an equivalence relation (reflexive, symmetrical and transitive) – on the assumption, at any rate, that instantiation is a *reflexive* relation, which has at least some plausibility. However, I do not propose to pursue this line of speculation any further in the present study. (Observe that if instantiation is alternatively conceived to be an *irreflexive* relation, the conjunct '$Y \neq X$' may of course be omitted at each of its occurrences in the definitions of *individual* and *sort* proposed earlier.)

According to the definitions of *individual* and *sort* suggested above, what distinguishes the individual *Dobbin* from the species or sort *horse* is that Dobbin has no instances (except, quite possibly, himself) whereas the horse does. That is, 'horse' *divides its reference* but 'Dobbin' does not. It is indivisibility of *reference* rather than *material* indivisibility which, it seems clear, the notion of 'individuality' implies. Dobbin is of course not indivisible in the sense that he cannot be cut into pieces, merely in the sense that nothing (apart from Dobbin himself) – such as any of these pieces – qualifies as an *instance* of Dobbin. There is no plurality of different 'Dobbins', in the way that there are many different horses. (Of course, in *another* way there *are* many different Dobbins, but only in the sense that many different individual horses may be called by the same name, 'Dobbin'. These different individuals are not however, *instances* of some one individual, Dobbin). It might be wondered whether these considerations apply equally in the case of an individual like a lump of gold, since each piece it is divided into (down to a certain level) is again a lump of gold; but even here it it not the case that each such piece is an *instance* of the original lump, as opposed to a *part* or *portion* of it.

Nonetheless, the definitions proposed are still arguably not entirely satisfactory, because they apparently fail to take into account the possibility of *infimae species* lacking individual instances. An *infima species*, or lowest species, if there can be such a thing, would be a sort without any distinct sub-sort instantiating it. There are various ways in which one might seek to evade this difficulty. One, which superficially seems quite plausible, would simply be to deny the possibility of *infimae species*, on the grounds that any sortal term 'ϕ' whatever can be suitably qualified or restricted so as to generate another (albeit complex) sortal term 'ψ' such that 'ψ is ϕ' is a true instantiation sentence: e.g., 'Boiling water is water', 'A wild horse is a horse', etc. The trouble with this proposal is that it misconceives the semantics of complex sortal terms (which, as I have said, I shall discuss more fully in a later chapter); specifically, it makes the mistake of supposing that an expression like 'boiling water' denotes a *kind* of water. Without this sort of supposition the proposal will not work, since it merely appeals to the *syntactical* fact that sortal terms can be adjectivally qualified *ad infinitum*.

Another possibility would be simply to regard individuals precisely *as* lowest species. This suggestion may quite attract some metaphysicians, on account of its economy and simplicity; but it has little *prima facie* plausibility and I shall not pursue it further.[13]

Yet another possibility would be to employ *modal* expressions in the definitions of 'individual' and 'sort', saying something to the effect that X is an individual only if X *cannot* have instances (other than itself). The trouble with this is that there may perhaps be some *sorts* which cannot have individual instances, such as the mythological sorts *centaur*, *mermaid* and *dragon*, individual instances of which would arguably be at least *physically* impossible objects. However, here I am strongly inclined to retort that precisely because they would lack individual instances there cannot really *be* any such sorts as these at all: mythological sortal terms like those mentioned very arguably fail of reference, just as do mythological proper names like 'Pegasus' and

---

[13] But compare Leibniz's contention that 'what St. Thomas [Aquinas] assures us on this point of angels or intelligences (*quod ibi individuum sit species infima*) is true of all substances' (*Discourse on Metaphysics*, trans. P.G. Lucas and L. Grant (Manchester: Manchester University Press, 1961), p. 14).

'Hercules'.[14] In short, the position I am inclined to adopt is that there cannot be *infimae species* lacking individual instances, not because there cannot be *infimae species*, but because there cannot be species or sorts *at all* that altogether lack individual instances. (There can, of course, be species like the *dodo* no individual instances of which still exist, but that is a different matter.) If this is correct, then the definitions of *individual* and *sort* proposed earlier may be allowed to stand, without any need to introduce modal considerations.

---

[14] Cf. Geach, *Reference and Generality*, 3rd edn, p. 217.

4

The Absoluteness of Identity: A Defence

I shall devote this chapter to examining in some detail two arguments presented by Geach purporting to show that a sentence of the form '*a* is the same ϕ as *b*' (where '*a*' and '*b*' are non-empty particular or individual terms and 'ϕ' is a sortal term or, in Geach's terminology, a 'substantival general term') is never analysable as '*a* is (a) ϕ and *b* is (a) ϕ and *a* is the same as *b* (or *a* is identical with *b*)', the implication of which would seem to be that 'there is no such absolute identity as logicians have assumed.'[1] On Geach's own view, '*a* is the same as *b*' can itself only be understood as elliptical for some sentence of the form '*a* is the same ϕ as *b*'. Moreover, according to Geach, '*a* is the same ϕ as *b*' may be true while '*a* is the same ψ as *b*' is false. As he says, 'On my own view of identity I could not object in principle to different [ψs] being one and the same [ϕ].'[2] This contention has now become known as the thesis of the *relativity of identity*.[3]

The two arguments of which I speak occur separately in successive editions – the second and third – of Geach's book

---

[1] P.T. Geach, *Reference and Generality*, 3rd edn (Ithaca: Cornell University Press, 1980), p. 216.
[2] Ibid., p. 181.
[3] See David Wiggins, *Sameness and Substance* (Oxford: Blackwell, 1980), p. 16.

Reference and Generality.[4] The argument of the third edition is expressly intended to replace that of the second; though it would appear from Geach's remarks in the Preface to the third edition that he has not been persuaded to regard the earlier argument as being in any way fallacious, but rather sees it as involving unnecessary complications concerning the distinction between count and mass nouns.[5]

My overall strategy will be as follows. I shall begin by presenting and discussing the argument Geach offers in the *third* edition of *Reference and Generality*, suggest a way of rebutting it, and examine how Geach may be expected to react to this sort of rebuttal. I shall then argue that if Geach does take this expected line of counter-attack his position lays itself open to *another* sort of objection which can in fact also be directed at the argument he originally presented in the *second* edition of *Reference and Generality*.

So let us consider first of all the argument that Geach presents in the third edition of *Reference and Generality*, which I shall call (for reasons which will become plain) his 'men and heralds' argument. (I shall call the other, second edition argument his 'water and rivers' argument.) Geach invites us to consider the following two sentences:[6]

1 Lord Newriche discussed armorial bearings with some herald yesterday and discussed armorial bearings with the same herald again today

and

2 Lord Newriche discussed armorial bearings with some man yesterday and discussed armorial bearings with the same man again today.

---

[4] Geach, *Reference and Generality*, 3rd edn and 2nd edn (Ithaca: Cornell University Press, 1968).
[5] See ibid., 3rd edn, p. 14.
[6] Ibid., pp. 174f. I have altered Geach's numbering.

Now, both (1) and (2) contain expressions of the form 'the same φ', where 'φ' is a sortal term, namely, 'the same herald' and 'the same man' respectively. (I am assuming here for the sake of argument that 'herald' qualifies as a genuine sortal term, though doubt will be thrown on this assumption later.) Geach evidently considers, and he is surely right, that if '*a* is the same φ as *b*' were always analysable as '*a* is (a) φ and *b* is (a) φ and *a* is the same as *b*', then (1) and (2) would have to be analysable as equivalent to the following two sentences respectively:

1* For some x, x is a herald and Lord Newriche discussed armorial bearings with x yesterday and discussed armorial bearings with x again today

and

2* For some x, x is a man and Lord Newriche discussed armorial bearings with x yesterday and discussed armorial bearings with x again today.

However, Geach argues that (1) and (2) *cannot* be analysed as being equivalent to (1*) and (2*) respectively, for the following simple reason. It is clear that

3 Whatever is a herald is a man

is true, and is moreover equivalent to

3* For any x, if x is a herald, then x is a man.

However, (1*) and (3*) together entail (2*), whereas (1) and (3) certainly do *not* entail (2), since (2) may well be false even though (1) is true (e.g., if there has been an overnight change of personnel in the College of Heralds). Hence, Geach concludes, it cannot be the case that (1) and (2) are equivalent to (1*) and (2*) respectively, and so cannot be the case that '*a* is the same herald (man) as *b*' is analysable as '*a* is a herald (man) and *b* is a herald (man) and *a* is the same as *b*'. Moreover, the implication seems to be that '*a* is the same φ as *b*' is *never* thus analysable, whatever sortal term 'φ' may be, since the man/herald example was, it appears, in no way peculiar.

When Geach concludes that (1) and (2) are not analysable as (1*) and (2*) respectively, he rests this conclusion on an extremely important assumption, which we have so far ignored. This is that these two analyses 'stand or fall together'.[7] (To say this is just to say that (1) is analysable as (1*) *if and only if* (2) is analysable as (2*).) Geach mentions this in passing, but oddly enough without attempting to justify the claim. Clearly, without this assumption, the most that Geach would be entitled to infer from the fact that (1*) and (3*) entail (2*) while (1) and (3) do not entail (2) is that *either* (1) is not analysable as (1*) *or* (2) is not analysable as (2*). I mention this because it seems that one very obvious line of attack on Geach's position will be to say that while (1) is *not* analysable as (1*), (2) certainly *is* analysable as (2*). On this view, there is a very significant difference between a sentence of the form '*a* is the same *herald* as *b*' and one of the form '*a* is the same *man* as *b*', such that the latter *is*, while the former *is not*, analysable in the way Geach rejects quite generally for sentences of the form '*a* is the same φ as *b*'. Also, on this view, there is a related difference between a sentence of the form '*a* is a herald' and one of the form '*a* is a man'.

What these differences amount to, according to this anti-Geachian view, is just this. To say that *a is a herald* is not to say what *sort* or *kind* of thing *a* is, in the way that to say that *a is a man* standardly is; rather, it is to say that *a* occupies a certain heraldic office, carrying with it certain titles and duties (and accordingly, on this view, 'herald' is not in fact a genuine sortal term). Correspondingly, to say that *a* and *b*

---

[7] Ibid., p. 176.

are the *same* herald is only to say that (presumably at different times) they occupy or have occupied the same heraldic office. Hence, when it is said (as in (1)) that Lord Newriche discussed armorial bearings with *the same herald* on two successive days, it is not, on this view, implied (as in (1*)) that there is *any single individual object of any sort* with which Lord Newriche stood in some relation on both of these two successive days. But precisely this *is* implied, according to this view, when it is said (as in (2)) that Lord Newriche discussed armorial bearings with *the same man* on two successive days. (Observe that on this view – which I am personally strongly inclined to endorse – it may certainly be allowed that, while 'herald' is not a genuine sortal term, only *things of a certain sort* may be heralds – i.e. may occupy heraldic offices – namely, *men*. This indeed is what (3) may be understood as affirming. Thus it may certainly be allowed that 'a is a herald' *implies* 'a is a man'. Allowing this is, in particular, quite consistent with a denial of the Geachian assumption that the two analyses 'stand or fall together'. For, while accepting the analysis of (2) as (2*), it may be urged that (1), instead of being analysed as (1*), should be analysed as, say, 'For some x, y and z, Lord Newriche discussed armorial bearings with x yesterday and with y today, z is an heraldic office, and x occupied z yesterday and y occupied z today'.)

So, if this view is tenable, all that Geach's argument succeeds in showing is that 'a is the same herald as b' is not analysable as 'a is a herald and b is a herald and a is the same as b'; which is something that holders of the view in question would want to urge anyway. Unless Geach can prove that the two analyses really do 'stand or fall together', he has therefore done nothing whatever to give us reason to think that a sentence of the form 'a is the same ϕ as b' is never analysable in the way he rejects. Adherents of the view I have just outlined may contend that such a sentence is in fact always thus analysable *provided that* the entailed sentence 'a is (a) ϕ' is used to state what *sort* or *kind* of thing a is, i.e.

provided that '*a* is (a) φ' is what I have earlier called an *instantiation sentence*.

In order to rebut objections of the foregoing kind, Geach clearly has to argue that sentences of the forms '*a* is a herald' and '*a* is a man' are *logically isomorphous*: that 'is' is not used here in two quite different senses. Now, Geach does in fact advance the view that, quite generally, a sentence of the form '*a* is (a) φ', where 'φ' is a term like 'man' or 'herald', is to be analysed as meaning '*a* is the same φ as *something*',[8] and it may be thought that this has some bearing on the isomorphism issue. However, even someone subscribing to the anti-Geachian view that I have just outlined can in fact accept that '*a* is a herald' and '*a* is a man' are at least *logically equivalent* to '*a* is the same herald as something' and '*a* is the same man as something' respectively, without in any way compromising his contention that '*a* is a herald' and '*a* is a man' are not logically isomorphous: for he can insist that '*a* is the same herald as something' and '*a* is the same man as something' are *themselves* not logically isomorphous, on the grounds that 'same herald' and 'same man' do not function logically in the same way. In fact, of course, that '*a* is (a) φ' is *logically equivalent* to '*a* is the same φ as something' is just trivially true, in virtue of the logical truth that any φ is the same φ as *itself*. Geach's view does, it is true, involve the more substantial claim that '*a* is a man' (for instance) is a 'derelativization' of '*a* is the same man as something', in much the way that '*a* is a mother' is a derelativization of '*a* is the mother of someone',[9] the implication being that sentences of the form '*a* is the same φ as something' are logically and semantically prior to ones of the form '*a* is (a) φ'. However, this more substantial claim itself relies upon the very success of his argument that '*a* is the same φ as *b*' is not to be analysed as '*a* is (a) φ and *b* is (a) φ and *a* is the same as *b*', which is precisely here in question. Altogether, then,

---

[8] Ibid., p. 213.
[9] Ibid., p. 214.

nothing that Geach has to say regarding the relationship between 'a is (a) φ' and 'a is the same φ as something' can go any way at all towards showing, what he needs at present to show, that 'a is a herald' and 'a is a man' are logically isomorphous, so that we may dismiss this line of thought completely.

What, I think, needs to be made clear is that Geach's commitment to the logical isomorphism of 'a is a herald' and 'a is a man' carries with it a certain *ontological* commitment. This is that the ostensibly sortal term 'herald', no less than the sortal term 'man', really designates a *sort* or *kind* of concrete, physical object. Geach, it seems, must take the view that a heraldic name such as (to use one of his own examples) 'Bluemantle' denotes a concrete, physical object of which a series of different men may be successive 'temporal phases'. Such an object may, moreover, have an intermittent or interrupted existence, since there may be intervals during which no man is (i.e. is the same herald as) Bluemantle. As Geach himself puts it, 'a herald like Bluemantle has not even spatio-temporal continuity over the years.'[10] So Geach's ontology apparently includes, in addition to men, a further sort or kind of object, namely heralds. Geach can, it seems, have no sympathy at all for the view that to be a herald is just to occupy some heraldic office. To speak of heraldic offices is to speak of *abstract* entities of a certain kind; what Geach is doing, in effect, is to reject talk of these in favour of talk of a (hitherto unrecognized!) kind of *concrete* entity. (Geachian heralds are *concrete*, inasmuch as their existence is spatiotemporally bound, albeit not necessarily continuous; they are moreover *physical*, because made of flesh and blood.)

Is anything to be said in favour of Geach's ostensibly uncommonsensical ontology? There are, I think, serious

---

[10] Ibid., p. 206. See also Geach's paper 'Existential or Particular Quantifier?', in P. Weingartner and E. Morscher (eds), *Ontology and Logic* (Berlin: Duncker & Humblot, 1979), pp. 146–7.

difficulties in it, not least in connection with the notion of intermittent or interrupted existence, which it seems committed to endorsing. However, I do not want to go into these problems here, interesting though they are.[11] What I want to try to show now is that *even if we grant* Geach these ontological flights of fancy, his argument still goes no way at all towards showing that 'a is the same φ as b' is never analysable as 'a is (a) φ and b is (a) φ and a is the same as b'. This is because, as I shall try to explain, if we concede that 'a is a herald' and 'a is a man' (as it is standardly used) *are* logically isomorphous, then it turns out in fact that Geach's premise

3* For any x, if x is a herald, then x is a man

must be false. The consequence of this will be, of course, that the truth of (1*) is quite as consistent with the falsehood of (2*) as is the truth of (1) with the falsehood of (2), so that there will be, after all, *no* evidence to deny that (1) and (2) may be analysed as (1*) and (2*) respectively (accepting still Geach's ontological revisions).

In order to make my argument plainer, it will be helpful to move at this point to a consideration of Geach's argument concerning water and rivers in the *second* edition of *Reference and Generality*.[12] This is the argument which is replaced in the third edition by the men and heralds argument. In the water and rivers argument, Geach again presents us with two groups of three sentences, corresponding to sentences (1), (2) and (3) and (1*), (2*) and (3*) above. The sentences in question are as follows. First, the counterparts of (1), (2) and (3) respectively are:

4 Heraclitus bathed in some river yesterday, and bathed in the same river today,

---

[11] I discuss some of them in my 'On the Identity of Artifacts', *Journal of Philosophy* 80 (1983), pp. 220–32.

[12] See Geach, *Reference and Generality*, 2nd edn, pp. 150–1.

5   Heraclitus bathed in some water yesterday, and bathed in the same water today

and

6   Whatever is a river is water.

Secondly, the counterparts of (1*), (2*) and (3*) respectively are:

4* For some x, x is a river and Heraclitus bathed in x yesterday and Heraclitus bathed in x today,

5* For some x, x is water and Heraclitus bathed in x yesterday and Heraclitus bathed in x today

and

6* For any x, if x is a river, then x is water.

Now once again Geach's argument is that (4*) and (6*) entail (5*) whereas (4) and (6) do not entail (5), and similarly his conclusion is that (4) and (5) cannot be analysed as being equivalent to (4*) and (5*) respectively, the implication being that 'a is the same river (water) as b' is not analysable as 'a is a river (water) and b is a river (water) and a the same as b'.

The advantage of considering the water and rivers argument is that we may at least be able to agree that sentences of the forms 'a is a river' and 'a is water' *can* be interpreted in a sense in which they are logically isomorphous, whereas this was much more contentious with sentences of the forms 'a is a herald' and 'a is a man'. (As I explained earlier, in connection with the men and heralds argument, Geach's strategy – which is the same in both of his arguments – commits him on the logical isomorphism issue, since opponents who dispute that the relevant pairs of sentences are logically isomorphous may object to his arguments simply by denying that the relevant pairs of analyses 'stand or fall together'.) What we may be able to agree, then, is that both '*a* is a river' and '*a* is water' can be interpreted as being, in my terminology, *instantiation sentences*, and thus as saying of an individual *a* that it is a certain *sort* or *kind* of concrete, physical object. Certainly, this is a position to which I have already implicitly committed *myself*, in the previous chapter.

Now it is true, I concede, that others may question my assumption that '*a* is water' can be interpreted as an instantiation sentence on a par with '*a* is a river' – simply because they do not accept as I do that both count *and* mass nouns qualify as sortal terms, insisting instead that they have a different logical grammar. But on this view '*a* is water' and '*a* is a river' *cannot* be interpreted as logically isomorphous at all, from which it will follow that (4*) and (5*) cannot, as Geach requires, be assumed to 'stand or fall together' as analyses of (4) and (5) respectively: someone holding such a view might accept that (4) is analysable as (4*) but not that (5) is analysable as (5*). (I imagine that it was precisely in the light of such possible objections that Geach replaced the water and rivers argument by one involving only count nouns.) This, then, is a view that we are not *obliged* to take into account here, inimical as it is both to Geach's water and rivers argument *and* to an assumption that I myself am inclined to make in arguing against Geach. Nonetheless, it is in fact possible, I believe, to modify both Geach's argument and my response to it in a way which will neither do any injustice to Geach nor conflict with my own principles but which will at the same time accommodate the sensitivities of those holding the sort of view I have alluded to. This may be done by utilizing the fact that 'water' is used in English not *only* as a mass noun but *also* as a count noun. (The *Shorter Oxford English Dictionary* includes the following entries under 'water', both of which exemplify a count noun use: 'Water regarded as collected in seas, lakes, etc., or as flowing in rivers or streams' and 'A body of water on the surface of the earth'.) Thus one may quite properly speak of *a* water and of water*s*, meaning thereby a *body* or *bodies* of water. The only modification to Geach's water and rivers argument required in order to exploit this point of grammar is the replacement, in sentences (6), (5*) and (6*), of the predicate '— is water' by the predicate '— is *a* water'. I shall therefore assume, henceforth, that just such a replacement may be taken as read.

Of course, I would want to say, very much as I imagine Wiggins would, that each of the sentences '*a* is a river' and '*a* is (a) water' can *also* be used in distinctive *constitutive* senses: '*a* is a river' as saying that *a* (which may be a certain body of water) *constitutes* a river, and '*a* is (a) water' as saying that *a* (which may be a certain river) *is constituted by* water.[13] Geach, though, would naturally *not* want to acknowledge such a plurality of senses: indeed, the issue between Geach (the relativist) and Wiggins (the absolutist) turns in the present case very much on the question of whether an 'is' of constitution has to be recognized, so of course its existence cannot at this stage just be assumed. However, all I am proposing at the moment is that the sentences '*a* is a river' and '*a* is (a) water' can at least both be interpreted as *instantiation* sentences, and in this way (but only in this way) be seen as logically isomorphous, as Geach's argument requires.

But now there immediately arises a difficulty for Geach. If, in (6*), '*x* is a river' and '*x* is (a) water' *are* thus interpreted as logically isomorphous, it soon becomes apparent that under such an interpretation (6*) *cannot be true*. This, at bottom, is because rivers and waters have *different criteria of identity*, and an individual of one sort or kind cannot also belong to another sort or kind with a different criterion of identity from that of the first. I shall argue this point in detail in a little while, but before doing so I want to broaden the perspective of the discussion somewhat. Let us begin, then,

---

[13] See Wiggins, *Sameness and Substance*, p. 30.

by asking quite generally when precisely it is that an individual x can simultaneously be an instance of each of two sorts or kinds, ϕ and ψ. There must be *some* restriction here, and what it is, I suggest, is this. An individual x may be an instance of each of two distinct sorts ϕ and ψ only if *either* ϕ and ψ are related as species to genus *or else* there is some further sort χ, instantiated by x, such that χ is a sub-sort of both ϕ and ψ.[14] Formally, we seem to have the following principle as a logical truth:

$$x/\phi \ \& \ x/\psi \rightarrow \phi = \psi \vee \phi/\psi \vee \psi/\phi \vee (\exists \chi)(x/\chi \ \& \ \chi/\phi \ \& \ \chi/\psi).$$

For example, Fido may be an instance of both the dog kind and the mammal kind, since dogs are a species of mammal. But Fido could not be an instance of both the mammal kind and the amphibian kind, for not only are mammals and amphibians not related as species to genus, but also there is not even any *sub*-species of mammal that is also a *sub*-species of amphibian to which Fido might belong (thus there is not, for instance, any *hybrid* kind related to mammals and amphibians in the way, say, that tigons are related to tigers and lions). To this it might be objected that one and the same individual x may at one time be, say, a caterpillar and at another a butterfly, even though caterpillars are not a *kind* of butterfly nor butterflies a *kind* of caterpillar, nor do they have any common sub-kind. But then mightn't this be precisely why x cannot be both *at the same time*, which is all that the principle implies? So it seems that we don't have a counterexample here at all, but *if anything* further confirmation. (It may be noted, incidentally, that sortal terms like 'caterpillar' and 'butterfly' are what Wiggins calls *phased* sortals.[15] Their special peculiarities do not at present concern me, but I shall say more about them shortly. I should add, though, that what I *shall* say will in fact undermine the

---

[14] Cf. ibid., pp. 201–4. Wiggins's objections to principles excluding the possibility of 'cross-classification' do not seem to touch the principle that I enunciate here.
[15] Ibid., p. 24.

suggestion that sortal terms like these are proper substituends for the sortal variables 'ϕ', 'ψ' and 'χ' in the formal principle I have proposed, thus further undercutting the alleged counterexample.)

Now, in view of the principle just stated, how could a single individual x be both an instance of the river kind and an instance of the water kind? For rivers are surely not a *kind* or *species* of water (in the way, say, that heavy water is), nor water(s) of rivers; nor does it appear that we can even say that there is any sub-species of river that is also a sub-species of water. However, I imagine that some may feel that what I say here turns on an equivocation in my use of the sortal term 'water', in particular an equivocation over its use as a mass noun and its use as a count noun. When I say that rivers are not a *kind* of water in the way that heavy water is, it seems clear that I must be using 'water' as a *mass* noun, to speak of a sort of *stuff*. But may it not be urged that when 'water' is used as a *count* noun, it is after all extremely plausible to say that rivers are a kind of water, other such kinds being lakes, seas and oceans? To this I would reply as follows. I am prepared to concede the point that what I said earlier illicitly traded on an ambiguity, but at the same time I am not prepared to concede that rivers after all *are* a kind of water – *not, at least, in a sense that offers any comfort to Geach*. Let me explain. It seems clear that *even used as a count noun* 'water' has two quite distinct senses. In one of these senses, a water is something with *the same criterion of identity* as a river, but in the other sense not. In the first sense, a water is something whose identity through time (i.e. whose continuing to be the *same* water) is not impugned by the addition to it or removal from it of various quantities of water. (This is the sense in which the Cumbrian lake Wastwater is *a water*.) In the second sense this is not so. But, of course, it is the *second* sense that must be at work in the (modified) water and rivers argument, since in the *first* sense there is no pressure at all to say that Heraclitus bathed in the same river but *not* the same water on two successive days.

However, in this second sense of 'water', it is very far from platitudinous to say that a river is a kind of water: indeed, I think it is plainly false. And hence one may still appeal to the principle formulated earlier in order to deny that any individual x could be both an instance of the river kind and an instance of the water kind (in the relevant sense of 'water kind').

However, I doubt whether the foregoing argument would make much impression on anyone not already favourably disposed towards its conclusion: a pro-Geachian would be only too ready to attempt to reverse it into a refutation of the formal principle previously enunciated. It would be more satisfactory, therefore, to tackle the issue head-on, and try to show quite generally that whenever an individual x belongs to each of two different sorts ϕ and ψ, these sorts cannot (as rivers and waters – in the relevant sense – clearly do) have different criteria of identity. (Observe that a demonstration of this would not in itself amount to a validation of the formal principle proposed earlier, though it would at least vindicate the proposition that sorts which stand in the species–genus relationship must share the same criterion of identity. Evidently, the formal principle itself is far stronger than anything that can be established by considerations merely involving criteria of identity, since – as we saw earlier – that principle imposes its restrictions even with regard to sortal terms which share the *same* criterion of identity, such as 'mammal' and 'amphibian'.)

Now, an argument of the kind we seek is not in fact particularly difficult to find. Suppose, for the purposes of a *reductio*, that an individual x *did* belong to each of two sorts ϕ and ψ whose respective criteria of identity, C_ϕ and C_ψ, were different. Then it seems that we could not in general rule out *a priori* the possibility that there should arise circumstances in which, according to C_ϕ (say), x would *cease to exist*, whereas according to C_ψ it would *not*; so that anyone asserting that x instantiated both ϕ and ψ would be laying himself open to the intolerable possibility that circumstances should arise in which he would be obliged to say that *x both did and did not* cease to exist. This presupposes, of course, that the criterion of identity for a sort φ determines conditions under which individuals of that sort will continue or cease to exist (their *persistence* conditions) – which, however, seems uncontroversial, at least in the case of contingent, concrete individuals such as presently concern us. (I do not claim, thus, that this sort of argument is *directly* applicable to abstract individuals like sets; though to the extent that the argument vindicates the absolutist conception of identity in the case of concrete individuals, it renders unattractive and uneconomical any adherence to the relativist conception in the case of abstract individuals.)

As far as I can see, the only way to evade the conclusion of this argument would be to attempt to relativize the very concept of *existence* itself to sortal distinctions – saying, for instance, that *x* might cease to exist *qua* φ but continue to exist *qua* ψ. I need hardly say how unpalatable are the prospects of attempting to defend such a conception of existence; indeed, it is not a conception that I can even begin to comprehend. (It should not surprise us, incidentally, that an adherence to a relativist conception of identity should carry with it an implicit commitment to a relativist conception of existence, since the notions of identity and existence are intimately related. On one quite plausible view, to say that *a* exists is indeed just logically equivalent to saying that there is something which is (i.e. is identical with) *a*: $E!a \longleftrightarrow (\exists x) x = a$. To discuss this view adequately, however, would require a digression on the role of quantifiers which would take us too far afield at present.)

Perhaps, though, it will not be immediately apparent that the prospects of relativizing existence really are as repugnant as I say. After all, we are happy to talk about someone ceasing to be a boy but continuing to be a human being (or, again, of something ceasing to be a caterpillar but continuing to be an insect). But we should be careful here not to suppose that 'ceasing to be a boy' means 'ceasing to be, *qua* boy' in the sense that a relativist conception of existence would demand. For, of course, an absolutist in matters of existence and identity can quite happily handle the former sort of expression. In fact, it seems clear that a so-called phased sortal like 'boy' is just a syntactically simple but *semantically complex* sortal term, being analysable as synonymous with some such semantically *and* syntactically complex sortal term as 'young, male human being'. As such it does not, in my view, denote a distinct *sort* or *kind* of individuals at all (a point I shall argue for in a later chapter); moreover, although it does have a criterion of identity associated with it, the criterion in question is just that associated with the unqualified sortal term 'human being'. For these reasons, then, it should not for a moment be imagined that examples like that of someone ceasing to be a boy but continuing to be a human being support a relativist notion of something ceasing to exist *qua* ϕ but continuing to exist *qua* ψ where ϕ and ψ have different criteria of identity.

Let me now just illustrate the general argument advanced above by reference to the particular case of rivers and waters, which plainly do (in the relevant sense of 'water') have different criteria of identity. Without attempting to *state* these criteria, we can at least say that the criteria in question are such that should *part* of a water be destroyed or removed (e.g. by molecular dissociation or by evaporation), then *that* water ceases to exist and what remains is a *different* water; whereas in these same circumstances (destruction or removal of some quantity of water in it) a *river* by no means ceases to exist, but merely becomes diminished in volume. This, however, means that 'Scamander', say, cannot denote an individual which is *both* a water *and* a river, since if it did we should have to say, in the circumstances just envisaged, that Scamander *both did and did not* cease to exist, which is absurd.

A philosopher of Geach's persuasion might urge at this point that it is allowable to say that the river Scamander *is (a) water* even though the proper name 'Scamander' has associated with it *only* the criterion of identity associated with the sortal term 'river' and not that associated with the sortal term 'water', i.e. that it is erroneous to suppose that where x is both (a) φ and (a) ψ, x must comply with the criteria of identity of *both* of these sorts or kinds.[16] *But I can agree with this*. I only maintain that where this is so and the criteria of identity in question are thus different, it follows that the two occurrences of 'is' in 'x is (a) φ' and 'x is (a) ψ' are not univocal: they cannot *both* be the 'is' of instantiation. This is because it is abundantly clear that if 'x is (a) φ' *is* used to say that x is an instance of the kind φ (i.e. if the 'is' is that of instantiation), then x must indeed comply with the criterion of identity of φ. In short, the supporter of Geach cannot have it both ways: he cannot claim *both* that 'x is (a) φ' and 'x is (a) ψ' may both be true where φ and ψ have different criteria of identity *and* that the two occurrences of 'is' in these sentences are univocal. (I shall, however, attempt to eliminate any lingering doubts there may be about this matter in the next chapter.)

Let me now make fully explicit what my objection to Geach's water and rivers argument is. In order that (4*) and (5*) should 'stand or fall together' as analyses of (4) and (5) respectively, it is necessary that 'x is a river' as it appears in (4*) should be logically isomorphous with 'x is (a) water' as it appears in (5*). So in order that (4*) and (6*) should entail (5*) it is necessary also that 'x is a river' and 'x is (a) water' *as they appear in* (6*) should be logically isomorphous (since otherwise the inference from (4*) and (6*) to (5*) would simply involve a fallacy of equivocation). But if 'x is a river' and 'x is (a) water' as they appear in (6*) *are* interpreted as logically isomorphous, i.e. as both being open instantiation sentences, then, for the reason already explained, (6*) *must be false*, contrary to what Geach requires. (6*) can only be regarded as true under an interpretation which does *not*

---

[16] Geach himself says something along these lines: see his *Reference and Generality*, 3rd edn, pp. 216f.

treat both its antecedent and its consequent as open instantiation sentences, e.g. under an interpretation which treats '*x* is a river' as an open instantiation sentence but '*x* is (a) water' as involving an 'is' of constitution, in Wiggins's sense. But under such an interpretation any inference from (4*) and (6*) to (5*) must involve a fallacy of equivocation, with '*x* is (a) water' having different senses in (5*) and (6*), since it is evident that no one holding that (5) is analysable as (5*), while also denying that (4) implies (5), would want to say that '*x* is (a) water' *as it appears in* (5*) involves an 'is' of constitution. It is clear then that an argument from (4*) and (6*) to (5*) is no more available than is an argument from (4) and (6) to (5), and hence that Geach's objection to analysing (4) and (5) in terms of (4*) and (5*) respectively fails.[17]

I am now in a position to relate my criticism of the water and rivers argument to the men and heralds argument. The lesson we may draw is that, even if we concede, for the sake of argument, that there *is* a use of a sentence like '*a* is a herald' in which it is logically isomorphous with one like '*a* is a man', namely, a sense in which each of these sentences says of something *a* that it is a certain *sort* or *kind* of thing, it is nonetheless clear that the sorts or kinds in question must have *different criteria of identity*,[18] and hence that (3*), when both its antecedent and its consequent are interpreted in *this* way, must be false. For even if we allow Geach his strange ontology of heraldic entities, with their intermittent or interrupted existence, it is plain enough that no individual instance of *this* sort of thing could *also* be an individual instance of the sort *man*, any more than an individual instance of the river kind can also be an individual instance of the water kind. After all, men, unlike Geach's heralds, do *not* have an intermittent existence extending (potentially, at

---

[17] This diagnosis of the flaw in Geach's water and rivers argument is close to that favoured by Michael Dummett: see his *Frege: Philosophy of Language* (London: Duckworth, 1973), p. 575.

[18] Geach himself concedes as much when he says 'There is no one criterion of identity for men and for heralds' (*Reference and Generality*, 3rd edn, p. 206).

least) over many centuries: on the contrary, they are born, live out their allotted span of some three score years and ten (without interruption!), and then die. Hence nothing can *be* both a man and a Geachian herald, in that sense of 'be' which corresponds to the 'is' of instantiation. Yet, clearly, it is precisely this sense of 'is' that has to be seen in '*x* is a herald' and '*x* is a man' *as they appear in* (1*) *and* (2*) *respectively*, by anyone attempting to defend against Geach the view that the latter two sentences are equivalent, respectively, to (1) and (2), while also accepting that (1) does not imply (2). And from this it will follow, just as in the water and rivers case, that only under an interpretation under which it is *false* can (3*) be seen as conjoinable with (1*) to give (2*). (I should emphasize, however, that I myself do *not* want to defend the view that (1) is analysable as (1*), but only the view that (2) is analysable as (2*).)

It will be recalled that the lesson that Geach himself wanted to draw was that '*a* is the same ϕ as *b*' is never to be analysed as '*a* is (a) ϕ and *b* is (a) ϕ and *a* is the same as *b*'. But now I don't see why we shouldn't say just this (provided that 'ϕ' is a genuine sortal term). We can still concede (as Wiggins would also have it) that any identity sentence of the form '*a* is the same as *b*' (or '*a* is identical with *b*') must in principle be expandable into the form '*a* is the same ϕ as *b*'.[19] But we should see this now as telling us not so much something about *identity* (e.g. that there is no such thing as *the* identity relation, but only a family of sortally relativized identity relations), as something about the individuation of particulars. As I have already stressed, particulars are only individuable at all *qua* instances of given sorts or kinds: so *any* use of a singular or individual term '*a*' presupposes the existence of some sort ϕ of which *a* is an instance.[20] Hence,

---

[19] See Wiggins, *Sameness and Substance*, pp. 15ff.

[20] Such a use, though, need not presuppose that the user of '*a*' has a *specific* sortal term in mind: cf. ibid., p. 48. The user must, however, grasp whatever criterion of identity is associated with '*a*', according to my contentions of the previous chapter.

more specifically, given any significant *identity sentence* '*a* is the same as *b*', there must at least be certain sorts φ and ψ (the same or different) which *a* and *b* respectively instantiate. So the truth of '*a* is the same as *b*' will imply that there is a true sentence of the form '*a* is (a) φ and *a* is the same as *b*' (and, equally, one of the form '*b* is (a) ψ and *a* is the same as *b*'). But, by Leibniz's law, '*a* is (a) φ and *a* is the same as *b*' implies '*a* is (a) φ and *b* is (a) φ and *a* is the same as *b*', which is just equivalent (on the proposed analysis, rescued now from Geach's attack) to '*a* is the same φ as *b*'. (The appeal to Leibniz's law here begs no question against the relative identity theorist, since I am only trying to show that the absolutist can explain, on his own terms, why '*a* is the same as *b*' should be expandable in the way suggested; and the absolutist does of course accept Leibniz's law.) So we can very readily understand why every identity sentence of the form '*a* is the same as *b*' must be expandable into one of the form '*a* is the same φ as *b*', *without* this implying that '*a* is the same as *b*' is somehow elliptical, or that '*a* is the same φ as *b*' is in any sense the logically prior form. We can retain the classical view that there is just *one*, univocal identity relation. And then, of course, we must also discard the thesis of the relativity of identity.[21]

I should just mention in passing that Geach apparently has, at least by implication, *another* argument against the proposed analysis of '*a* is the same φ as *b*', in addition to the pair I have just been criticizing (the men and heralds and the water and rivers arguments). What Geach actually says is this. Having concluded, for the reasons we have been examining, that '*a* is the same φ as *b*' is not analysable as '*a* is (a) φ and *b* is (a) φ and *a* is the same as *b*', he remarks:[22]

> We have already by implication rejected this analysis; for it would mean that 'the same *F*' always made sense, for any

---

[21] See further the Appendix at the end of this chapter.
[22] Geach, *Reference and Generality*, 3rd edn, p. 176; my emphasis. I have used '*F*' in place of Geach's '*A*'.

predicable term '*F*'; and in introducing the notion of substantival terms we explicitly denied this view, *which would make all predicable terms substantival*.

But nothing said here invalidates my argument of the previous paragraph. To say, as I have said, that '*a* is the same φ as *b*', where 'φ' is a *sortal* (or 'substantival') term, *does* submit to this analysis isn't to imply that '*a* is (an) *F*' and '*b* is (an) *F*' and '*a* is the same as *b*', where '*F*' is *any* predicable term (e.g. 'red thing'), can always sensibly be combined to give '*a* is the same *F* as *b*'. So this second objection of Geach's has no force, and the absolute conception of identity remains unscathed.

Appendix: Some Formal Principles and Arguments

In this appendix I shall present in a formal way some of the theses that have been under debate in this chapter, with a view to displaying their logical relationships as perspicuously as possible. There are in particular three important theses to be considered, which are as follows. First, there is what may be called, for obvious reasons, the *Sortal Expandability Thesis*,

(S) $a = b \longleftrightarrow (\exists \phi)(a =_{\phi} b)$

according to which to say that *a* is the same as *b* (where '*a*' and '*b*' are *individual terms*, such as the proper names 'Cicero' and 'Tully' or 'Hesperus' and 'Phosphorus') is to say that *a* is the same *something* as *b* – as it might be, the same *man* or the same *planet* or whatnot. A formula of the form '$a =_{\gamma} b$' (a notation I borrow in slightly modified form from Wiggins) may be read as '*a* is the same γ as *b*', where 'γ' is a *sortal term* (like 'man' or 'planet'). In (S), 'φ' is a *sortal variable*. I take (S) to be a relatively uncontroversial thesis that can be accepted by absolutist and relativist alike (but see further my remarks at the end of this appendix).

The second important, but controversial, thesis we have to consider may be called, again for obvious reasons, the *Reducibility Thesis*,

(R) $a =_\gamma b \longleftrightarrow (a/\gamma \,\&\, b/\gamma \,\&\, a = b)$

according to which to say that a is the same γ as b is just to say that a is (a)γ and b is (a)γ and a is the same as b. (As hitherto, I use '/' to express the 'is' of instantiation.) And, finally, there is the *Absoluteness Thesis*,

(A) $(a =_\gamma b \,\&\, a/\delta \,\&\, b/\delta) \to a =_\delta b$

according to which if a is the same γ as b and a is (a) δ and b is (a) δ, then a is the same δ as b. To deny the validity of (A) is, of course, to uphold the thesis of the relativity of identity.

Concerning these theses, the following observations may be made. First of all, if (S) is true, we must surely accept that (R) holds in the *left-to-right* direction, i.e. that

(R_1) $a =_\gamma b \to (a/\gamma \,\&\, b/\gamma \,\&\, a = b)$

is true. For, surely, '$a =_\gamma b$' entails both 'a/γ' and 'b/γ'; and also obviously entails '$(\exists \phi) (a =_\phi b)$', which by (S) is equivalent to '$a = b$'. But it doesn't follow that (R) holds in the *right-to-left* direction, i.e. that this is true:

(R_2) $(a/\gamma \,\&\, b/\gamma \,\&\, a = b) \to a =_\gamma b$

However, if not only (S) but also (A) is true, then clearly (R_2) *must* be true. Proof: assume as hypothesis (i) $a/\gamma \,\&\, b/\gamma \,\&\, a = b$. By (S) it follows that (ii) $a/\gamma \,\&\, b/\gamma \,\&\, (\exists \phi) (a =_\phi b)$. Let $\phi = \delta$ (say): then we have (iii) $a/\gamma \,\&\, b/\gamma \,\&\, a =_\delta b$. But then by (A) it follows that (iv) $a =_\gamma b$. So (i) implies (iv), which is what (R_2) states: Q.E.D. We may thus conclude that anyone accepting both (S) and (A) must also accept (R).

THE ABSOLUTENESS OF IDENTITY

But what happens if one accepts both (S) and (R) – must one then also accept (A)? Clearly one must. Proof: assume as hypothesis (i) $a =_\gamma b$ & a/δ & b/δ. By (R) it follows that (ii) a/γ & b/γ & $a = b$ & a/δ & b/δ and hence that (iii) a/δ & b/δ & $a = b$. But again by (R) this implies (iv) $a =_\delta b$. So (i) implies (iv), which is what (A) states: Q.E.D. (Observe, however, that this proof does not in fact appeal to (S) at all.) We see, then, that, given the truth of (S), (R) is true *if and only if* (A) is true. Hence we can understand Geach's strategy which, as we saw in the present chapter, is to argue against (A) by arguing for the falsehood of (R).

So far I have not had any occasion to refer to *Leibniz's law* in this appendix, though that law has an obvious bearing on the debate between absolutism and relativism. Notice, then, that if Leibniz's law is accepted, (A) follows straightforwardly from (S). Proof: assume as hypothesis (i) $a =_\phi b$ & a/δ & b/δ. From this it follows that (ii) $(\exists\phi) (a =_\phi b)$ and hence by (S) that (iii) $a = b$. Now, presumably, it also follows from (i) that (iv) $a =_\delta a$ and hence, conjoining (iii) and (iv), that (v) $a = b$ & $a =_\delta a$, whence, by Leibniz's law, we may infer (vi) $a =_\delta b$. Thus – assuming Leibniz's law – (i) implies (vi), which is what (A) states: Q.E.D. We see, thus, that the relativist is committed to rejecting Leibniz's law (at least in its classical, unrestricted form).

There is one further principle which is of considerable interest and importance in the present context, and that is what might be called the *Sortal Individuation Thesis*,

(I) $(\forall x) (\exists\phi) (x/\phi)$

i.e. the thesis that every individual instantiates some *sort* or other (that everything is some *kind* of thing – there are no 'bare particulars'). It is worth mentioning that we can prove (S) if we assume (I), (R) and Leibniz's law. To prove that (S) holds in the left-to-right direction, assume as hypothesis (i) $a = b$. By (I) we know that $(\exists\phi)a/\phi$. Let $\phi = \gamma$ (say): then we have (iii) a/γ, and from (i) and (iii) by Leibniz's law there follows (iv) b/γ, so that we now have from (i), (iii) and (iv) that (v) $a = b$ & a/γ & b/γ. But from (v) by (R) there follows (vi) $a =_\gamma b$ and hence (vii) $(\exists \phi) (a =_\phi b)$. So (i) implies (vii), and the first half of the proof is complete. To prove the converse, assume as hypothesis (viii) $(\exists \phi) (a =_\phi b)$. Again let $\phi = \gamma$ (say): then we have (ix) $a =_\gamma b$ and from this by (R) there follows (x) a/γ & b/γ & $a = b$ and hence (xi) $a = b$. So (viii) implies (xi). Q.E.D. The significance of this result is that it shows that the absolutist, who is committed of course to the Reducibility Thesis (R) and to Leibniz's law, can establish the Sortal Expandability Thesis (S) *merely by appeal to the Sortal Individuation Thesis*, (I), and hence is in a position to *explain* the validity of (S) without having to concede that its validity implies the logical or conceptual priority of sortally restricted identity relations over the non-restricted variety: in short, without having to concede that (S) has to be understood as providing a *definition* of the unrestricted identity relation '='. (This is just the point I made more informally at the end of the present chapter.) The result is obviously quite vital, because without it it could be objected that (R) does not effect a genuine *reduction* or *analysis* of sortally restricted identity statements, on the grounds that the conjunct '$a = b$' on the righthand side of (R) can itself only be understood as a shorthand way of writing '$(\exists \phi) (a =_\phi b)$', which of course employs a sortally restricted identity relation.

5

Identity and Constitution

What I hope to have made clear, so far, is that Geach at least has offered no persuasive reason for thinking that the absolutist account of identity is untenable. However, it may not yet be quite so fully clear that the relativist account is not a viable alternative. It may be suspected that the two rival accounts are each internally consistent and coherent, and moreover that they present compensating advantages and disadvantages as regards their respective ontological commitments and their respective conceptions of the logic of identity and predication. Thus on the ontological side it may be pointed out that the relativist can eliminate commitment to such abstract entities as heraldic offices in favour of further commitment to merely concrete ones (Geachian heralds) – but only at the expense of having to countenance the notion of intermittent existence. And on the logical side it may be pointed out that the relativist economizes on the number of senses of 'is', eschewing the notion of an 'is' of constitution – but again only at the expense of having to countenance a logic of identity and predication considerably complicated by the absence of Leibniz's law in its classical form. However, this irenic picture of healthy rivalry is not one that I can endorse, since I do *not* consider that the relativist conception of identity is coherent. Indeed, I believe that I have already shown, by implication, that it is not. For the relativist conception is void of interest without a commitment on its part to the *thesis of the relativity of identity* – the thesis, that is, that a may be the same φ as b and yet not the same ψ. But putative examples of such relativity will, it seems clear, only arise where the sortal terms 'φ' and 'ψ' are conceived as having associated with them *different criteria of identity* (as in the case of 'river' and 'water'). And we have seen that in such cases it is not in fact possible to say that either a or b is (univocally) both (a) φ and (a) ψ. However, to make the case against relativism still clearer, by showing that recognition of a distinctive 'is' of constitution really is unavoidable, it may be helpful at this point to examine an intriguing paradox which Geach has recently presented as calling for a relativist solution. (Subsequently I shall go on to say a little about how I think the 'is' of constitution should be understood.)

In § 110 of the third edition of his book *Reference and Generality*, Geach presents the following puzzle or paradox. We are to suppose that a certain cat, Tibbles, is sitting on a mat; moreover, Tibbles is the only cat sitting on the mat. Since Tibbles is, we suppose, a normal cat, it has at least one thousand hairs. Geach continues:[1]

> Now let c be the largest continuous mass of feline tissue on the mat. Then for any of our 1,000 cat-hairs, say h_n, there is a proper part c_n of c which contains precisely all of c except the hair h_n; and every such part c_n differs in a describable way both from any other such part, say c_m, and from c as a whole. Moreover, fuzzy as the concept *cat* may be, it is clear that not only is c a cat, but also any part c_n is a cat: c_n would clearly be a cat were the hair h_n plucked out, and we cannot reasonably suppose that plucking out a hair *generates* a cat, so c_n must already have been a cat. So, contrary to our story, there was

---

[1] P.T. Geach, *Reference and Generality*, 3rd edn (Ithaca: Cornell University Press, 1980), p. 215.

not just one cat called 'Tibbles' sitting on the mat; there were at least 1,001 sitting there!

Geach concedes, of course, that this conclusion is absurd, but it is interesting to observe wherein he professes to detect the fallacy. He explains:[2]

> Everything falls into place if we realize that the number of cats on the mat is the number of *different cats* on the mat; and c_{13}, c_{279} and c are not three different cats, they are one and the same cat. Though none of these 1,001 lumps of feline tissue is the same lump of feline tissue as another, each *is* the same cat as any other: each of them, then, is a cat, but there is only one cat on the mat, and our original story stands.

Now I concede that this manoeuvre of Geach's saves the truth of the original story; but, as he says, there is a price to pay. 'The price to pay is that we must regard "——— is the same cat as . . ." as expressing only a certain equivalence relation, not an absolute identity restricted to cats.'[3] Geach, of course, is happy to pay this price, since he considers that it 'must be paid anyhow, for there is no such absolute identity as logicians have assumed',[4] and in defence of this contention he refers us to the earlier arguments in his book which we have already examined and found unsatisfactory. What I want to do now is to explain why I think that the truth of the original story can be saved far more plausibly without having to pay this price; and at the same time I shall try to show that Geach's resolution of the puzzle is in fact untenable.

Let me then say at once what my own solution to the paradox is. What I would say is that it is not merely *not* 'clear' (as Geach claims), but is in fact just *unintelligible* to suggest that the lump of feline tissue c (or any of the other lumps mentioned) *is a cat* – at least in the sense in which it is

---

[2] Ibid., p. 216.
[3] Ibid.
[4] Ibid.

correct to say that *Tibbles* 'is a cat'. *None* of the 1,001 lumps of feline tissue is a cat in this sense, so there is not even a *prima facie* case for saying that there are at least 1,001 cats sitting on the mat. The reason why I say this, of course, is that the sortal terms 'lump of feline tissue' and 'cat' have *different criteria of identity* associated with them, and as I have explained, I consider that no individual of a sort φ can intelligibly be said also to belong to a sort ψ if φ and ψ have different criteria of identity.

That these two sortal terms do indeed have different criteria of identity associated with them, and that Geach implicitly recognizes the fact, are things not difficult to show. For it is clear on the one hand that the criterion of identity for cats, however it might be framed in detail, is such that it implies that the removal or destruction of one of a cat's hairs is not as such sufficient for the termination of that cat's existence. By contrast, however, it is equally clear that Geach is using the expression 'lump of feline tissue' in such a way that the removal or destruction of the hair h_n would suffice to terminate the existence of the lump of feline tissue c of which the tissue in that hair formed a part. For after the removal or destruction of h_n what would remain would be the lump of feline tissue c_n, which Geach has made clear he regards as being a *different* lump of feline tissue from c (as indeed it obviously is); so that after such destruction or removal the lump of feline tissue c could no longer be said to exist, since there would no longer be in existence any lump of feline tissue which could properly be said to be the *same* lump of feline tissue as c.[5] In short, after the destruction or removal of h_n, c cannot survive as c_n since that has been acknowledged not to be the same lump of feline tissue as c; but if c cannot survive as c_n, it equally clearly cannot survive as any of the other lumps of feline tissue still remaining after

---

[5] Geach has in fact conceded in print that 'We need different criteria to decide whether Tibbles, who exists at time t, still exists at time t', and whether a lump c of feline tissue, which coincides with Tibbles at time t, still exists at time t'': see his 'Reply to Lowe's Reply', *Analysis* 42 (1982), p. 32.

the removal or destruction of h_n. The only way to try to evade this conclusion (that the removal or destruction of h_n would suffice to terminate c's existence) would be, once more, to try to relativize the very notion of *existence*, saying perhaps that although c might cease to exist *qua* lump of feline tissue, it could continue to exist *qua* cat (on the grounds, presumably, that after the removal or destruction of h_n there would still remain a cat, namely Tibbles, which was the same *cat* as c, even though there remained no lump of feline tissue which was the same *lump of feline tissue* as c). But I have already dismissed this sort of proposal as being of doubtful coherence, and in any case it is one which Geach himself clearly does *not* wish to endorse.[6] (Of course, what I have just been saying here concerning the criteria of identity for cats and lumps of feline tissue closely parallels what I said earlier about the criteria for rivers and waters; here, as before, I presuppose, what seems uncontroversial, that the criterion of identity for φs is a determinant of the *persistence conditions* of φs, provided at least that φs are contingent, concrete entities.)

Geach, we have seen, wants to say of the lump of feline tissue c (and equally of each of the other such lumps) that it *is a cat*. Moreover, it is crucial to his position that there is no ambiguity as between saying of c that it *is a cat* and saying of Tibbles that it *is a cat*. (For Geach, the predicate '— is a cat' is an *unambiguous* 'derelativization' of the predicate '— is the same cat as something'.) Once ambiguity is conceded the game is up for the relativist, since the case for a distinction between an 'is' of identity and an 'is' of constitution can then be made out. But such ambiguity *must* be conceded, as I shall now attempt to prove.

My reasoning is simple. Compare the sentences 'Tibbles is a cat' and 'c is a cat'. Let us grant that each sentence *is* true in *some* sense. It nonetheless must be the case that they are true in *different* senses. For the implication of saying that

---

[6] See ibid. for Geach's repudiation of any such proposal.

Tibbles is a cat is clearly that Tibbles complies with the criterion of identity associated with the sortal term 'cat' (and thus, for example, that Tibbles will not cease to exist merely upon the removal or destruction of a single hair). But, evidently, no such implication can attach to saying that c is a cat, in any sense in which this can be interpreted as true (since, for example, c *will* cease to exist upon the removal or destruction of a single hair – assuming again that we reject, as Geach himself does, a relativized notion of existence). So it seems that we must have here *two* different senses of '— is a cat', one of which demands that the subject of this predicate names something which complies with the criterion of identity associated with the sortal term 'cat', and the other of which does not. But once this is granted Geach's theory becomes untenable, and we are driven, as I have said, towards one like Wiggins's, which distinguishes between an 'is' of identity and an 'is' of constitution: c is a cat only in the sense that c *constitutes* a certain cat, namely, Tibbles.[7] (Moreover, it is worth pointing out here that once this is conceded it becomes most implausible to suppose that, prior to the removal or destruction of any hairs, any of the *other* lumps of feline tissue mentioned by Geach, such as c_n, *is a cat* even in the sense that c is. For none of these other lumps *does* (wholly) constitute Tibbles, though any of them might *come* to constitute Tibbles upon the removal or destruction of a certain hair. Geach is right in saying, in the passage quoted earlier, that 'c_n would . . . be a cat were the hair h_n plucked out', but only in the sense that c_n would then *constitute* a cat; however, once this is understood we can easily discern the fallacy in his going on to say 'and we cannot reasonably suppose that plucking out a hair *generates* a cat, so c_n must already have been a cat.' What plucking out a hair does is to bring it about that c_n, instead of c, is a cat, in the constitutive sense; but c_n's beginning to be a cat in this

---

[7] Leslie Stevenson offers a somewhat different argument for the same conclusion in his 'The Absoluteness of Identity', *Philosophical Books* 23 (1982), pp. 1–7.

sense obviously doesn't amount to the generation of a cat, i.e. the coming into existence of a cat.)

Is there any way in which a defender of Geach could respond to the foregoing objection? What seems undeniable is that 'Tibbles is a cat' implies that Tibbles complies with the criterion of identity associated with the sortal term 'cat', while '*c* is a cat', in any sense in which it can be interpreted as true, does *not* imply that *c* complies with this criterion. Now, I have assumed that the difference between the implications of these two sentences must be attributed to an ambiguity in the predicate '— is a cat'. But could it not instead be attributed to a difference in sense between the two names 'Tibbles' and '*c*'? After all, it may be said, any proper name, say '*N*', has associated with it the criterion of identity associated with a certain sortal term, the implication being that *N* must comply with that criterion. So it may be pointed out that 'Tibbles' and '*c*' differ precisely in that the former has associated with it the criterion of identity associated with the sortal term 'cat', while the latter has associated with it the criterion of identity associated with the sortal term 'lump of feline tissue'. Now, may it not be argued that the reason why, for instance, 'Tibbles is a cat' implies that Tibbles is something complying with the criterion of identity associated with the sortal term 'cat' has nothing to do with the sense of the predicate '— is a cat', but everything to do with the sense of the proper name 'Tibbles' (and the same, *mutatis mutandis*, as regards '*c* is a cat')? If so, it would seem to follow that '— is a cat' as it appears in these two sentences is *not* ambiguous.

My answer to this line of argument is as follows. I can *accept* (as will be clear from chapter 3) that the proper names 'Tibbles' and '*c*' have associated with them the criteria of identity associated with the sortal terms 'cat' and 'lump of feline tissue' respectively. However, I would urge that the very fact that proper names *do* have associated with them the criteria of identity associated with certain sortal terms, far from subserving the Geachian view that the predicate '— is a cat' is univocal, actually undermines that view. The point is that it is not as though (most) proper names wear their associated criteria of identity on their sleeves. ('Tibbles' is perhaps an atypical example in this respect, in that it is, purely by convention, rarely used as a name for *anything but* a cat.) Therefore we *need* a way of conveying to others *which particular sortal term's* criterion of identity is associated with the use of a given proper name, say 'N'. Suppose the sortal term in question is 'cat': then what *better* way of conveying this information is there than by saying 'N is a cat'? Natural language must possess a relatively simple way of conveying this important information, and there is, I think, no good reason to doubt that in English it is done by a certain use of the predicate '— is a cat'. But if so, and if it is *also* claimed that a sentence like 'c is a cat' may be interpreted as true even though 'c' does *not* have associated with it the criterion of identity associated with the sortal term 'cat', but another and incompatible criterion, it must inevitably follow that the predicate '— is a cat' is *not* being used in this latter sentence in the same way as it was in the sentence 'N is a cat', and hence that the predicate is, contrary to the Geachian view, ambiguous. For, clearly, in the sense of the predicate '— is a cat' in which it is used to convey the information that a proper name figuring as its subject has associated with it the criterion of identity associated with the sortal term 'cat' (i.e. as it was used in our sentence 'N is a cat'), it must be true to say that c is *not* a cat, given that 'c' does *not* have that criterion associated with it. And from this it follows, on pain of contradiction, that '— is a cat' must have two different senses, in one of which it is, *ex hypothesi*, truly predicable of c but in the other of which it is not. (Of course, my own view is that the predicate '— is a cat', as it is used in a sentence like 'Tibbles is a cat', is used to say what *sort* or *kind* of thing an individual is, i.e. that such a sentence may be classified as what I have previously called an *instantiation* sentence. But what I have been trying to do in the last few paragraphs is to argue against Geach without appealing to a semantic classification of my own, which might have appeared question-begging. This was less important in the previous chapter, where I was more concerned to defend absolutism than to attack relativism.)

One aspect of Geach's theory to which I have not so far alluded, but which might be thought to be relevant to the argument that I have just developed, is his distinction between a name 'for' a ϕ and a name 'of' a ϕ.[8] A name is a name 'for' a ϕ, in Geach's sense, if and only if that name has associated with it the criterion of identity associated with the sortal term 'ϕ'; but he takes the view that a name may still be a name 'of' a ϕ even though it has associated with it another criterion of identity. Thus, according to Geach, 'Tibbles' is both a name *for* and a name *of* a cat; but though it is not a name *for* a lump of feline tissue, it is nonetheless a name, albeit a 'shared' one, *of* all the various lumps of feline tissue $c_1, c_2, \ldots c_n$ and c on the mat. Equally, each of the names 'c_1', 'c_2', etc. is a name *for* and *of* a lump of feline tissue; but though none of them is a name *for* a cat, each of them is still a name *of* a cat, namely, Tibbles.[9]

But when, exactly, according to Geach, is a name a name 'of' a ϕ? The answer, it seems, is that it is so just in case there is some ϕ *that it names*. Thus he says: 'A proper name is a name *of* a cat if it is not an empty name but does actually name a cat',[10] and this is presented as definitional. The problem, however, is that I see no good reason to think that 'c', for instance, *names* a cat at all: all it names, in my view, is a certain lump of feline tissue. Certainly, it seems clear that the suggestion that a name 'for' a ϕ may nonetheless be a name 'of' a ψ, where ϕs and ψs have different criteria of identity, is not one that can be motivated independently of an argument in favour of the relativist conception of identity; for the only reason one could have to suppose that 'c', say, is a name 'of' a cat is just that c allegedly *is the same cat*

---

[8] See Geach, *Reference and Generality*, 3rd edn, p. 70.
[9] See further ibid., p. 216.
[10] Ibid., p. 70.

as Tibbles, which of course presupposes relativism. Moreover, I see nothing in this suggestion which offers a means of escape, for the relativist, from my foregoing argument to the ambiguity of the predicate ' — is a cat'. For the central claim of that argument was that there must be a distinctive sense of ' — is a cat' which is tied to its use in conveying the information that a name figuring as its subject has associated with it the criterion of identity associated with the sortal term 'cat', i.e. that such a name is, in Geach's terminology, a name 'for' a cat. And this can scarcely be denied. But then, *whether or not* it is supposed that '*c*' is a name 'of' a cat, given that it is not a name 'for' a cat it cannot be true to say that *c is a cat* in the sense just distinguished; so that if it *is* nonetheless true to say that *c* is a cat, it must be in some other sense – hence ambiguity. Finally, it is in any case highly questionable whether Geach's doctrine concerning names really makes much sense. For consider some condition which is true of Tibbles the cat but not true of *c* the lump of feline tissue – such as that it will not cease to exist merely if a single hair is removed or destroyed. The problem now is that if, as Geach holds, '*c*' is a name 'of' Tibbles, i.e. *names* Tibbles, then it is hard to see why the false sentence '*c* will not cease to exist merely if a single hair is removed or destroyed' should not also be *true*, since its subject allegedly names something (*viz.* Tibbles) of which its predicate is undoubtedly true. Perhaps in an artificial or regimented language this difficulty could be overcome by the exploitation of appropriate technical devices, but at least it seems clear enough that *natural* languages like English do not work in the way Geach's doctrine demands.[11] Altogether, then, it appears that this doctrine concerning names is one which a relativist should regard as more of an embarrassment than a

---

[11] Geach himself seems to recognize this sort of difficulty, though he rather makes light of it: see ibid., p. 218. The best attempt that I have seen to develop Geach's ideas on a formal basis is by Toomas Karmo, 'Relative Identity: A Working-Out of a *Prima Facie* Consistent Position Broadly Faithful to Geach' (unpublished).

strength, and which he would do well to eschew if possible. (I do not in fact see that a relativist *must* be committed to the doctrine, as Geach appears to think.)

Having argued that the distinction between the 'is' of identity and the 'is' of constitution is well motivated, I shall now go on briefly to say something positive about the latter sort of 'is', but also to comment on a rival absolutist theory which appears to offer a way of diminishing the importance of any such 'is'. I shall approach the matter by returning to Heraclitus's famous problem. Heraclitus, of course, is commonly supposed to have held that one cannot bathe (or 'step') in the same river twice.[12] This is no place to enter into questions of Presocratic exegesis, which I am not in any case equipped to answer. However, the relevant Heraclitean text, whatever precisely we are to make of it, is just this:[13]

> Upon those that step into the same rivers different and different waters flow . . . It scatters and . . . gathers . . . it comes together and flows away . . . approaches and departs.

Now Geach, as we have seen, implicitly charges the absolutist with being committed to the paradoxical view which I have described as being commonly attributed to Heraclitus: that one cannot bathe in the same river twice – unless indeed in doing so one were to bathe in the same *water* twice, which, given the mutable nature of rivers one is unlikely to do. I have defended the absolutist against this charge, arguing with Wiggins that the right response to make to Heraclitus's alleged claim is just to refuse to *identify* a river with the water which, at any given time, may properly be said to *constitute* it. As Wiggins himself puts it:[14]

---

[12] Plato at *Cratylus* 402 A attributes this opinion to Heraclitus: see G.S. Kirk & J.E. Raven, *The Presocratic Philosophers* (Cambridge: Cambridge University Press, 1957), p. 197, and their ensuing discussion, pp. 197–9. See also Jonathan Barnes, *The Presocratic Philosophers*, 2nd edn (London: Routledge and Kegan Paul, 1982), pp. 65ff.
[13] See Kirk & Raven, *The Presocratic Philosophers*, p. 196.
[14] David Wiggins, *Sameness and Substance* (Oxford: Blackwell, 1980), p. 35.

Rivers are indeed waters but this means that water goes to make them up. 'Same water' is not therefore a covering concept for an identity statement identifying a river with something.

What he means by this last assertion is just that where the individual terms '*a*' and '*b*' refer to *rivers* (and hence, as I should say, have the criterion of identity associated with the sortal term 'river' incorporated in their sense), the identity statement '*a* is the same as *b*' *cannot* be expanded as '*a* is the same *water* as *b*' in the way that it *can* be expanded as '*a* is the same *river* as *b*'. With '*a*' and '*b*' thus understood, the sentence '*a* is the same water as *b*' might indeed conceivably be *true*, but only if interpreted not as an *identity* statement concerning *a* and *b* but rather as merely affirming that the same water constitutes both *a* and *b*. My only dissatisfaction with Wiggins derives not from his views on these matters, with which I very substantially agree, but only from what is in my opinion a failure on his part to present a completely adequate defence against the relativist opposition. (Wiggins's defence places rather too much reliance on appeals to Leibniz's law in its classical form, which the relativist may fairly object to as question-begging; he is furthermore hampered, I consider, by his failure to recognize a distinctive 'is' of *instantiation*. It will become clear in a later chapter that on issues other than that of the correctness of absolutism I am often by no means in agreement with Wiggins, and in particular consider that as an absolutist he takes a mistaken line on the question of personal identity.)

I spoke a moment ago of a *rival* absolutist theory which makes no significant appeal to an 'is' of constitution. The theory in question is Quine's. Quine is an absolutist who equally believes that he can avoid the paradoxical 'Heraclitean' position that one cannot bathe in the same river twice. What he actually says, however, is this:[15]

---

[15] See W.V. Quine, 'Identity, Ostension and Hypostasis', in his *From a Logical Point of View*, 2nd edn (Cambridge, Mass.: Harvard University Press, 1961), p. 65.

> The truth is that you *can* bathe in the same *river* twice, but not in the same river stage [. . .] A river is a process through time, and the river stages are its momentary parts.

He goes on to explain:[16]

> Let me speak of any multiplicity of water molecules as a *water*. Now a river stage is at the same time a water stage, but two stages of the same river are not in general stages of the same water. River stages are water stages, but rivers are not waters. You may bathe in the same river twice without bathing in the same water twice, and you may, in these days of fast transportation, bathe in the same water twice while bathing in two different rivers.

From what Quine says, it does not appear that he would positively *reject* the notion of an 'is' of constitution, though it would seem clear that it cannot play any very fundamental theoretical role for him in the resolution of problems like that of Heraclitus. It is open to Quine, perhaps, simply to *define* 'Water x constitutes river y at time t' as meaning something like 'There is some water stage z of x such that z is a river stage of y at time t'.[17] However, when Quine blithely asserts that 'A river is a process through time, and . . . river stages are its momentary parts', I am immediately impelled to ask: but just what *are* these 'river stages' to which he so readily refers? *Rivers* are a species of thing with which we are all quite familiar, but hardly so *river stages*. Why indeed should Quine feel the slightest need to resort to the apparent extravagance of introducing such peculiar entities in response to Heraclitus's problem? The only reason I can suggest is that he assumes that when I bathe in a certain

---

[16] Ibid., pp. 65–6.
[17] This cannot in fact quite do as it stands, because it fails to have the surely correct implication that if water x constitutes river y at time t, then river y does *not* constitute water x at t. Whether securing this required asymmetry really presents any *less* of a problem for a Quinean approach to defining constitution than it does for me is not a matter that I shall pursue here, since Quine is under no *obligation* to produce such a definition at all.

river and at the same time in a certain water (i.e. a certain 'multiplicity of water molecules'), then since these individuals are *different* things (and in this we may agree with Quine, though not of course with Geach), there must be some *one* thing that I bathe in (distinct both from the river and from the water) by virtue of bathing in which I may be said to bathe both in the river and in the water, *because this one thing is a 'common part' of both the river and the water*. (An obvious analogy, I suppose, would be with the way that I can stand in both of two distinct shadows, because they have a common *spatial* part; but Quinean thing-stages are of course intended to be *temporal* parts of things.) Only this assumption seems to explain why Quine introduces 'river stages' and 'water stages', namely, so that he can then go on to *identify* entities of these sorts despite the fact that we cannot, he agrees, identify rivers and waters themselves. (As we saw him put it, 'River stages are water stages, but rivers are not waters' – and the 'are' here is plainly the 'are' of *identity*.)

But why should we accept the assumption? I can see no reason, because we can reach Quine's common-sense conclusion ('You may bathe in the same river twice without bathing in the same water twice, and . . . in the same water twice while bathing in two different rivers') without countenancing any sorts of entities other than ordinary rivers and waters. The fact in virtue of which I may be said to bathe simultaneously in a certain river *and* in a certain water (despite their distinctness) need not be that these two individuals have some 'common part' in which I bathe, but quite simply that they *exist simultaneously in the same place* at the time and place at which I bathe. And it is, moreover, precisely because they are *non-identical* that these two individuals nonetheless need not *always* coincide spatially, thus securing for us our common-sense answer to Heraclitus's problem. But since these are facts that Quine himself is committed to recognizing, it seems that he gains nothing by additionally postulating the existence of 'river stages' and 'water stages'. (Certainly, no reason has been given, and I don't see how one could, for supposing that two individual things can only exist in the same place at the same time if they share a common 'temporal part'.)

However, here it may be protested on Quine's behalf that by introducing mention of river stages and water stages he effects the considerable economy of doing away with any reliance on an undefined 'is' of constitution. That would be a fair objection against anyone who, rejecting the doctrine of temporal parts (as we may call Quine's theory of thing-stages), took the 'is' of constitution to be logically primitive. But such is not my own position. We saw indeed that for Quine defining an 'is' of constitution *may* be a relatively trivial matter, give his acceptance of river stages and water-stages. But while anyone who, like myself, looks askance at the doctrine of temporal parts will for that very reason find a definition of that sort quite unilluminating, it does not follow that such a person should reject altogether the prospect of achieving a reductive analysis or explication of constitution statements. Indeed, one element required in such an analysis has already become apparent, at least in the case of concrete, physical entities: simultaneous existence in the same place. If x is to be constituted by y at a certain time – say a river by a water – then at that time the spatial locations of x and y must exactly coincide. Of course, there must evidently be *more* to constitution than just this, not least because constitution is an asymmetrical relation (if x is constituted by y, then y is *not* constituted by x), whereas spatiotemporal coincidence is symmetrical. Another essential feature of constitution has also already emerged from previous discussion: that if x is to be constituted by y, then x and y must have different, and incompatible, criteria of identity, as do rivers and waters – though this still does not, of course, explain the asymmetry of constitution. Now, quite how to fill out the logically necessary conditions mentioned so far into a logically *necessary and sufficient* condition for x to be constituted by y is not something I have a settled view about at present – though one promising line of thought would obviously be to introduce some notion of the 'supervenience' of some or all of x's properties upon those of y. The notion of supervenience is, however, a far from simple one, as the considerable literature on the topic amply testifies; and I have no intention of attempting to contribute to the debate here. But what I feel reasonably confident about is that in some such terms as these a reductive analysis or explication of constitution statements *can* be achieved, without recourse to the doctrine of temporal parts.[18] Nor need we wait upon such an achievement before availing ourselves of the notion of constitution and its distinctive 'is', which can quite adequately be introduced by way of illustrative examples of the sort we have been discussing.

We are, then, under no pressure to follow Quine's lead in attempting to change the ontological category of things like rivers and waters from that of *continuants* to that of *processes*. Continuants, on my understanding of the term, may have spatial but not temporal parts (but need not necessarily even have the former, if we allow for the conceptual possibility of non-extended Cartesian egos). Processes, by contrast, seemingly must have temporal parts but may not necessarily have spatial parts even if they take place over an extended region of space. (A particular performance of a play would be an example of a process not *obviously* having any spatial parts despite occupying an extended spatial region.) Quine's proposed ontological revision, so blithely advanced by him, is in fact one of enormous magnitude and of highly questionable intelligibility; certainly, then, it is not one even to be contemplated so long as the prevailing 'common-sense' ontological scheme can be seen to be viable, as I believe it can. My own view about the doctrine of temporal parts, I should say, is that in fact no clear sense can

---

[18] For other and more detailed proposals for the analysis of constitution statements, with whose spirit I can agree, see F.C. Doepke, 'Spatially Coinciding Objects', *Ratio*, 24 (1982), pp. 45–60 and Peter Simons, *Parts: A Study in Ontology* (Oxford: Clarendon Press, 1987), pp. 237ff.

be made of the notion that something like a river has such parts, and that attempts by philosophers to give sense to this notion are implicitly parasitic upon a prior understanding of what I have called the category of continuants; but since satisfactory arguments to this effect have, to my mind, been developed elsewhere, I shall not attempt to add to them here.[19] Altogether, then, the cost at which the Quinean theory eliminates any special appeal to an 'is' of constitution is far too high; and the elimination is in my view more cosmetic than real, for at best what is provided is merely a superficially simple way of defining the 'is' of constitution which in fact only serves to disguise the substantial underlying task of philosophical explication that requires to be tackled.

I shall say more about the *parts* of continuants in the next chapter, but only about their *spatial* parts, which in my view are the only kind of parts they have.

---

[19] See, in particular, D.H. Mellor, *Real Time* (Cambridge: Cambridge University Press, 1981), pp. 127ff. My own suspicion has long been that the doctrine of temporal parts rests on an unspoken identification of continuants with their *life-histories*. Of course the *life-history* of a tree (say) has its early, middle and late stages: but the tree itself doesn't have such stages. Nor am I able to make much sense of the notion of an 'object-at-a-time' as a way of thinking of a temporal part or 'time-slice' of an object like a tree or a man (e.g., Napoleon-in-July-1798): for objects like trees and men don't have temporal *locations* (i.e. dates) at all, in the way that *events* do. Events in the life of a tree or a man (e.g. a man's birth) have dates, but no 'part' of a man has a date any more than the man himself does. Of course, a man's *existence* will extend over some definite period of time and so its beginning and end will be datable; but a *man* is no more to be identified with his own 'existence' than he is with his own life-history. Moreover, even if a notion like that of a 'man-at-a-time' *did* make sense, our understanding of it would in any case still be parasitic upon that of the notion of a 'man' *simpliciter*, in terms of which it is expressed. For further discussion of these issues, see my 'Substance, Identity and Time', *Proceedings of the Aristotelian Society*, supp. vol. LXII (1988).

6

Parts and Wholes

It is often said that certain 'wholes' are 'greater than the sum of their parts'. Since it is not entirely clear what 'greater than' means in this context, I would prefer to say simply that some wholes are *distinct from* the sum of their parts – or, more accurately, distinct from *any* sum of their (proper) parts, since there may be more ways than one of individuating a thing's 'parts', and so no such thing as *the* sum of its parts. But this is not true of all wholes. By a 'whole', I should explain, I just mean a (concrete) thing which *has* (proper) parts, or is 'composite'. (Henceforth I shall drop the parenthetical qualification 'proper', and so should be understood to be using 'part' in a sense, or senses, in which it is *not* the case that any thing is, trivially, a part of itself.) I shall begin by defending the claims I have just made; later I shall go on to examine their implications for the views of certain other philosophers, in particular those who adhere to a relativist conception of identity.

Consider again our old friend Tibbles the cat. Tibbles is a composite thing: he certainly has parts. Tibbles's tail, call it 'Tail', is a part of Tibbles. But is there an object which is, so to speak, Tibbles *minus* Tail? I rather think there is, and that this object is also a part of Tibbles, albeit a very large part. Let us, following Noonan, call this part 'Tib'.[1] (Many may

---

[1] See Harold W. Noonan, *Objects and Identity* (The Hague: Martinus Nijhoff, 1980), p. 22.

find the suggestion that there *is* such an object highly dubious; and to some extent I sympathize, as I shall explain subsequently.) Now, granted all this, it seems that we may affirm the following identity, appropriately understood:

1   Tib = (Tibbles − Tail).

But the use of the minus sign here, even if legitimate, is a distinctly peculiar one, because it apparently doesn't conform to the laws of arithmetic! For we cannot derive from (1) anything like

2   Tibbles = (Tib + Tail).

The problem is not that '(Tib + Tail)' does not denote an object – I think that it does: it denotes the 'sum' of two parts of Tibbles, the object which is Tib *plus* Tail. The problem rather is that this object is *distinct from Tibbles*. Of course one could just *stipulate* that the plus sign in (2) has whatever sense is required to make (2) simply an alternative way of writing (1). But then my point would be that this sense would have to differ from any sense we could intuitively attach to it in talking about a 'sum' of an object's parts, and hence that the intuitive notions of 'subtraction' and 'addition' at work in the present context are not very closely related to the arithmetical notions going by the same names. It may legitimately be inquired here what bearing these remarks have on the logistical system known as 'mereology', or the 'calculus of individuals', and I shall indeed address this question in due course.

That (Tib + Tail) is distinct from Tibbles may be shown in the following familiar way. If Tail were to be annihilated (but no other part of Tibbles), Tibbles would continue to exist, but (Tib + Tail) would cease to be. A sum of certain parts ceases to be when one of those parts ceases to be. Suppose this were denied: suppose it were claimed that even if Tail were annihilated, (Tib + Tail) would continue to exist. This seems to lead to absurdity. For, clearly, if Tail were annihilated, *Tib* at least would (*ceteris paribus*) continue to exist, and Tib is distinct from (Tib + Tail). But if *both* Tib *and* (Tib + Tail) were to continue to exist after the annihilation of Tail, what would then distinguish Tib from (Tib + Tail)? Perhaps it could be answered: their different past histories (for instance, things that happened to Tail were included in the history of (Tib + Tail) but not in that of Tib). But this puts the cart before the horse, for the question at issue is precisely whether (Tib + Tail) *has* a history subsequent to the time of Tail's annihilation. I think it is clear that it does not.

The next question is this: is Tib a cat? Indeed, is (Tib + Tail) a cat? If the answer is 'Yes' in either case, we are of course in trouble, because we are obliged to deny both

3   Tibbles = Tib

and

2   Tibbles = (Tib + Tail)

so that, it seems, we must have in one and the same place at one and the same time two, or even three, different cats. One putative remedy, as we saw in the previous chapter, is to reject the notion of absolute identity and say that Tibbles, Tib and (Tib + Tail) are all the same *cat*, but that Tibbles and Tib are different *lumps of feline tissue* while Tibbles and (Tib + Tail) are different relative to some other appropriate sortal distinction. But I hope I have already shown that this remedy is a desperate one indeed.

Why, however, should we be at all *tempted* to suppose that either Tib or (Tib + Tail) is a cat? (By 'is a cat' I mean of course exactly what I mean in saying that *Tibbles* 'is a cat'; that is, I am using the 'is' of instantiation.) Well, consider Tib. There are readily conceivable circumstances in which Tib would continue to exist if Tail were annihilated, as would Tibbles. But, it may be urged, Tib and Tibbles would then be spatially indistinguishable (despite differing in their past histories): and hence, since Tibbles would still be a cat, so too would Tib then be a cat.[2] And if Tib would be a cat after the annihilation of Tail, then why not also before that?

But this argument is unsatisfactory. The mere spatial indistinguishability (i.e. exact spatial coincidence) of two objects at a given time is by no means sufficient to show that they fall under the same sortal concepts at that time, much less at other times. This is a lesson which we should by now have learned from the discussions of the preceding two chapters. Nor should we be unsettled by the fact that, according to the view I am defending, we may not simply be able to tell *by looking* that Tibbles is a cat but that Tib is not. For sortal concepts like that of a cat are just not in this sense purely observational.

But what then *is* Tib subsequent to the annihilation of Tail, given that it is not then (much less previously) a *cat*? My answer is that Tib remains what it was before, namely a *part* of the cat Tibbles – albeit a part which now *wholly composes* Tibbles ('wholly composes' Tibbles in the sense that Tibbles has no other part which is not materially included in Tib). It really should not surprise us that an object can come to be wholly composed by a part of it which at one time only partially composed it, as the following somewhat macabre example should help to make clear. It is at least conceivable that Tibbles should meet with a dreadful accident, in which his body and legs are run over, and have to be amputated from his head which (through the miracles of modern science) can be kept alive on a life-support machine. (Never mind if this is not really quite feasible with today's technology.) Tibbles will (I suggest) have survived the accident, albeit terribly maimed, having lost everything except his head. Call this 'Head'. Are we then to say that

4   Tibbles = Head

[2] Cf. ibid.

is true in these circumstances? Surely not. A cat cannot be identical with a cat's head, even though it may *have* no more than a head. A cat's head cannot be a *cat*, but at most only a *part* of a cat, even though it may be the *largest* remaining part in certain extreme circumstances. In like manner, then, if it is conceded that Tib is indeed a genuine object and a cat-part (something which I shall examine more closely later on), it *remains* only a cat-part after the annihilation of Tail, and is not a *cat* either before or after that.

Tibbles, then, is the sort of 'whole' that is distinct from any sum of its parts. But not all wholes are like this. (Tib + Tail) is not, since it *is* the sum of its parts – relative, of course, to that way of individuating its parts that identifies these as Tib and Tail. (But it should also be said, however, that Tib and Tail are not 'parts' of (Tib + Tail) in anything like the same sense in which they are 'parts' of Tibbles.) Objects such as *heaps* and *lumps* may, at least on one reading of these terms, apparently be likened to (Tib + Tail). One might call such objects *aggregates*. Thus it seems that a heap of sand in this sense is (i.e. is identical with) the sum of the individual grains of sand in the heap, and that a lump of butter is (i.e. is identical with) any sum of individual butter-portions into which it may be completely divided without remainder (though there are some problems involved in spelling this out clearly). To this it may be objected that the heap of sand ceases to exist if all the grains in it are *scattered* (or indeed if only one grain is removed, whereupon we have a *different* heap), whereas the sum of the grains continues to exist provided each grain does. In answer to this we may either distinguish two different senses of 'sum', one of which permits scattering while the other does not, or else (rather more simply) we may concede the point and just say that aggregates, while *consisting* of the sum of their (appropriately individuated) parts, are not after all to be *identified* with such sums because an additional constraint on their persistence conditions is set by the requirement of adhesion of parts. I shall adopt the second of these responses. (Note here that our preceding discussion of the case of (Tib + Tail) in fact left it open whether we were talking of an aggregate or merely of a sum, in the sense just adopted: for though I said that (Tib + Tail) would cease to exist upon the *annihilation* of Tail, I didn't address the question of whether it would continue to exist if Tail were simply removed from Tibbles and preserved separately.)

Let us then say that a summative object, or *collective*, is a composite object which is identical with a certain sum of its parts (as individuated in a certain way), while an *aggregate* consists of a collective whose (appropriately individuated) parts are united by adhesion. (It is not necessary that every such part adhere directly to every other, so long as any two parts which do not adhere directly to each other belong to a single chain of parts adjacent members of which do adhere directly to each other. Just what counts as 'adhesion' need not trouble us for present purposes: it may amount to little more than contact in the case of a heap of sand, or to something much more robust in the case of something like a lump of stone.) A collective, I should perhaps point out, is not as I understand the term the same as a *set*: for collectives are *concrete* objects while sets are *abstract*. And the distinction between collectives and aggregates resides in the fact that the former are, while the latter are not, 'scatterable', in the sense that they can survive the separation of their (appropriately individuated) parts.

Now, in contrast with both collectives and aggregates we have objects like Tibbles the cat, which we may call (for want of a better word) *integrates*. Integrates are composite objects which are *not* identical with any sum of their parts, nor with any aggregate consisting of any sum of their parts. Thus one mark of an integrate is that it may survive the destruction or removal of at least some of its parts and their replacement by new ones, however these parts may be individuated – though, obviously, some parts of an integrate may play such a vital role in its make-up that their removal or replacement is effectively precluded. (Notice too that some integrates may be scatterable: those that are artefacts, e.g., clocks and ships, certainly often are, for they may be taken to pieces and put together again without ceasing to exist during the time in which their parts are separated.[3]) By contrast, the mark of a collective is that it cannot survive the destruction of any one of the parts of which it is the sum, and the mark of an aggregate is that it cannot even survive the separation of any of the parts of whose sum it consists. And corresponding to these different persistence conditions there are of course different *criteria of identity* for objects in these different categories (though even within each category there may also of course be objects with different criteria of identity: thus not all integrates share the same criterion).

Observe, incidentally, that even a collective or an aggregate *may* survive the destruction or removal of one of its parts, provided that that part is not one of those the sum of which the collective is identical with or the aggregate consists of. For instance, a heap of sand, which consists of the sum of a number of grains of sand, clearly contains as a part (in *some* sense of 'part') an atom of silicon in one of those grains; but the removal or destruction of that atom is surely consistent with the survival of the heap, provided it is consistent with the survival of the grain. (I might add here that we can certainly allow that there is *another* sense of 'heap' according to which heaps belong to the category of integrates: in this sense, the *same* heap of sand may grow or diminish by addition or removal of various grains of sand.)

I turn now to the implications of these conclusions for the views of certain other philosophers. I have already indicated what I regard as the main issue: the debate between 'absolute' and 'relative' identity theorists. A number of arguments for the relativist position can be scotched by appeal to the distinctions I have drawn. Consider, for instance, Ze-

---

[3] See further my 'On the Identity of Artifacts', *Journal of Philosophy* 80 (1983), pp. 220–32.

mach's argument to the conclusion that 'the overwhelming majority of the objects actually referred to [by us], objects such as Jimmy Carter, this shirt, the man on my right, etc., are *not* ontologically complete'[4] – by which he means that, for such an object, it is *not* the case that 'with respect to every property F, either it has it, or it does not have it'.[5] The following passage will give us the flavour of his position:[6]

> Does the referent of 'this table' include, e.g., the nail and thumb tack which were driven into it? Does it, or does it not, include the paper pasted on it? Yet surely table A, which includes nail, thumb tack and paper, is a very different object (it has a different weight, history, mass, etc.) from table B which does not include them as parts.

For Zemach, then, there are at least two (and in fact many more than two) distinct 'ontologically complete' objects in the region occupied by this table, all of which are *tables*, but all of which may be counted as the *same* table. (This is how his argument leads to a version of the relative identity theory.) 'This table', however, denotes an 'ontologically incomplete' or 'schematic' object, of which it may not be true to say (for instance) either that it weighs more than fifty pounds or that it does not weigh more than fifty pounds.

Here again I think we see some confusion concerning the relations between parts and wholes. Let us suppose (for the sake of argument) that the nail, thumb tack and paper are indeed parts of a certain ('complete') object, which we shall continue to call 'table A', on the understanding that this object really is a *table*. (I shall however query this assumption in a moment.) Now tables are *integrates* in my terminology: they are not identical with any sum of their parts, and they may lose and gain at least some parts without ceasing to

---

[4] Eddy M. Zemach, 'Schematic Objects and Relative Identity', *Nous* 16 (1982), pp. 295–305: see p. 295.
[5] Ibid.
[6] ibid., p. 297.

be. So, in particular, table A may presumably lose the nail, thumb tack and paper that (we have assumed) are parts of it, and continue to exist without them. We may also agree that there is an object which is table A *minus* the nail, thumb tack and paper, an object which Zemach calls 'table B'. But is table B a *table*? I think not, *given that table A is*: B is just a very large part of table A, and a part of a table, no matter how large a part, is not a table. (I exclude here as irrelevant the special case of tables made by joining together smaller tables.) We should not be misled by the fact that if the nail, thumb tack and paper are removed table A will become spatially indistinguishable from the object we have called 'table B', any more than we should be misled by the comparable circumstance in the case of Tibbles and Tib.

In fact, however, I think that we were mistaken to suppose that the nail, thumb tack and paper (or at least the latter two items) could really be *parts* of a *table* (certainly in the way in which one of its legs is, or even the knob on one of its drawers). There may indeed be an object which is the sum of a table, a nail, a thumb tack and a piece of paper, but such an object is *not* a table, because it is not even an integrate. (Such an object ceases to be if, say, the thumb tack is destroyed, but no *table* can cease to exist merely for such a reason.) Equally, an aggregate consisting of the sum of these items does not qualify as a table.

I conclude that there can be no such two objects as Zemach calls 'table A' and 'table B' *both* of which are tables. Either table A is a table, in which case 'table B' is just a large table-part; or else (as seems much more plausible) table B is a table and 'table A' is just an *aggregate* which consists of the sum of table B, the nail, the thumb tack and the paper – and such an aggregate cannot be a table. And so it will be with regard to any other ('complete') objects Zemach cares to identify in this case (table C, table D, . . .): only one of the objects can be a *table* – others will either be *parts* of that table or else *aggregates* of such table-parts or of such table-parts and other objects which are not table-parts. For instance, if table B is indeed a table, the object which is table B *minus* the bottom half-inch of one of its legs will be a table-part (albeit a large one). It may perhaps be the case that it is to a degree arbitrary precisely how we individuate the table (and consequently that there is 'no fact of the matter' as to whether, say, there is a table in the room weighing more than fifty pounds): all I am claiming is that *not more than one* object in the location can simultaneously qualify as a table – tables can't 'overlap'. And therefore we don't need to resort to the relative identity theory to justify the common-sense conviction that there is only *one table* in the room: that is, we don't have to say that different objects, all of them tables, may be one and the same table – because we don't have to concede that more than one of these objects *is* a table.[7]

It may be wondered why I have made no use in this chapter of the so-called *calculus of individuals*, in one or other of its versions, since that is usually regarded as providing the classic treatment of the part–whole relation.[8] The reason is that this calculus is plainly quite inadequate for my purposes. For instance, according to the calculus, an individual x is a *sum* of the individuals y and z if and only if y is a part of x and z is a part of x and every part of x has a part in common with either y or z. But on this definition it would appear that Tibbles *is* a sum of Tib and Tail: for Tib is a part of Tibbles and Tail is a part of Tibbles and every part of Tibbles has a part in common with either Tib or Tail, i.e., no part of Tibbles is such that no part of it is either a part of Tib or a part of Tail. (This is true even if, as the calculus demands, we regard Tibbles himself as

---

[7] David Wiggins has said some things with which the view I have here developed is broadly in sympathy: see his 'Mereological Essentialism: Asymmetrical Essential Dependence and the Nature of Continuants', in E. Sosa (ed.), *Essays on the Philosophy of Roderick M. Chisholm* (Amsterdam: Rodopi, 1979).

[8] See, e.g., H.S. Leonard and N. Goodman, 'The Calculus of Individuals and its Uses', *Journal of Symbolic Logic* 5 (1940), pp. 45–55; N. Goodman, *The Structure of Appearance*, 3rd edn (Dordrecht: D. Reidel, 1977), pp. 33ff.; and A. Tarski, *Logic, Semantics and Metamathematics*, 2nd edn (Indianapolis: Hackett Publishing Co., 1983), pp. 24–9.

a part of Tibbles.) However, precisely what I *deny* is that Tibbles is a sum of Tib and Tail. My conclusion must therefore be that *either* the 'is a part of' relation utilized by the calculus under its intended interpretation does not correspond to the ordinary sense of this expression as it is used to say (for example) that Tail *is a part of* Tibbles, *or else* the notion of 'sum' defined in the calculus does not correspond to the notion that I have invoked in characterizing collectives as being 'sums' of certain of their parts. (Nor is this disjunction exclusive.) Either way, it is clear that I cannot accept that the calculus provides an adequate framework for discussion of the issues raised in this chapter. For it fails to provide the resources wherewith to articulate the very distinctions that I have been trying to draw between what I call *integrates* on the one hand and *aggregates* and *collectives* on the other. Furthermore, it takes no proper account of the fact, emphasized throughout this chapter, that there may be more ways than one of individuating a thing's 'parts'. (To speak unrestrictedly of *the* parts of a thing is not to speak fully determinately because the general term 'thing which is a part of *a*', where *a* is some individual, is only what I have earlier called a 'dummy sortal': it conveys no criterion of identity and hence, though grammatically a count noun, carries with it no principle for counting.)

I do not pretend to have rendered perfectly transparent, in this chapter, all the subtle distinctions that can be drawn concerning our ways of talking about 'parts' and 'wholes' (much less to have *defined* the expression 'is a part of', which I don't even regard as being univocal): but at least I hope I have made it clear that the concepts involved are considerably more complex and sophisticated than any that can be handled purely in terms of the calculus of individuals, or 'mereology', a least in its classical, extensional form.[9]

---

[9] Cf. Peter Simons, *Parts: A Study in Ontology* (Oxford: Clarendon Press, 1987), passim. I find myself in substantial agreement with Simons's critique of standard extensional mereological theory, and indeed with much else in his overall ontological viewpoint (especially his repudiation of the idea that continuants have 'tem-

Finally I turn to an interesting question which I have so far set on one side. Is there *really* an 'object' which is the cat Tibbles 'minus' his tail? Many will view the suggestion with suspicion: and their suspicion is, I think, partly well founded – though not completely so. I think that Tib – that is, (Tibbles − Tail) – *is* a genuine object, though nonetheless a logically rather peculiar one. It is significant that both Tibbles and Tail are uncontentious objects of quite familiar sorts – a *cat* and a *cat's tail* respectively. But what sort of thing is Tib? I suggest that what is logically peculiar about Tib is that, to the extent that we can individuate this object *at all*, we can only do so precisely as the 'difference' of two *bona fide* objects, Tibbles and Tail; Tib is not *independently* individuable as a *bona fide* object of any sort. And this fundamentally is why, even after the annihilation of Tail, Tib cannot be *identified* with Tibbles; for even then Tib is *still* only individuable in a way which presupposes the independent individuability of Tibbles the cat – Tib is still only a 'logically dependent' object, as we might call it, in contradistinction to Tibbles the cat (even though they now coincide spatially). An object which is introduced to us as a logically dependent one cannot subsequently become a logically independent one: an object cannot change its logical status. I believe that the puzzles set by Noonan, Zemach and others partly trade upon a blurring of this distinction. (I might add, however, that while I am prepared to countenance the existence of objects like Tib, no positive thesis of mine hinges upon this acceptance, and I am fully open to persuasion that no such objects do in fact exist.)

Perhaps a geometrical example will help to clarify the distinction I have just drawn. Suppose AB is the straight line interval between A and B which includes A and B as its end-points; and suppose X is a point somewhere within AB.

---

poral parts'). However, I am not entirely convinced by Simons's account of the basic logical principles which, as he contends, constitute 'the minimum we can require of a relation if it is to be one of proper part to whole' (p. 362). For instance, I am not convinced that such a relation must necessarily be transitive.

Then XB is, like AB, a straight line interval with two end-points, X and B. But if we consider the straight line interval, call it I, obtained by *subtracting XB* from AB (i.e., the interval which is the set of all points that are in AB but not in XB), it is obvious that this interval does *not* have two end-points (it is a 'half-open' interval, i.e., closed at only one end). Hence I is not to be identified with the closed interval AX, even though I and AX have the same length. Now I itself is, in our sense, a logically dependent object, inasmuch as it can only be individuated as the 'difference' between two closed intervals or, alternatively, as the 'difference' between a closed interval and a point, i.e., as what 'remains' when the point X is 'subtracted' from the closed interval AX. And though that closed interval can in turn be individuated as the result of 'adding' that point to I, it can nonetheless *also* be individuated independently of I and without appeal to any operation of 'addition', namely as the closed interval whose end-points are A and X.

7

Persons and their Bodies

What is the relationship between a living organism and the collection of material particles composing it at any given time? What is the relationship between a person and his body? Is either of these relations simply that of *identity*? If not, are we at any rate faced with the *same* relation in each case? Questions like these are amongst the most difficult and interesting that arise in metaphysics, and I hope to cast some light on them in the course of this chapter, making full use of the semantic and logical findings of the preceding chapters.

7.1 Matter and Organisms

I have, of course, already implicitly answered our first question, 'What is the relationship between a living organism and the collection of material particles composing it at any given time?': this relationship is one of *constitution* rather than *identity*. It cannot be one of identity simply because living organisms and collections of material particles have *different criteria of identity* and so cannot be identified, for reasons which I have tried to make clear in previous chapters. That the relevant criteria are different is something that Locke must be credited with having understood particularly clearly (though where he would have elected to stand on the modern debate between absolutists and relativists is a moot point, since he does not raise the issue explicitly and says things in different places which could be interpreted as favourable now to the one position and now to the other). Indeed, we can still look with much profit at what Locke says on the subject in the opening sections of chapter XXVII ('Of Identity and Diversity') of Book II of the *Essay Concerning Human Understanding*.

In § 3 Locke gives us what is effectively a criterion of identity for what he calls a 'body', 'mass' or 'parcel of matter' (such as a lump of gold), as follows:[1]

> whilst [a number of atoms] exist united together, the Mass, consisting of the same Atoms, must be the same Mass, let the parts be never so differently jumbled: But if one of these Atoms be taken away, or one new one added, it is no longer the same Mass or the same Body.

Locke, then, understands a 'mass' or 'parcel of matter' to be, in my terminology, *an aggregate of atoms*, and the criterion of identity he provides for such objects may simply be stated thus:

> If x and y are *parcels of matter*, then x is identical with y if and only if x and y consist of the same atoms united together.

Now we may of course query Locke's assumption that the criterion of identity for parcels of matter should imply that matter is *atomic*, rather than, say, infinitely divisible; for this is surely not inherent in the very concept of matter, i.e. is not a semantic fact about the term 'matter' as we ordinarily use it, but rather just a thesis advanced by a currently favoured scientific theory concerning the *nature* of matter. (Though here, to be quite fair to Locke, we should not

---

[1] John Locke, *An Essay Concerning Human Understanding*, ed. P.H. Nidditch (Oxford: Clarendon Press, 1979) Book II, ch. XXVII, § 3.

perhaps assume that *he* was concerned to state a purely semantic principle.) We may agree that parcels of matter have the ontological status of *aggregates*, and as such consist of 'sums' of certain of their 'parts', but need to examine further precisely which of the constituents of a parcel of matter (say, a lump of gold) are to *count* as its 'parts' for the purposes of framing an appropriate criterion of identity for such an object. (Does an electron, for instance, qualify? Clearly not.)

What I myself am inclined to say is that the relevant parts of a lump of gold are just the various smaller *lumps of gold* into which it may be divided (and not, thus, the atoms or smaller particles composing it); though of course there are infinitely many different ways of carrying out such a division. For clearly, we *are* inclined to say that it is a purely semantic fact that if any *part* of the gold in a lump of gold is removed or replaced, what remains is a different lump; but to make determinate sense of this assertion we need to specify what *sort* of 'part' we are talking about, and the obvious answer is that we are talking about any part which itself would qualify as a lump of gold – though, strictly speaking, we should no doubt also include such 'parts' as are 'sums' of *separate* parts each of which would qualify as a lump of gold. (An *atom* of gold does not of course qualify on this specification, since for something to be a lump of gold it must be *golden*, i.e. consist of gold, and gold atoms do not consist of gold but rather of protons, neutrons and electrons.)

What I am suggesting, then, is that we ordinarily conceive of a lump of gold as being an aggregate of (smaller) lumps of gold; a conception which we no doubt acquire from our experience of being able to join and divide such lumps to make larger or smaller ones (if not in the case of gold itself, then at least in the case of lumps of commoner sorts of stuff, such as clay). However, this creates a problem when we seek to frame a *criterion of identity* for lumps of gold, because it looks as though any such criterion would have to involve a circularity: it would scarcely do, for instance, to say that if x

and y are *lumps of gold*, then x is identical with y if and only if x and y are aggregates of (or are divisible into) *the same lumps of gold*. And there are, besides, other difficult questions about lumps of matter or stuff: for instance, if two separate lumps of gold x and y are conjoined and their united matter is thoroughly mixed (say, by melting and stirring), do x and y continue to exist? Indeed, more generally, to what extent do we want to say that all the lumps of gold into which a given lump is divisible *actually* exist prior to any actual division (or can we intelligibly speak of their merely 'potential' existence)?[2] Again, what do we say about mixtures of *different* sorts of stuff, homogeneous or otherwise (e.g. gold and silver, flesh and bone)?[3]

Perhaps in the light of these awesome problems Locke's corpuscularian prejudices saved him a good deal of trouble, and at least freed him to discern the crucial fact that parcels of matter, whatever their precise criterion of identity, do *not* share the same criterion as living organisms. This, too, is the only fact that I would wish to emphasize at this point, for the purpose of pursuing the questions raised at the outset of this chapter; and so I shall attempt no further resolution at present of the problem of framing an adequate criterion of identity for 'parcels of matter'. (In fact, I should point out, I deliberately formulated those initial questions in terms of 'collections of material particles' rather than of 'parcels of matter' partly in order to deflect the latter problem; Locke might have been advised to do likewise, since the criterion of identity which he gives for parcels of matter is of course much more acceptable as a criterion rather for collections of material particles, or more precisely for aggregates of atoms.)

Having given us a criterion of identity for parcels of matter, Locke goes on to make the following observation:[4]

---

[2] Some of these questions are interestingly addressed by Eli Hirsch, in his *The Concept of Identity* (Oxford: Oxford University Press, 1982), pp. 113ff.

[3] For an interesting discussion of some of the issues, see Richard Sharvy, 'Aristotle on Mixtures', *Journal of Philosophy* 80 (1983), pp. 439–57.

[4] Locke, *An Essay Concerning Human Understanding*, Book II, ch. XXVII, § 3.

> In the state of living Creatures, their Identity depends not on a Mass of the same Particles; but on something else. For in them the variation of great parcels of Matter alters not the Identity.

The point he is making, of course, is quite simply that living organisms, such as an oak tree, can lose and gain material particles (e.g. through metabolic processes) while retaining their identity, i.e. without thereby ceasing to exist, and that *therefore* living organisms must have a *different* criterion of identity from the one that he has just assigned to what he calls parcels of matter. He even goes so far as to suggest what this criterion might be in § 4, where he writes:

> We must therefore consider wherein an Oak differs from a Mass of Matter, and that seems to me to be in this; that the one is only the Cohesion of Particles of Matter any how united, the other such a disposition of them as constitutes the parts of an Oak; and such an organization of those parts, as is fit to receive, and distribute nourishment, so as to continue, and frame the Wood, Bark, and Leaves, *etc.* of an Oak, in which consists the vegetable Life.

This is slightly obscure, and perhaps has a misleading air of circularity, inasmuch as the very sortal term 'oak' is itself used in an attempt to explain the criterion of identity associated with that sortal term. Nonetheless, two obviously important features of the continuing identity through time of a living organism do emerge from Locke's remarks: the maintenance of a certain *form* or *organization of parts*, and the maintenance (by virtue of that organization) of certain *biological functions* serving to preserve that organization or form. Actually, of course, we must be prepared to be quite flexible in talking about the preservation of 'form' here, in view of the sort of alterations that can take place as a sapling grows into a mature tree. What is more fundamental than mere continuity of form is the maintenance of a system of biological functions (e.g. photosynthesis, respiration) which contribute to their own preservation, rendering the organism relatively autonomous despite the constant interchange of matter between it and its environment, precisely by conferring upon it some considerable *control* over that process of interchange. (In short, a living organism is a *homeostatic* mechanism.) Locke seems to understand that this is the the crucial point, as he subsequently proceeds to advance the following criterion of identity for *man*, conceived purely as a species of animal, i.e. as a kind of living organism:[5]

> the Identity of the same *Man* consists [. . .] in nothing but a participation of the same continued Life, by constantly fleeting Particles of Matter, in succession vitally united to the same organized Body.

Spelling this out more in line with my own style and terminology, we might say that Locke is here endorsing a criterion of identity for living organisms (and so, more specifically, for 'men' or human beings) which might be stated thus:

> If x and y are *living organisms*, then x is identical with y if and only if x and y are constituted by collections of material particles participating of the same continued life,

where the notion of 'participation of the same continued life' is to be explained in terms of the engagement of material particles in the metabolic and other vital processes that together constitute the workings of the sort of self-sustaining (homeostatic) system of biological functions discussed earlier. (It is perhaps worth remarking, incidentally, that though the last quoted passage from Locke may not make it quite clear, other passages indeed indicate that for Locke it is not so much *organisms* as the *material particles* constituting them that are to be said to 'participate of life'; not that I think a great deal turns on this terminological point, since it

---

[5] Ibid., § 6.

is easy enough to define organisms as sharing 'the same life' just in case their constituents do.) The only awkward feature of Locke's proposal as he himself states it – apart from its undoubted vagueness – is his use of the phrase 'the same organized Body': for this can only be understood to mean something like 'the same living organism' (plainly it cannot be taken just to mean 'the same *body*', in the sense of 'the same *mass*, or *parcel of matter*') – but then circularity again threatens, since 'man' is here being understood precisely to denote a species of *living organism* and hence something with precisely the latter's criterion of identity. However, I consider Locke's use of the offending phrase as superfluous for his purposes, as will appear from my suggested paraphrase of his proposed criterion.

An objection which might be raised against the foregoing proposal is that it would not permit us to rule out *a priori* one and the same living organism changing from being an organism of one kind or species, say a dog, to being one of another, say a cat (or even, more radically, from being an animal to being a vegetable or *vice versa* – unless perhaps 'life' can be understood in different senses as applied to animals on the one hand and to vegetables on the other). However, in my view it would indeed be wrong to see such changes as being *conceptually*, as opposed merely to physically or naturally, impossible. (And who, after all, would have thought, prior to experience, that caterpillars might change into butterflies? If such inter-specific changes had been excludable *a priori*, surely this change equally would have been.) The sort of change that clearly *would* be conceptually impossible is – to use an example of Wiggins's – one such as a human being becoming a pillar of salt, as is said to have happened to Lot's wife (and even then only if we understand 'becoming' as implying 'continuing to exist'). But this of course is just because living organisms and parcels of matter have different criteria of identity. Incidentally, these considerations again serve to show that it would be mistaken to place too much emphasis on the preservation of *form* as far as the identity of living organisms is concerned (though, no doubt, *sudden* changes of form are naturally inimical to the homeostatic mechanisms that are essential to life). Of course, I do not mean to deny that an organism's form is relevant to a consideration of what *species* or *kind* of organism it is (something with four legs and a tail could scarcely qualify as an oak tree); the question is only whether such considerations bear upon that individual's *criterion of identity*, and I do not think that they really do.

My own view, I should say, is that the criterion of identity for living organisms that I have ascribed to Locke is one that is *broadly* along the right lines, though it suffers from a certain amount of vagueness over what constitutes 'the same life' and consequently may leave the answers to some important identity questions – especially certain 'synchronic' ones – undetermined. (For example, do Siamese twins share 'the same life' and so constitute a single living organism? Do a pregnant woman and her unborn child? To answer that 'inseparable' Siamese twins do, or that a woman and her 'non-viable' foetus do, is merely to invite further questions.) However, I shall not attempt to render the notion and hence the criterion more precise here, since my main concern once more is merely to emphasize the *difference* that must obtain between any adequate criterion of identity for living organisms and any adequate criterion of identity either for 'parcels of matter' or for collections of material particles – the consequence of this difference being, of course, the *non-identity* of individuals of the sorts or kinds in question.

A further implication of this difference is, as we have seen, that we must allow that two or more different individual things not only may, but very often do, exist in the same place at the same time: the 'parcel of matter' occupying the region of space occupied by an oak tree at a given time, and that oak tree itself, are two such individual things. To this a relativist in matters of identity might object that it makes no determinate sense to speak of 'two things' existing in the same place at the same time unless we can specify what *sort* or *kind* of thing they are supposedly two distinct instances of – which, of course, we cannot do with the present example. He may claim that it makes sense to talk of two different *oak trees*, or two different *parcels of matter*, but not of two different 'things', one an oak tree and the other a parcel of matter. But this objection rests on a confusion. Certainly, counting only makes sense where we have countable sorts of thing: we cannot simply count 'things', but only things of this or that countable sort. But it doesn't follow that we can only count relative to a *single* sortal distinction.[6] 'How many things?' is an indeterminate question, unlike 'How many ϕs?'; but it doesn't follow that 'How many ϕs and ψs?' is indeterminate, even where there is no sort χ of which both ϕ and ψ are (disjoint) sub-species, i.e. even where the answer 'There are n ϕs and ψs' cannot be recast in the form 'There are n χs' (in the way, say, that 'There are ten boys and girls' can be recast as 'There are ten children'). All that is required for the question 'How many ϕs and ψs?' to make determinate sense is that nothing should qualify as *both* a ϕ *and* a ψ (which is why 'How many dogs and animals?', say, lacks determinate sense), i.e. ϕ and ψ should be *disjoint* sorts or kinds. And this of course *is* the case with the sorts *oak tree* and *parcel of matter*. It is not necessary that there be some *higher* sort or kind χ of which both ϕ and ψ are sub-kinds.

Another objection which might be raised is that Locke himself seems to rule out simultaneous existence in the same place in §§ 1–2 of chapter XXVII of Book II of the *Essay*. In fact, however, he is careful to say there only that it is impossible that 'two things *of the same kind* should exist in the same place at the same time',[7] and indeed specifically allows that different sorts of substances 'do not exclude one another out of the same place'.[8] Nonetheless, it may be

---

[6] Compare Jonathan Bennett and William Alston, 'Identity and Cardinality: Geach and Frege', *Philosophical Review* 93 (1984), pp. 553–67.
[7] Locke, *An Essay Concerning Human Understanding*, Book II, ch. XXVII, § 1, my emphasis.
[8] Ibid., § 2.

conceded that in making this latter remark the 'sorts of substances' he has in mind are God, 'finite intelligences', and bodies, and he insists indeed that different *bodies* cannot exist in the same place at the same time. However, by 'body' here he just means, of course, 'parcel of matter', and he has not so far extended his discussion to a consideration of 'organized bodies', i.e. living organisms or 'living creatures'. So nothing that Locke says in §§ 1–2 about simultaneous existence in the same place implies that he would have been obliged to *deny* that an oak tree and a parcel of matter existing in the same place could be distinct objects, even though the question does not seem to have occurred to him. Moreover, it might in any case be pointed out that it is in fact questionable whether the existence in the same place at the same time even of two different *parcels of matter* can be ruled out *a priori*, as Locke seems to think when he asserts 'could two Bodies be in the same place at the same time; then those two parcels of Matter must be one and the same.'[9] Certainly, if parcels of matter are conceived to be, as Locke would have it, *aggregates of atoms*, it is not at all obvious why it should be logically impossible for one such aggregate to pass intact through another, provided at least that there are interstices between the 'atoms' (or perhaps even if there are not): we allow, after all, that water may seep through earthenware without loss of identity. It is true that this observation does not apply to the supposed 'atoms' themselves, but even with them it is not obvious why temporary merging should be ruled out *a priori*; for it might even be empirically detectable by, say, a doubling in density.

A living organism, then, such as an oak tree, and the parcel of matter or collection of material particles existing in the same place at a given time, are distinct individuals, the latter of which *constitutes* the former at that time but may not do so at another time during the organism's life. And here it may be observed that when an individual x of one

[9] Ibid.

sort, φ, is constituted at a certain time by another individual *y*, it is not in general a purely contingent affair as to what *sort of thing y itself is*, even though it *is* contingent that it should be *y*, as opposed to some other individual *z* of the same sort, that constitutes *x* at that time. There will then in general exist some non-contingent (possibly even *a priori*) principle to the effect that φs are constituted by ψs. For instance, it is not contingent that rivers are constituted by water, nor that human beings are constituted by flesh and bone, nor that trees are constituted by wood. Perhaps not all such necessities can plausibly be regarded as purely *a priori*, however, because due scope must be allowed to empirical scientific investigation in such matters. None the less, it *is* I suggest an *a priori* truth that, say, living organisms are constituted by matter, the reason being that this is implied by the very *criterion of identity* for living organisms. This is why, though we can *perhaps* conceive of discovering that 'oak trees' are after all composed of some synthetic substance imported from Mars (provided, of course, that this is consistent with still regarding them as being *alive*), the notion of an 'immaterial' oak tree is just incoherent and absurd. (If departed oak trees have ghosts, their ghosts certainly aren't *trees*!) Living organisms are *essentially* material. For if a living organism were to lose *all* its matter without replacement, the very criterion of identity for living organisms implies that it would thereby cease to exist. (By an 'essential' property of an individual, I should say, I mean in the present context a property which that individual *cannot lose without thereby ceasing to be*. There is another notion of 'essence' according to which an 'essential' property of an individual is one which that individual *could not have lacked*, or which it 'possesses in all possible worlds in which it exists'. But this distinction does not presently concern me.[10])

Notice, however, that though I allow that certain *a post-*

---

[10] I discuss the history of the distinction in my chapter on 'Substance' in *An Encyclopaedia of Philosophy*, ed. G.H.R. Parkinson (London: Routledge, 1988).

eriori necessary truths of constitution may also obtain – truths that are not derivable purely from criteria of identity – such as that human beings are constituted by flesh and bone, such necessities only attach to the sorts or kinds in question, not directly to individuals instantiating them. For while it may be necessary that φs are constituted by ψs, it may not be necessary that a given individual, which is now a φ, should *always* be constituted by a ψ – provided the necessity is not one that arises from that individual's very criterion of identity; though, of course, should that individual cease to be constituted by a ψ, it will no longer qualify as a φ. Thus, though human beings are necessarily constituted by flesh and bone, it is not perhaps *inconceivable* that an individual that is now a human being should come in time to be constituted by synthetic materials, though that individual would thereby cease to be a human being. What *is* however inconceivable is that such an individual might cease altogether to consist of *matter*, or cease to be *alive*, and yet continue to exist; for this is contrary to its very criterion of identity.

7.2 Organisms and Persons

We are now in a position to begin looking at the second question raised at the outset of this chapter: what is the relationship between a person and his body? By 'body' here I mean what Locke would call 'organized body', and what I have hitherto called 'living organism'. I am concerned, then, as is Locke himself, with the relationship between *person* and *man*, the latter being understood as a species of animal and so of living organism. There are two issues to be dealt with: (1) can an individual man or human being be *identified* with an individual person, and (2) if not, may we at least say that an individual man or living human organism can *constitute* an individual person, or even that the collection of material particles or parcel of matter constituting an individual man at a given time may *also* constitute an individual person at that time? I shall argue that both answers should be negative. The relation between a person and his 'organized body' and its constituents is *neither* that of identity *nor* that of constitution.

If previous arguments of mine are correct, the most direct way to establish that an individual person is identifiable neither with his 'organized body' nor with the parcel of matter constituting that body at any given time is simply to show that *persons do not have the same criterion of identity either as living organisms or as parcels of matter*. Of course, determining what precise criterion of identity persons have (if indeed they have any, which cannot just be assumed) is no easy matter; though fortunately it may not be necessary to do so in order to show that they do *not* have either of the other criteria of identity under consideration. Let us begin, however, more optimistically by inquiring how we should approach the problem of finding a criterion of identity for persons, if one exists. Here Locke is again surely right in saying that we should start from a consideration of the meaning of the sortal term 'person'. As he puts it:[11]

> This being premised to find wherein *personal Identity* consists, we must consider what *Person* stands for; which, I think, is a thinking intelligent Being, that has reason and reflection, and can consider it self as it self, the same thinking thing in different times and places; which it does only by that consciousness, which is inseparable from thinking, and as it seems to me essential to it: It being impossible for any one to perceive, without perceiving, that he does perceive.

And I largely agree with Locke's characterization of the concept of a *person* here. A person is, essentially, something that acts and perceives and knows that it does so: it is a perceiving, self-conscious agent, or, alternatively, an active, self-conscious percipient. (By 'acting' I mean, of course, performing *intentional* actions. I should also stress that I

[11] Locke, *An Essay Concerning Human Understanding*, Book II, ch. XXVII, § 9.

demand of persons only a *capacity* of action, perception and self-reflection, not a continual exercise of such capacities.)

However, turning aside for the moment from the quest for a criterion of personal identity, we can I think say already that if the foregoing characterization of persons is even approximately correct, it does *not* follow that a person must be something embodied or material. And indeed there is *not* apparently an absurdity in speaking of an immaterial person, in the way that there is in speaking of an immaterial oak tree or river. At least, if there *is* any incoherence here, it must be buried very deep – which would in itself be enough to set 'person' apart from biological sortals like 'animal'. I say this in view of the long history in human thought of the notions of survival after bodily death and of the supposed existence of immaterial spirits, demons and gods, which testify to the fact that our concept of a person is not one which *obviously* excludes, *a priori*, the possibility of an individual person existing without a body.[12] (I point to this, however, without prejudice as to the question of whether such existence is an empirical *scientific* possibility.) And when we consider what sort of evidence we look for if we want to detect the presence of a person, we see that we do *not* in fact necessarily look for bodily characteristics of any sort: we look for *intelligent activity*, and where we find it we attribute its source to a *person*. Thus if we hear a message tapped out on a wall, we assume the presence of a person responsible for it; we may well, of course, *also* assume the presence of an 'organized body' associated with that person and through which that person acts, but this is *not*, I would urge, a *conceptual* requirement without which we cannot make sense of the notion of a person's presence and agency.

---

[12] One well-known attempt to demonstrate the incoherence of the notion of disembodied personal existence is by Terence Penelhum, in his *Survival and Disembodied Existence* (London: Routledge and Kegan Paul, 1970). But I do not find his arguments convincing. They are vitiated, not least, by an assumption that 'person' must *have* a criterion of identity and that in the absence of a 'bodily' criterion a 'memory' criterion would have to suffice – which, he argues, it could not. If, as I suspect, 'person' denotes a *basic* sort, such arguments are beside the point.

Persons are not, I repeat, essentially material in the way that oak trees are.¹³ But then for this very reason persons cannot be regarded as *a species of living organism*, since living organisms *are* essentially material.¹⁴ (Another reason for denying that persons are a species of living organism would of course be that we can plausibly envisage certain non-living mechanisms – 'robots' – as embodying persons; I won't say as *being* persons, for reasons that will become plain.¹⁵)

I should emphasize that in saying that persons are not essentially material, I do not want to deny that they can be bodily beings *at all*, i.e. to deny that they can genuinely have bodily characteristics. I certainly do not want to draw the inference (which would be fallacious) that persons are essentially *non*-material or *im*material and hence have a status somewhat akin to that of Cartesian egos. From 'φs are not essentially *F*' we cannot legitimately infer 'φs are essentially non-*F*'. I do not even want to accuse Descartes of committing this fallacy, for though he clearly regarded the *mind* as being essentially non-extended, it is implausible to represent him as regarding the terms 'mind' and 'person' as synonymous. On the other hand, while the inference I have just mentioned would be fallacious, that in itself does not of course exclude the possibility that its conclusion *might* be true; though my own view is that it is false and that persons

---

¹³ I cannot then accept David Wiggins's claim that 'A person is material in the sense of being essentially constituted by matter': see his *Sameness and Substance* (Oxford: Blackwell, 1980), p. 164.

¹⁴ Hence I cannot accept Wiggins's view that 'by *person* we mean *a certain sort of animal*', ibid., p. 187.

¹⁵ Wiggins writes of 'our [. . .] conviction that [. . .] such artifacts as robots and automata have no title to any kind of civil right', of 'the depth and passion of most people's resistance to the idea that automata can approximate to life or sentience' and of '[our belief] that, to have genuine feeling or purposes or concerns, a thing must *at least* be an animal of some sort' (ibid., pp. 174–5). But to the limited extent that we *do* have any such convictions, they can be explained (I suggest) by a proper reluctance to allow that one might *identify* a person with a robot; the evidence of people's reactions to science-fiction stories and films is, *pace* Wiggins, that we find it *only too easy* to suppose that automata might nonetheless *embody* persons. There is, in my view, no *deeper* mystery in understanding how *electronic* mechanisms could be involved in sentience than there is in understanding how *biological* mechanisms could be.

can indeed *have bodily characteristics*, in a strict and literal sense.[16]

Now if what I have just been saying about the concept of a person is right, then even without endeavouring to formulate a precise criterion of identity for persons, we can at once see that any such criterion would have at least to *differ* from the criteria for either living organisms or parcels of matter. This is because the latter criteria imply that anything answering to them is *essentially* material, so that if persons are not essentially material they cannot answer to those criteria. But from this of course we can immediately conclude, for now familiar reasons, that no person can be *identified* either with any living organism or with any parcel of matter. And indeed this is a conclusion to which we are plausibly driven quite independently of my contention concerning the status of persons as beings that are not essentially material. For if the Lockean account of the concept of a person advanced earlier is even remotely correct, it is clear that this concept so *differs* from either that of a living organism or that of a parcel of matter that, in view of the intimate semantic linkage between sortal concepts and their associated criteria of identity, there is really no good reason to suppose that the criterion of personal identity *should* be the same as either of the other criteria at issue (and certainly the burden of proof lies entirely with those who think otherwise). But then, once more, difference in criteria of identity is sufficient for a denial of any possibility of *identifying* individuals answering to those different criteria.

Here, however, it may be objected that it is just *absurd* to deny that a particular man or living organism may be a person: for cannot a living organism *act* and *perceive* and engage in *self-reflection*? – in which case it can surely have

---

[16] To a considerable extent, then, though not entirely, I can agree with P.F. Strawson's characterization of persons in his *Individuals: An Essay in Descriptive Metaphysics* (London: Methuen, 1959), chapter 3. Here it is worth recalling that Strawson does allow for the conceptual possibility of disembodied personal survival (pp. 115–16).

all that is required to make it a person, according to the Lockean conception. Various responses might be made to this objection. First of all, *is* it in fact especially obvious that a *living organism*, as opposed (as I should say) to the *person* that it embodies, may act and perceive and have self-consciousness? Not, I suggest, unless we confuse these properties with certain properties which living organisms obviously *do* have, that is, with certain physiological phenomena. After all, action and perception are very arguably not just *the same* as bodily movement and sensory stimulation, nor is self-consciousness plausibly just *the same* as any neurological activity in the brain. (Again, it is surely the *person* that thinks, feels, desires and so on, not his body or any part of it such as his brain.) It is currently fashionable, of course, to distinguish in this context between 'type–type' and 'token–token' identity theories, the suggestion being made, for instance, that though there may be no *kind* (or 'type') of neurological activity which is identifiable with a given *kind* (or 'type') of mental activity, such as self-reflection or perceptual experience, nonetheless particular *instances* (or 'tokens') of the former kind might be identifiable with particular *instances* of the latter.[17] My response to this suggestion is that I do not, of course, concede that questions concerning the identity or diversity of *particulars* can in this way be so divorced from questions concerning what *kind* of particulars they are. Mental and physical *events* and *processes*, no less than those particulars that belong to the category of *continuants* (like persons and their bodies), can only be individuated and identified as particulars of some kind, and their criteria of identity will be determined by the kinds of particulars that they are.[18] Unless, therefore,

---

[17] See, e.g., Colin McGinn, 'Anomalous Monism and Kripke's Cartesian Intuitions', *Analysis* 37 (1977), pp. 78–80, and his *The Character of Mind* (Oxford: Oxford University Press, 1982), p. 27.

[18] Donald Davidson, of course, has proposed a quite general criterion of identity for events, according to which events are identical if and only if they have the same causes and effects: see his 'The Individuation of Events', in his *Essays on Actions and Events* (Oxford: Clarendon Press, 1980), p. 179. But, though not explicitly

mental typology and physiological typology can be shown to be capable of being appropriately matched, the proposal that one might ('barely', as it were) *identify* particulars of the relevant types (mental and physical) is devoid of determinate sense; and in the absence of the required arguments, such an 'identity theory' of mind and brain amounts to nothing more than an empty gesture, which may give emotional satisfaction to the committed materialist but has no intellectual substance to it.[19]

The general objection that I have been addressing, it will be recalled, was that a living organism might qualify as a person simply by virtue of possessing the requisite properties

---

circular, this proposed criterion dissatisfies me because questions of event identity will arise in determining the identities of causes and effects, these being events themselves: see further J.E. Tiles, 'Davidson's Criterion of Event Identity', *Analysis* 36 (1976), pp. 185–7. I agree with Tiles's suggestion that 'there is no single criterion of identity for everything that may be called "an event"' (ibid., p. 185). Thus there seems to me to be no more sense in the idea that one might set about counting the *events* that have occurred in this room during the last hour than there is in the idea that one might set about counting the *things* now in it. What one *may* intelligibly count are *sorts* of event, e.g., one might well count how many *door-shuttings* have occurred in this room during the last hour. (The search for a general criterion of identity for *actions* is similarly misconceived, even if one does not construe actions to be events, as I do not.)

[19] It is often argued that a token-token identity theory may be supported on empirical grounds together with some plausible assumptions about causal relations between mental and physical events (see, e.g., Christopher Peacocke, *Holistic Explanation* (Oxford: Clarendon Press, 1979), pp. 134ff., and Robert Kirk, 'From Physical Explicability to Full-Blooded Materialism', *Philosophical Quarterly* 29 (1979), pp. 229–37). Very roughly, the sort of argument I speak of goes like this: we must accept (on pain of an implausible epiphenomenalism) that mental events sometimes cause certain physical events, e.g. bodily movements; but it is plausible to suppose that empirical scientific investigation will eventually show such physical events to be fully accountable for by wholly physical causes, e.g. neural events in the brain; therefore, on pain of allowing a most implausible systematic causal overdetermination of the physical effects in question, we must accept that their mental causes just *are* (i.e. are identical with) certain of their physical causes. The weak link in this argument is the bland assumption that empirical investigation *can* show what is alleged prior to a resolution of the very identity question at issue: for, while it is still an open question whether the accepted mental causes of a given physical effect are distinct from any physical events, empirical investigation cannot establish that a *wholly physical* causal account of that effect exists, since any complete causal account of the effect must acknowledge the causal contribution which, *ex hypothesi*, the mental events in question make. See further my 'Against an Argument for Token Identity', *Mind* 90 (1981), pp. 120–1.

– a capacity to act, perceive and engage in self-reflection. However, quite apart from my response of the previous paragraph, I would point out that, according to my own precepts, if *persons* constitute a genuine *kind* of entities at all then the general term 'person' is to be construed as a *semantically simple sortal term*, and as such not reducible by analysis or definition to some complex general term incorporating a conjunction of 'defining characteristics'. That is to say, when I announced earlier my sympathy with the Lockean conception of a person, I was not proposing to endorse (even if Locke was) any such suggestion as that the sentence '*a* is a person' might be *analysed as meaning* either '*a* is a thing which acts and perceives and is self-conscious' or even '*a* is a φ which acts and perceives and is self-conscious', where 'φ' is some sortal term. On the first of these analyses, of course, 'person' is not a genuine sortal term at all, since 'thing' is not; on the second, it is a semantically complex sortal term (see again chapter 3 of the present work). Now, to adopt the first proposal is fairly radical, and flies in the face of our apparent readiness to *individuate*, *distinguish* and *count* persons.[20] I suppose it might conceivably be argued that some of the bizarre clinical evidence arising from pathological cases of 'multiple personality', such as the famous case of 'Miss Beauchamp',[21] supports this radical view; and a similar appeal might be made to some of the evidence arising from cases of so-called 'split-brain' patients.[22] But on the

---

[20] One philosopher who has recently been prepared to deny that 'person' is a genuine sortal term is Bernard Williams, in his *Ethics and the Limits of Philosophy* (London: Fontana, 1985), on the grounds that 'The category of person, though [. . .] it looks like a sortal or classificatory notion [. . .] in fact [. . .] signals characteristics that almost all come in degrees – responsibility, self-consciousness, capacity for reflection, and so on' (p. 114). But though these characteristics 'come in degrees', this is no reason to suppose that *being a person* is a matter of degree, unless one presupposes, as I do not, that being a person is *definable* in terms of possessing these characteristics. And, in any case, the existence of borderline cases is not incompatible with a general term's being a genuine sortal.
[21] For discussion, see Kathleen V. Wilkes, 'Multiple Personality and Personal Identity', *British Journal for the Philosophy of Science* 32 (1981), pp. 331–48.
[22] See, e.g., Thomas Nagel, 'Brain Bisection and the Unity of Consciousness', in his *Mortal Questions* (Cambridge: Cambridge University Press, 1979). I shall

whole I am most reluctant to allow our responses to pathological cases to dictate to us concerning the meaning or use of well-entrenched concepts, like that of a person. The second proposal, however, is also seriously flawed: and there the difficulty resides in deciding in a principled way precisely *what* sortal term 'ϕ' should figure in the analysis. 'Living organism' will *not* do, for reasons which we have already discussed (persons are arguably not essentially material and, less contentiously, are at any rate not essentially *alive*, in the literal, biological sense).[23] To suggest that any of a range of unrelated sortal terms may do service for 'ϕ', or to hold that '*a* is a person' means 'For *some* ϕ, *a* is a ϕ which acts and perceives and is self-conscious', is again to give up a well-entrenched idea, namely, that persons, even if they may divide into different species, do not form a heterogeneous class of entities governed by a variety of different criteria of identity and hence by different principles for counting.

My own view, then, is that pending satisfactory arguments to the contrary, 'person' should be accepted at its face value as being a semantically simple sortal term, and hence *unanalysable*.[24] When I announced my sympathy for the view that persons are *essentially* active, self-reflective percipients I was not, then, advancing the case of any particular semantic analysis, and so to the extent that the general objection that I have been considering presupposes otherwise it is misconceived. And here I would add that, in my

---

review the evidence later, however, and argue that it at most creates problems for individuating *minds* rather than *persons*.

[23] I reject, then, what Wiggins calls the 'animal attribute view' of persons, according to which '*person* is a non-biological qualification of *animal*' (Wiggins, *Sameness and Substance*, p. 171). But I reject it for a reasons diametrically opposed to Wiggins' reasons for rejecting it; he does so because he apparently thinks that 'person' is a wholly biological concept – that 'by *person* we mean *a certain sort of animal*' (ibid., p. 187) – whereas I do so because I think it is not essentially biological at all.

[24] Wiggins also seems to endorse this view (ibid., pp. 173ff.); where I differ from him is in refusing to accept that 'persons are a class of organisms' (ibid., p. 187).

opinion, any attempt to confer upon something the status of 'person' by trying to ascertain *first* whether it can act, perceive and engage in self-reflection is, in any case, inevitably going to be implicitly question-begging. For positive answers to these questions very arguably *presuppose* personhood. For instance, in deciding whether in speaking of a robot device as 'seeing' (intelligently) with its electronic eye or 'acting' (intentionally) with its mechanical arm, we can interpret our words *literally* or only *metaphorically*, we very arguably have to come to a decision precisely as to whether or not the subject of our descriptions has the status of a *person* (though if we decide that it *does*, then of course I would urge that it is not after all the *robot* that perceives and acts, but rather *the person that it embodies*). The reason for this is that ascriptions of agency, perception and self-consciousness to a subject cannot be made *independently* either of each other or of ascriptions to it of indefinitely many other appropriately related states, such as beliefs, desires and intentions, together going to make up the complex network of phenomena necessary to constitute the mental life of a single *person* (so that, for example, a subject cannot genuinely be said to *perceive* unless it can also be said to believe, intend, imagine and so forth). In short, what we have to contend with is the *holism of the mental*.[25]

How we *are* to come, in a principled way, to a decision that something is (or embodies) a person is, I confess, no easy question to answer: though of course in practice we make many such decisions every day, whenever indeed we meet a new face. One lesson which we can however learn from these practical encounters is that our decision to confer the status of 'person' is not, apparently, one that is arrived at by observing the satisfaction of any determinate list of necessary and sufficient conditions (and to this extent my suggestion that 'person' is unanalysable gains some empiri-

---

[25] I borrow the phrase, of course, from Donald Davidson: see his 'Mental Events', in his *Essays on Actions and Events*, p. 217.

cal support). Of course we *do* decide on the basis of *observational evidence* (evidence precisely of agency, perception and self-consciousness, I should say), but that evidence is apparently quite non-uniform and moreover always *defeasible*. The basis for such decisions cannot then be captured, it seems, in any algorithm or rote procedure; and indeed our very ability to make them is just one sign of our own personhood – persons recognize other persons.

I have been arguing that a person can never be *identified* with the living organism that is his 'organized body' (if he has one), much less with the parcel of matter or collection of material particles that constitutes that organism at any given time. This of course raises the question: what then *is* the relationship between a person on the one hand and his 'organized body' and its constituents on the other? Before addressing that question, however, a minor point needs clearing up. My contention, in Lockean terms, is that a *person* is never identifiable with a *man*. Put this way, it does indeed seem rather paradoxical, since we often use 'man' and 'person' pretty well interchangeably.[26] And we have no hesitation in saying, for instance, that if 'John Smith' (say) is the name of a *man* then it is *ipso facto* the name of a *person*. But I take such facts only to show that 'man' in ordinary usage is *not* employed simply to denote a certain species of animal and so of living organism: in fact it means something like 'adult, male, human person', i.e. (as I should say) 'person who has an adult, male, human body'. Used in this sense, then, 'man' is a semantically complex sortal term governed by no other criterion of identity than that (if there is one) associated with the semantically simple sortal term 'person'. Here it may be asked why, this being so, we do not have names *both* for persons *and* for the human organisms that I refuse to identify with them. The answer is that, being persons, our primary interest lies with the assignment of

[26] Locke addresses this objection in much the way that I do, in his discussion of his imaginary example of the prince and the cobbler (*An Essay Concerning Human Understanding*, Book II, ch. XXVII, § 15).

personal names, but that we have at the same time a simple and satisfactory method of uniquely referring to human organisms which dispenses with the need for a distinctive set of names for them: we simply speak of '*N*'s body', where '*N*' is a personal name – relying on the empirical fact that, in the common experience of the vast majority of us, there is a one-to-one relation between persons and human organisms. The very existence and ubiquity of this form of expression, '*N*'s body', testifies indeed to our common-sense refusal to identify a person and his 'organized body': a refusal which we have seen to be wholly justified.

Returning now to the question raised previously, can we perhaps say that the relationship between a person and a living organism which is his 'organized body', like that between this organism and a parcel of matter spatiotemporally coincident with it, though not one of *identity*, is one of *constitution*? Is a person constituted by his body (if he has one), in anything like the way in which a river is constituted by water? Plainly *not*, if my earlier remarks about constitution were correct. For I pointed out earlier that it is never in general a purely *contingent* affair that things of a sort φ are constituted by things of a sort ψ. (I concede that in the case of artefacts like tables it is contingent whether they are constituted by wood or metal, say; but even here it isn't contingent that they are constituted by *matter* of some sort.[27]) So if persons were *constituted* by living organisms, it ought surely to make as manifestly little sense to speak of disembodied or even non-living persons as it does to speak of an immaterial oak tree or river: but it doesn't. Furthermore, the relation of constitution would appear to be *transitive*: if x is constituted by y and y by z, then x is constituted by z. So if persons were constituted by living organisms they would

---

[27] It has of course been argued by Kripke that in the case of a *particular* table it is not even contingent that it is (or, at least, was originally) constituted by wood, if that is what it is (or was originally) constituted by – though I am not really convinced by his arguments. See further Saul A. Kripke, *Naming and Necessity* (Oxford: Blackwell, 1980), pp. 113–14.

equally be constituted by the matter constituting those organisms, and hence be essentially material, which I have denied they are. Nor can we plausibly suppose that there might be various different *kinds* of differently constituted persons, e.g. human persons that are constituted by living organisms, artefactual persons that are constituted by electronic machines, and disembodied persons that have no physical constitution at all: for these three 'kinds' would seemingly by implication have to have different criteria of identity (in view of the known intimate connection between such criteria and necessities of constitution), and hence it would be improper after all to speak of them as species of a single genus, *person*. The supposition that one and the same human person might survive bodily death as a disembodied person would also have to be manifestly absurd, as would the supposition that a person with a human body might, through successive artificial replacements, eventually come to have a wholly artefactual body. Yet, surely, neither of these suppositions *is* manifestly absurd.

Altogether, then, I can see no prospect at all of successfully modelling the relationship between persons and living organisms on that between living organisms and their material constituents. Persons stand to their 'organized bodies' and to the matter constituting those bodies *neither* in the relation of identity *nor* in that of constitution (indeed, I don't believe that persons are *constituted* by anything at all). I can see little alternative, in fact, to recognizing a *sui generis* relationship of *personal embodiment*, because I cannot see that the relation between a person and his body (whether the latter be human, animal but non-human, or indeed altogether non-biological) is remotely like that between objects of any other two sorts. This should not, however, be seen as a concession to obscurantism (or even to Cartesian dualism), since I am by no means denying that facts about a person's body (whether they be biological facts or facts pertaining to some other branch of physical science, such as electronics) can cast light on and help to explain psychological facts concerning that person; though, of course, I am committed to repudiating the possibility of the 'reduction' of psychology to any of the physical sciences (biology, chemistry, electronics or what not), either separately or conjointly. And it may even be that in the light of such psychophysical explanations we may some day come to establish that the existence of disembodied (or even non-living) persons, though a conceptual possibility, is not an empirical scientific possibility; though I would add that such a day is, in my view, still a long way off.

7.3 Is There a Criterion of Personal Identity?

It will be appreciated that these conclusions, though turning on considerations involving criteria of identity, have been arrived at without any attempt so far actually to formulate a criterion of personal identity: the quest for such a criterion was deferred quite early on in the present discussion. My reason for proceeding in this indirect fashion is that, as I have indicated previously, I am rather doubtful whether this quest can succeed. I suspect that persons do not in fact *have* an (informative) criterion of identity: that they may constitute a 'basic' sort, in the terminology of chapter 2 of the present work. To see why this might be so, we must return to Locke. (It should be observed, incidentally, that the non-existence of a criterion of personal identity would not vitiate those arguments of the preceding part of this chapter which turned on the non-identity of individuals belonging to sorts not sharing the same criterion of identity, since two sorts can fail to share the same criterion not only by having different criteria but also because one of them has a criterion while the other does not. Wherever I speak, earlier, of sorts differing in their criteria of identity, I should be understood to include this possible source of difference.)

Now, I agreed earlier with Locke that in order to discover a criterion of personal identity or, as he puts it, to 'find wherein *personal Identity* consists', we needed to examine the concept of a person, or 'what *Person* stands for'; and I substantially agreed with him also as to what persons essentially are – thinking, self-conscious beings with a capacity for perception and action. (Locke himself is not perfectly explicit about the need for perception and agency, though I think he is implicitly committed to considering them as essential characteristics of persons, and certainly I believe that they are such.[28]) Let us then look at the criterion of personal identity that Locke himself proposes, since if any proposal can be satisfactory it must I think be one along broadly Lockean lines. (We have of course already seen that no 'bodily' criterion of personal identity can hope to succeed.) The criterion he proposes is stated in his own words as follows:[29]

> since consciousness always accompanies thinking, and 'tis that, that makes every one to be, what he calls *self*; and thereby distinguishes himself from all other thinking things, in this alone consists *personal Identity*, *i.e.* the sameness of a rational Being: And as far as this consciousness can be extended backwards to any past Action or Thought, so far reaches the Identity of that *Person*; it is the same *self* now as it was then; and 'tis by the same *self* with this present one that now reflects on it, that that Action was done.

And a little later he puts it thus:[30]

> *personal Identity* consists [. . .] in the Identity of *consciousness* [. . .] If [. . .] *Socrates* waking and sleeping do not

---

[28] In the very section (*An Essay Concerning Human Understanding*, Book II, ch. XXVII, § 9) in which Locke characterizes a *person* as 'a thinking intelligent Being, that has reason and reflection, and can consider it self as it self, the same thinking thing in different times and places', he goes on to speak of both perceptions and actions as properties of persons, quite as a matter of course. And though Locke used 'perception' in a broad sense to include thinking, it is clear that in this section he also means to include *sense*-perception. Thus, having commented that it is 'impossible for any one to perceive, without perceiving, that he does perceive', he immediately adds, obviously as a gloss on this, 'When we see, hear, smell, taste, feel, meditate, or will any thing, we know that we do so.'
[29] Ibid., § 9.
[30] Ibid., § 19.

partake of the same *consciousness*, *Socrates* waking and sleeping is not the same Person.

It is clear, as this last passage may suggest, that Locke was to some extent modelling his criterion of personal identity on his earlier criterion of identity for living organisms, with the notion of 'participation of the same consciousness' playing a role analogous to that of the notion of 'participation of the same life'. At one point he even draws a direct parallel, in these words:[31]

> Different Substances, by the same consciousness (where they do partake in) being united into one Person; as well as different Bodies, by the same Life are united into one Animal, whose *Identity* is preserved, in that change of Substances, by the unity of one continued Life.

It would *appear* that the 'different substances' referred to by Locke at the beginning of this passage are understood by him to be different *immaterial* or *spiritual* substances, or (perhaps) 'souls'; these apparently being the entities which, as he *here* supposes, may 'participate of the same consciousness' by analogy with the way in which different *material* substances (bodies, or particles of matter) may 'participate of the same life'. I do not know to what extent he intended this analogy to be taken seriously, since he frequently openly admits our almost total ignorance concerning spiritual substances, saying that we are 'in the dark concerning these Matters'.[32] Certainly, elsewhere he speaks as though it is *persons*, rather than souls or immaterial spiritual substances, that may be said to 'participate of the same consciousness' and thereby be the same person (witness the penultimate passage quoted above, in particular Locke's remark concerning Socrates waking and Socrates sleeping). And indeed it is in these terms that I propose to interpret Locke's

---

[31] Ibid., § 10.
[32] Ibid., § 27.

suggested criterion of personal identity, in common I think with most other commentators. For if the analogy mentioned earlier is taken too seriously, Locke cannot be represented as making a contribution of much value to our understanding of personal identity. Accordingly, I shall take it that the criterion that Locke wishes to endorse may be stated in my own style somewhat as follows:

> If x and y are *persons*, then x is identical with y if and only if x and y participate of the same consciousness at all times at which they are conscious (i.e. are 'co-conscious' at all such times).

Of course, interpreting what this criterion actually *amounts to* is a considerable problem in itself. But this much at least is clear enough: 'participation of the same consciousness' cannot be supposed to mean *possession of the same conscious states*, simply because the same person at different times possesses different conscious states – such states being transient whereas persons endure.[33] I therefore interpret it to mean (what I call) *co-consciousness*, a notion which demands that if x and y are conscious at times t_1 and t_2 respectively (where $t_1 \leq t_2$), then x and y are *co-conscious* at those times only if for any item z of which x is conscious at t_1,

---

[33] Butler is, I think, uncharitable to Locke on this issue, setting him up as something of a straw man at one point by suggesting this unsatisfactory interpretation: see Joseph Butler, 'Of Personal Identity', in John Perry (ed.), *Personal Identity* (Berkeley: University of California Press, 1975), pp. 102–3. Of course, I am not denying that if x and y *are* the same person, then any conscious state possessed by x must also be possessed by y: Leibniz's law demands this much. And, equally evidently, possession of the same conscious states by both x and y is logically sufficient for the identity of x and y, in virtue of the logically non-shareable nature of individual conscious states. However, it is obvious that no adequate *criterion* of personal identity can be grounded on these truths, because individual conscious states are only individuable by reference to the persons whose states they are (which is precisely why they are logically non-shareable). My criticism of Butler as 'uncharitable' turns on a quite different issue, namely, his imputation that on Locke's criterion persons could strictly speaking only be said to endure as long as their current state of consciousness. A similar criticism may be levelled at Thomas Reid's 'Of Mr. Locke's Account of Our Personal Identity' in Perry (ed.), *Personal Identity*, pp. 116–17.

y is (at least *potentially*) conscious of z at t_2 – so that, for example, where t_1 = noon on lst January 1805 and t_2 = now, if Napoleon and I were to be co-conscious at those times I would now be conscious of (or at least be *capable* of calling to consciousness) everything of which Napoleon was then conscious. (This then is a condition which may obviously be satisfied in respect of any such item z by the occurrence at *different* times of two distinct acts of consciousness, e.g. a perception of z at one time and an 'experiential memory' of z at a later time.) So, clearly, what is at issue *here* is not so much the identity of conscious states as the identity of objects of consciousness; though, of course, conscious states may *themselves* be such objects, and *must* be in any self-reflecting being such as Locke takes a person to be. (Recall Locke's assertion, quoted earlier, that it is 'impossible for any one to perceive, without perceiving, that he does perceive', which commits him at least to such higher orders of consciousness, seemingly indeed *ad infinitum*.) I also take it, however, that co-consciousness demands satisfaction of another condition which is harder to state clearly, but which might loosely be expressed in this way: if x and y are co-conscious at a certain time (so that this is the 'synchronic' case, in which $t_1 = t_2$), and w and z are items of which x and y respectively are conscious at that time, then x must be conscious of w and z 'together', as the object of a single act of consciousness, as must y also. (This might be called the 'unity of consciousness' condition.) No doubt much more could be said about the notion of co-consciousness that Locke seems implicitly to be operating with, but I have said enough for my present purposes (and I should in any case make it plain that I have no stake in claiming that the notion is ultimately either a very useful one or even a wholly coherent one).

Many commentators dwell on the *diachronic* implications of Locke's proposed criterion of personal identity (i.e. its implications for the identity of persons *through time*) and the problems arising therefrom, though of course it also has *synchronic* implications. (An adequate criterion of identity for any sort of *continuant* must, naturally, have both diachronic and synchronic implications.) But even in the case of synchronic identity-questions the proposal meets with difficulties. It is true that the so-called 'unity of consciousness' seems to play an important role in our understanding of what makes one person distinct from another at a given time: in general, one wants to say, I am *jointly* conscious of each of my present conscious states but not at all conscious (at least, not 'directly' conscious, or conscious 'from the inside') of any of your present conscious states. But then we have to contend with the evidence arising from the studies by Sperry and others of so-called 'split-brain' patients, who *seem* to be subject to a bifurcation of consciousness.[34] Interpreting this evidence is however a contentious issue, some holding that consciousness in fact only resides in the dominant left hemisphere of the brain,[35] others that even prior to commissurotomy there are two distinct centres of consciousness,[36] and yet others that a genuine bifurcation of consciousness is brought about by the operation, with one mind 'splitting' into two. However, whatever we are to say about the possibility of a 'split mind' or bifurcation of consciousness, what we surely *cannot* say is that *either* ordinary human beings *or* even those with 'split brains' embody two distinct *persons*. (It would be rash indeed to imagine that 'mind' and 'person' are co-designative, though this is apparently often tacitly assumed in philosophical discussions of 'split-brain' phenomena.) To suppose that all normal human beings embody two distinct persons simply runs completely counter to common sense and the well-entrenched usage of the term 'person'; moreover, genuinely distinct persons could not, I suggest, tolerate the degree of

---

[34] For a description and discussion of Roger Sperry's results, see Karl R. Popper and John C. Eccles, *The Self and its Brain* (London: Springer Verlag, 1977), pp. 313ff.

[35] Eccles suggests as much: see ibid., pp. 325ff.

[36] This is Sperry's own view: see ibid., p. 325.

mutual dependence that co-embodiment would impose upon them (a degree inestimably higher than that imposed even on inseparable Siamese twins). And this latter consideration also counts against the proposal that commissurotomy *divides one person into two*. In consequence, only the hypothesis that consciousness is restricted to the dominant left hemisphere permits the evidence to be interpreted in a manner compatible with a retention of Locke's co-consciousness criterion of personal identity; yet this hypothesis is not, in my view, a particularly plausible one, in the light of some of the patently intelligent actions that seem capable of being performed, in 'split-brain' patients, through the right hemisphere.

So the Lockean co-consciousness criterion of personal identity appears to fail even before we consider its application to diachronic questions. In this latter context Locke is of course usually interpreted as advancing a so-called 'memory' criterion of personal identity and, certainly, much of what he says supports that interpretation. I do not, however, propose to traverse once more this well-trodden area of debate, making all the now customary references to the objections of Butler, Reid and so on. I think it has been sufficiently shown, by recent writers like Wiggins and Parfit,[37] that many of the standard objections either fail or can easily be circumvented by modifications true to the spirit of Locke's views (e.g. by replacing the requirement that identical persons be co-conscious with respect to *all* different times at which they are conscious by one only demanding transtemporal co-consciousness – i.e. memory – with respect to times at most separated by some minimum interval; or again, by relaxing the requirement – if indeed Locke intended it – that memory embrace *all* of the items held in consciousness at some former time). What I shall do, rather, is to explain why I do not think that anything remotely along the lines of Locke's

---

[37] See further Wiggins, *Sameness and Substance*, chapter 6, and Derek Parfit, *Reasons and Persons* (Oxford: Clarendon Press, 1984), chapters 10 and 11. See also the useful anthology edited by John Perry, *Personal Identity*.

criterion of personal identity can hold out any hope of success. We have seen indeed that Locke's own co-consciousness criterion appears to fail on empirical grounds even in the synchronic case: but I am not now concerned with merely empirical reasons for dissatisfaction with a criterion along Lockean lines.[38]

It will be recalled from our general discussion of criteria of identity in chapter 2 that an adequate criterion of identity for things of a given sort ϕ must specify the truth-conditions of identity-statements concerning ϕs *in an informative way*; and, more particularly, that a putative criterion could not be deemed genuinely to inform us 'wherein identity consists' for ϕs if it made appeal (however tacit) to *ϕ-identity* in its expression of the relevant criterial condition C_ϕ. I also suggested that a criterion of identity for ϕs could only be thus informatively supplied in terms which presupposed the identity of things of one or more *other* sorts. This was certainly true of the criterion of identity for *sets* (which presupposes identity-conditions for their members), but it is equally true of the Lockean criteria for *parcels of matter* and for *living organisms*, to which I have given qualified endorsement in this chapter. Thus the criterion for parcels of matter presupposes an account of the identity of *atoms*, and the criterion for living organisms presupposes an account of the identity of *collections of material particles*. We saw, indeed, that a defect in the former was its presumption of atomism, but we also saw that it was no easy task to formulate an informative, non-circular criterion of identity for parcels of

---

[38] So what I want to contend is that there is a *defect of principle* in Lockean-type accounts of personal identity which cannot be overcome by any amount of tinkering with the details. And here I should remark that for my purposes I can lump in *Humean*-type accounts with Lockean ones, since both traditions attempt to provide an account of personal identity purely by reference to *psychological states and their interrelationships*; though Hume of course differs from Locke in thinking that personal identity is strictly 'fictitious', and perhaps more importantly in emphasizing the role of *causal* relationships between the psychological states of the 'same' person in contrast with Locke's emphasis upon *cognitive* relationships, especially those involving memory. See David Hume, *A Treatise of Human Nature*, ed. L.A. Selby-Bigge, 2nd edn (Oxford: Clarendon Press, 1978), Book I, Part IV, Section VI.

matter which did not presuppose atomism. And I suspect that similar difficulties would arise for atomism itself if it were pressed to provide an informative, non-circular criterion of identity for *atoms*. (I speak here, of course, of seventeenth-century atomism of the Locke/Boyle kind, not the modern theory in which 'atom' is a complete misnomer: today the problems arise instead with the latest candidates for the status of 'fundamental particles' – formerly protons and neutrons, now quarks.) Observe, here, that it would be naive indeed to suppose that mere considerations of 'spatiotemporal continuity' might settle such questions; first, because this ignores the thorny issue of interrupted existence, but more fundamentally because we must always be prepared to answer, in a non-question-begging way, the query 'spatiotemporal continuity of *what*?' Thus if, in the atomic case say, we appeal to the spatiotemporal continuity of the presence of *an atom*, we seem to be begging the question by *presupposing* an account of the identity-conditions of atoms; whereas if we appeal instead to the spatiotemporal continuity of 'atom-stages' we are committed to the dubious doctrine of temporal parts.[39] The lesson, I suggest, is that any system of ontology must take *some* sorts or kinds to be 'basic': these are the sorts or kinds for which informative identity-criteria *cannot be given*, simply because there are no other sorts or kinds of things available in the system whose identity can be presupposed in specifying the truth-conditions of identity-statements concerning things of these sorts.[40]

Now why might it be supposed that *persons* comprise a basic sort? First of all, it is to be observed that persons are not, plausibly, *constituted* by anything. We have seen already that they have no *material* constituents. Locke, it is true, seems to have toyed with the idea that persons have

---

[39] For more detailed discussion of the issues, see my 'Substance, Identity and Time', *Proceedings of the Aristotelian Society*, supp. vol. LXII (1988).
[40] The point I am making is, of course, closely related to Strawson's view that there must be a class of 'basic particulars': see Strawson, *Individuals*, pp. 38ff.

immaterial or *spiritual* constituents, in attempting to draw a parallel between the notion of 'participation of the same consciousness' and 'participation of the same life': but we saw that this analogy could not be taken seriously, simply because we have no knowledge of the existence of 'spiritual' substance of any sort. Now *if* persons had constituents, then of course they could not be expected to comprise a basic sort, since we would expect to be able to formulate their criterion of identity in terms presupposing the identity of these constituents, whatever they were. But it doesn't seem that they do: which, I think, is why we find it so difficult to comprehend how a *person* could split or divide, since only what has parts seems capable of division. (This, no doubt, is the element of truth in the Cartesian doctrine of the indivisibility of the soul.) Of course, though persons do not have constituents, they do have *states*, both mental and physical (though the latter only if they are embodied). So why may we not hope to supply an informative criterion of personal identity in terms presupposing only the identity of such states? The states in question would, of course, have to be *mental* ones, since a physicalistic criterion has already been ruled out. And indeed it is just such a criterion (one in terms of mental states) that Locke proposes (on the interpretation I have favoured). The co-consciousness criterion that he advances presupposes an account of the identity of *conscious states*. (I am not forgetting here my earlier denial that 'participation of the same consciousness' just *means* 'possession of the same conscious states', only pointing out that questions concerning the identity of conscious states require to be settled in arriving at ascriptions of co-consciousness, since the latter turn on questions involving the identity of *objects* of consciousness, some of which objects are themselves *conscious states*.) Thus, for example, on a Lockean-type account the answers to diachronic identity questions concerning persons will turn on such issues as whether a person at time t_2 remembers some conscious episode experienced by a person at some earlier time t_1 – such as a particular *pain*: and this presupposes that we have some grasp of how to individuate and identify particular pains.[41] (It is clearly not enough that the person at t_2 should remember a pain *qualitatively indistinguishable* from the one experienced at t_1 – he must remember *that very pain* if, by a Lockean account, he is to be identified with the person who originally experienced it.)

However, this is precisely why, quite apart from the question of its empirical satisfiability, the Lockean criterion (and more generally any criterion along broadly Lockean lines) cannot be deemed informative in the way required of any adequate criterion of identity. For conscious states (and indeed mental or psychological states quite generally) cannot themselves be individuated or identified save in terms which presuppose the identity of the persons (or conscious subjects) whose states they are.[42] Thus there is, for instance, no generally applicable way of identifying a particular *pain* save as the pain of such-and-such a character experienced on a given occasion *by a given person* (e.g. the toothache I experienced at noon yesterday). Character and occasion alone may clearly be insufficient to identify a pain uniquely (as an imagined example involving Siamese twins will testify). Nor will reference to the pain's *causes and effects* do more than (at best) to shift the question of identification on to other items in the same category as the pain itself (i.e. other mental or psychological states) – since no psychological state has purely non-psychological causes and effects (a

---

[41] Similarly, on a Humean-type account the answers to diachronic identity-questions concerning persons will turn on such issues as whether the particular psychological states of a person at t_2 are *causally related* in the right sorts of ways to the particular psychological states of a person at an earlier time t_1 – and this again presupposes a grasp of the identity-conditions of psychological or mental states.

[42] Cf. Strawson, *Individuals*, pp. 41ff. It is unfortunate that Parfit, while acknowledging the existence of Strawson's arguments to this effect, has elected to defer discussion of them (see Parfit, *Reasons and Persons*, p. 225); for unless he can counter these arguments, Parfit's entire approach to personal identity is vitiated. The same criticism may be made regarding John Perry: see his 'Personal Identity, Memory, and the Problem of Circularity', in Perry (ed.), *Personal Identity*, pp. 136–7.

fact which is once more connected with the so-called holism of the mental). And in the case of non-locatable conscious states such as thoughts and desires, the dependence of their identity upon that of the persons whose states they are is still more evident. Those modern philosophers who have felt sympathy for a mentalistic criterion of personal identity along broadly Lockean lines have, I suspect, been guilty of implicitly hypostatizing mental states and treating them effectively as the *constituents* of persons. (Hume, of course, did this quite explicitly, regarding a person as 'nothing but a bundle or collection of different perceptions'.[43]) But, clearly, the constituents of objects precisely *do* need to be conceived of as entities that are individuable and identifiable independently of the objects whose constituents they are, in a way in which we can now see that mental states could not in principle be. The tacit hypostatization of mental states confers upon them, however, an illusory ontological independence which, I suggest, has served to disguise this fatal flaw in the Lockean approach from friend and foe alike.

But perhaps it may be felt that my argument of the last paragraph has proceeded too swiftly. In particular, some may wish to urge that a *physicalist* in matters of the mental could overcome the difficulty I have been dwelling on by suggesting that each psychological state is identifiable *at least in principle* with some physiological state (albeit only on a 'token–token' basis), the latter being uniquely individuable by reference to its causes and effects as described in purely physical terms. However, quite apart from the fact that this proposal threatens to reduce what was intended to be a psychological account of personal identity to a physiological one, the phrase 'at least in principle' should certainly not be allowed to pass unchallenged. All that its employment really represents here is a pious hope that what I say cannot be done *might* somehow be achieved by a neuroscientist of the distant future. But, as I have already indicated earlier in this

---

[43] Hume, *A Treatise of Human Nature*, p. 252.

chapter, it would be utterly facile to suppose that such an achievement could issue purely from empirical inquiry. Clearly, before one can even *begin* to consider what empirical evidence there might be in support of the thesis that each or any psychological state is identifiable with some physiological state, one must not only have some grasp of the identity-conditions of *physiological* states (whether in terms of their physical causes and effects or in some other terms), one must also have some *independent* grasp of the identity-conditions of *psychological* states. So already we can see that the physicalist proposal now under consideration presents as such no *solution* to the current difficulty – that of circumventing the need to refer to the *persons possessing* psychological states in identifying the latter – since no reason has been offered to doubt that such reference will still be needed in order to specify *which* particular psychological state (if any) is supposedly identifiable with a given physiological state. (Recall that we are dealing here with a 'token–token' theory, so that no 'type–type' criteria will be available to be called in aid.) But furthermore this very fact threatens to vitiate altogether the ('token–token') physicalist thesis. For, as I have stressed so often before, individual items are *not even in principle identifiable* if they instantiate sorts governed by *different criteria of identity*, and this now appears to be precisely how matters stand with regard to psychological states and physiological states, since the former but not the latter appear to be governed by a criterion making reference to the persons possessing the states in question.

Another reason, however, why it may be felt that my condemnation of mentalistic criteria of personal identity along broadly Lockean lines has been too swift is that it may be thought that the sort of objection I raise fails to undermine the capacity of such a criterion to determine answers to *diachronic* identity-questions concerning persons, even if it shows that the answers to *synchronic* identity-questions concerning persons are presupposed in individuating and identifying mental states. But to adopt such a defence is effectively to endorse the approach of treating persons as four-dimensional 'spacetime worms'. According to this approach, what we should try to do in framing a criterion of identity for persons is to look for some relationship between *person-stages* ('time-slices' of persons) which is necessary and sufficient for their being *stages of the same person*.[44] I am, however, totally opposed to this approach to the diachronic identity of continuants quite generally, as I made plain in an earlier chapter. I wholly repudiate the 'four-dimensional view' which it embodies, since I find the notion that things like persons, trees and tables *have* 'stages' or 'time-slices' barely comprehensible and at best metaphysically extravagant.[45] More crucially, I see no reason whatever to suppose that the notion of a 'person-stage' can be introduced in a way which would make the individuation and identification of person-stages possible without reference to the persons whose stages they were, and in consequence see no prospect of there emerging an *informative*, *non-circular* criterion of personal identity framed in terms of person-stages.[46] If my scepticism on this point is warranted, then it provides an answer to the objection raised at the beginning of this paragraph: for the implication would be, contrary to the supposition of that objection, that *synchronic* identity-questions concerning persons (which, on the four-dimensional view, are tantamount to

---

[44] See, e.g., David Lewis, 'Survival and Identity', in his *Philosophical Papers, Volume I*, (Oxford: Oxford University Press, 1983).

[45] See further my 'Substance, Identity and Time' and also my 'Lewis on Perdurance versus Endurance', *Analysis* 47 (1987), pp. 152–4. That my view of the nature of time itself is antithetical to the 'four-dimensional view' may be gleaned from my 'The Indexical Fallacy in McTaggart's Proof of the Unreality of Time', *Mind* 96 (1987), pp. 62–70.

[46] One leading stage theorist, Sydney Shoemaker, concedes that by his own account the diachronic identity-conditions of continuants quite generally cannot be non-circularly specified: see 'Identity, Properties, and Causality' in his *Identity, Cause, and Mind* (Cambridge: Cambridge University Press, 1984). But I cannot agree that a circular specification, however *non-trivial*, may legitimately be presented as an account of what identity through time *consists in*: cf. Colin McGinn's review of *Identity, Cause, and Mind* in *Journal of Philosophy* 84 (1987), pp. 227–32. (I should perhaps emphasize that in insisting that adequate identity-criteria be 'informative' in my sense, I do not merely require that they specify identity-conditions non-trivially.)

identity-questions concerning person-stages) are not answerable independently of *diachronic* identity-questions concerning persons, and that, indeed, any acceptable criterion of identity for persons should be capable of delivering answers to *both* diachronic *and* synchronic identity-questions concerning them.

In connection, then, with the crucial point at issue, I suggest that any attempt to formulate identity-conditions for person-stages will be compelled to presuppose answers to diachronic identity-questions concerning persons: in short, that person-stages will (at best) only prove to be identifiable and distinguishable by reference to the *personal histories* to which they supposedly belong. This, at root, is because I consider that persons are *essentially* things with a past and a (potential) future. The essential historicity of persons promises to defeat, then, any attempt to see their careers as merely constructed compositionally from momentary elements, and hence promises to prevent us from seeing 'person-stages' other than as (at best) abstractions from the histories of persons. One way of making the point would be to deny that any genuine sense could be made of the notion that a *person*, or indeed anything even temporarily *simulating* a person, could exist for only the span of a few moments or minutes. The generation of a person is, I suggest, something that *necessarily* takes time, because it involves processes of education, socialization and the accretion of experience whose end-products *could not* even in principle be reproduced in any 'instantaneous' fashion. This is, admittedly, a large claim, which I cannot undertake to defend in depth just here. At the same time, the burden of proof in this matter lies if anything more with my opponents, since it is they who seek to invoke entities of a hitherto unheard of kind ('person-stages').

My overall conclusion, then, is that persons in all probability *do* comprise what I would call a basic sort, for which no adequate criterion of identity can be formulated – though it is true that I have arrived at this conclusion by the exhaustion of alternative possibilities rather than by the securer method of deduction from first principles.[47] However, if I am finally to embrace this conclusion it is plainly incumbent upon me to offer something in answer to the question as to how it is, in the supposed absence of a criterion of personal identity, that we are nonetheless able to identify and distinguish persons as relatively easily as we apparently do. The sort of response that is available to me will become clear when one recalls the distinction made, in the second chapter of this book, between criteria of identity proper, which are *semantic* principles, and merely *epistemic* or *heuristic* or *evidential* rules. There are many principles of the latter sort available to guide us in forming judgements as to the identity and diversity of persons. For instance, since we almost exclusively have dealings with human persons, and believe that a one-to-one relationship almost universally obtains between human persons and human organisms, we can in general rely on identity of human organism as a guide to personal identity. Thus, since apparently unique physical characteristics like fingerprints are a reliable guide to the identity of human organisms, they are derivatively also a reliable guide to personal identity; so that in an *evidential* sense of 'criterion', we can indeed legitimately speak of 'bodily criteria' of personal identity. And in the same evidential sense we may equally speak, say, of a 'memory criterion' of personal identity. The various 'puzzle cases' and

---

[47] One possibility which some readers may feel I ought to have explored is a 'bootstrapping' strategy whereby, say, we first individuate psychological states by reference to persons conceived of in a primitive, criterionless way but then go on to reconceptualize and reindividuate persons by reference to causal and/or cognitive relationships between the psychological states previously picked out (after which the cycle might be repeated a further number of times, resulting in a gradual tightening-up of the identity-criteria of *both* psychological states *and* persons through their mutual interaction). My own feeling is that this is a revisionary strategy which would only be appropriate in the case of entities of a highly theoretical status (such as those postulated by the advanced sciences) and hence not in the case of persons, given their conceptual centrality in both metaphysics and common-sense thinking. But, in any case, unless and until such a strategy is worked out in enough detail for its tenability to be properly evaluated, I cannot be expected to pass a definitive opinion to it.

thought-experiments beloved of writers on the subject of personal identity (beginning with Locke himself) only serve to show, what philosophical analysis more directly serves to show, that neither 'bodily' nor 'memory' criteria of personal identity can have the status of semantic principles, but at most only the status of rules of evidence (and defeasible rules at that): they do not tell us 'wherein personal identity consists', but only guide us (more or less reliably) in the formation of judgements of personal identity in the light of the empirical evidence available to us.[48] Wherein *does* personal identity consist, then? The only tenable answer that I can see at present is the perhaps rather perplexing one that *it consists in nothing but itself*: that personal identity is, as we might say, *primitive and ungrounded*.[49] If this really turns out to be so, the further implications for metaphysics and for psychology promise to be exciting and far reaching.[50]

---

[48] It may of course be wondered with what *justification* we can regard such rules of evidence as 'reliable' in the absence of any substantive account of what personal identity is supposed to consist in. To this query I would however be inclined to respond by saying that search for a justification at this level would be inappropriate, and that all we can or should look to is our complex network of practices in arriving at everyday judgements of personal identity or diversity. In short, I am inclined to reject any sort of *foundationalism* in the epistemology of personal identity, even though I am inclined to accept the semantic primitiveness of our concept of a person.

[49] Amongst recent authors, much the same conclusion is arrived at by Geoffrey Madell, in his *The Identity of the Self* (Edinburgh: Edinburgh University Press, 1981); though there are many aspects of Madell's position with which I cannot agree.

[50] On the side of metaphysics, I might mention that an additional reason for thinking that personal identity must indeed be primitive – a reason which may help to overcome one's initial perplexity at the very possibility of this – can be extracted from certain conceptual connections plausibly holding between the notions of personhood and time. If arguments developed in my 'The Indexical Fallacy in McTaggart's Proof of the Unreality of Time' are correct, then we regard time rather than space as the dimension of *change* because of certain constraints, asymmetrical with respect to space and time, on the spatiotemporal 'routes' which it is open to one and the same person to take. This, however, implies that the idea of personal identity is actually presupposed by our understanding of the nature of time, and hence that one cannot expect a perfectly non-circular account of what identity through time 'consists in' for persons.

8

Sortal Terms and Natural Laws

That there is a distinction of some importance to be made between 'nomic' and 'accidental' generalizations has long been recognized by philosophers of science.[1] There is disagreement, however, as to whether the source of the distinction lies in some subjective diversity of our attitudes towards statements bearing a single underlying form,[2] or in some objective difference between the truth-conditions of two types of statement. An important ontological question raised by the latter thesis is this: does the assertion of nomic or lawlike generalizations invoke entities which are not invoked by the assertion of accidental generalizations? In particular, does it presuppose a universe of discourse embracing more entities than just the 'actually existent individuals' countenanced by the nominalist, and if so, what is the character of these supplementary entities? Will it do, for instance, merely to expand the nominalist's ontology by the addition of *possible* individuals, or must entities of a quite different order be acknowledged? I shall argue in favour of the objectivist thesis that lawlike statements have distinctive truth-conditions and I shall suggest, without claiming to

---

[1] See, e.g., W. Kneale, *Probability and Induction* (Oxford: Clarendon Press, 1949), pp. 70ff.
[2] Cf. A.J. Ayer, *Probability and Evidence* (London: Macmillan, 1972), pp. 129ff.

offer firm proof, that a satisfactory answer to the ontological question will require us to invoke, as additional entities, not possible individuals but (actual) *sorts* or *kinds* as objects distinct from the individuals ordinarily said to instantiate or exemplify them. My approach will be, initially, through a consideration of the grammatical form of lawlike sentences in natural language. I justify this point of departure on the grounds that natural language is the basic vehicle of all human thought, at least at the level of sophistication which must concern us at present.

In a natural language natural laws are, I would claim, most naturally expressed as *dispositional predications with sortal terms in subject position*. Enough has already been said by way of introduction about sortal terms in previous chapters, but some brief reminders may be in order here. *Sortal terms* may be either *simple* or *complex*. (We may skirt, for the time being, my earlier distinction between syntactical and semantic simplicity or complexity, relying on the fact that for the most part the syntax may be expected to reflect the semantics.) In English the chief varieties of *simple* sortal terms are mass nouns (like 'wood' and 'water') and common or count nouns (like 'tree' and 'horse'). *Complex* sortal terms are formed from simple ones by the addition of adjectives or adjectival phrases (as in 'rusty iron', 'wild horse', 'wood which has been soaked in water' and 'tree which sheds its leaves in winter'). As I explained in a previous chapter, a plural suffix or the indefinite article may often appropriately be regarded just as a logically redundant part of a sortal term containing a count noun, so that I shall commonly describe simply as sortal terms noun-phrases of the form '*a* so-and-so' or 'so-and-so*s*' (e.g. '*a* tree' or 'wild horse*s*'). One widely applicable test for such logical redundancy, which I shall often exploit in what follows, is that it should be a matter of merely stylistic difference whether the singular or the plural form is used (as for example in the logically equivalent sentences 'A horse is a mammal' and 'Horses are mammals'). We may compare and contrast sortal terms with *individual terms*, which in a natural language like English may also be either simple or complex, simple ones being chiefly exemplified by proper names (like 'Dobbin' and 'Scott') and complex ones by definite descriptions (like 'the horse in Farmer Brown's stable' and 'the author of *Waverley*'), though also by demonstrative noun-phrases (like 'that horse' and 'this piece of salt').

Dispositional (as opposed to *occurrent*) predication is indicated, in English at least, either by certain conventions of tense or by certain conventions of adjective-formation. Thus compare the sentences 'Dobbin *eats* grass' and 'Dobbin *is eating* grass', the first of which is dispositional in force and the second occurent. Or again, compare the sentences, 'This piece of salt *dissolves* in water' and 'This piece of salt *is dissolving* in water'. In present-tense predications, as these examples show, English generally uses the continuous present to indicate occurent predication and the simple or absolute present to indicate dispositional predication. (In past-tense predications the corresponding distinction is between the continuous past, as in 'was eating' or 'was dissolving', and the habitual past, as in 'used to eat' or 'used to dissolve'.) Alternatively, English often uses the adjectival suffix '-able' (and variants of this) to denote dispositional predication, as in 'This piece of salt is water-soluble' (clearly equivalent to 'This piece of salt dissolves in water'). But some adjectives are ambiguous with respect to the dispositional/occurent distinction, most notoriously the English colour-adjectives: thus one may say that in blue light a (dispositionally) red object is (occurrently) black.

How the dispositional/occurrent distinction is ultimately to be explicated is a difficult issue, which I cannot yet go into in any detail. So far I have characterized the distinction for English in purely syntactical terms, but that there is an important underlying semantic distinction cannot be in doubt. Of course, one very popular theory is that disposition-statements may be analysed in terms of conditionals involving only occurrent predication. Thus 'This piece of salt is water-soluble' might be analysed in terms of the counterfactual 'If this piece of salt were in water, it would be dissolving'. Although I cannot go into my reasons at the moment, my own view is that *any* such attempt to eliminate dispositional predication in favour of the occurrent variety is doomed to failure, and thus it seems to me that Aristotle (if I interpret him correctly) was on the right lines in viewing the distinction between the 'actual' (or occurrent) and the 'potential' (or dispositional) as ultimate and irreducible.[3] Unfortunately this means that I cannot yet profess to explain, in any non-question-begging way, precisely in what the distinction consists (if I could, some analysis would be forthcoming permitting the replacement of distinctively dispositional modes of locutions by something else). Thus for present purposes I shall have to appeal to the reader's linguistic intuitions to corroborate any claim of mine that a certain predicate has dispositional or occurrent force. But I should emphasize that even if I am wrong about the irreducibility of the dispositional/occurrent distinction, nothing I have to say concerning the logical form or ontological status of natural laws need be compromised, since my views on the latter only presuppose such a distinction without presupposing anything about its ultimate nature. Nonetheless, in due course I shall offer some further speculations about the nature of the distinction: in particular, I shall suggest that the irreducibility of the dispositional/occurrent distinction is ultimately grounded in the irreducibility of the distinction between individuals and sorts.

In ordinary English, both individual and sortal terms may figure as the grammatical subjects of sentences, whether involving dispositional or occurrent predication. We have already seen how the individual terms 'Dobbin' and 'this piece of salt' may serve as the subjects both of the dispositional predicates '___ eats grass' and '___ dissolves in water' and of the corresponding occurrent predicates '___ is

---

[3] See Aristotle, *Metaphysics*, Book θ, passim.

eating grass' and '⎯⎯ is dissolving in water'. But sortal terms, such as 'a horse' and 'salt', may also serve as the subjects of these predicates, as in the (dispositional) sentences 'A horse eats grass' and 'Salt dissolves in water' on the one hand and the (occurrent) sentences 'A horse is eating grass' and 'Salt is dissolving in water' on the other. All of these sentences are well formed in English, and native English speakers will be well aware of circumstances in which their utterance would be appropriate.

We are now better placed to evaluate my claim that in a natural language natural laws are most naturally expressed as dispositional predications with sortal terms in subject position. This claim may be corroborated by the following commonplace examples of lawlike English sentences: 'Fire burns', 'Bread nourishes', 'Arsenic is poisonous', 'Ravens are black' (in which the colour-adjective has dispositional force), 'Lightning precedes thunder', 'Horses eat grass', 'Water dissolves salt' (or, equivalently, 'Salt is water-soluble'). At a further remove from everyday concerns and more clearly within the realms of natural science, we have: 'Sulphuric acid reacts with copper to form copper sulphate', 'Protons carry unit positive charge', 'A planet moves in an ellipse with the sun at one focus' (Kepler's First Law of Planetary Motion), 'A gas at constant temperature varies in volume inversely as the pressure exerted upon it' (Boyle's Law), 'A body upon which no external force is impressed continues in its state of rest or uniform motion in a straight line' (Newton's First Law of Motion), 'An electric charge attracts or repels another directly as their product and inversely as the square of the distance between them' (Coulomb's Laws). Inspection will show that all of these sentences contain sortal terms (sometimes complex and sometimes more than one) in subject position and verbs or adjectives having dispositional rather than occurrent force. (More complex scientific laws usually need to be expressed with the aid of mathematical symbols for the sake of clarity, but even these can in principle be formulated in the foregoing fashion.) For instance, take the sentence just cited as expressing Kepler's First Law: 'A planet moves in an ellipse with the sun at one focus'. The grammatical subject, 'A planet', is clearly a (simple) sort term, consisting of a common noun preceded by the (logically redundant) indefinite article. And the predicate is plainly dispositional in force, as may perhaps most clearly be seen by substituting the individual term 'Mars' for 'a planet' and comparing the resulting sentence, 'Mars moves in an ellipse with the sun at one focus', with the corresponding occurrent sentence, 'Mars *is moving* in an ellipse with the sun at one focus'. (Here, as explained above, I appeal to the reader's linguistic intuitions to corroborate my judgement.)

Even so, the claim I have just made concerning the natural expression of natural laws is insufficiently general in that it only accommodates lawlike sentences in which only sortal *terms* occur, neglecting those in which there appear sortal *variables* (or, more precisely, the quantifier expressions which in a natural language do the job of quantifiers with sortal variables). For example: we have already noticed the equivalence between 'Water dissolves salt' and 'Salt is water-soluble', and this should draw our attention to the corresponding equivalence between the simpler nomic generalization 'Salt is soluble' and '*Something* dissolves salt', where 'something' is a *sortal existential quantifier expression*, by which I mean that the sentence 'Something dissolves salt' is true provided that there is some true sentence differing from it only in that 'something' is replaced by a sortal term (such as 'water' or 'alcohol' or 'oil'). The use of sortal variables (or their natural language counterparts) is a natural and inevitable extension of the use of sortal terms (just as the use of individual variables is a natural and inevitable extension of the use of proper names and other individual terms).

We are now in a position to give a simple and straightforward (albeit somewhat contentious) answer to the question of the ontological status of laws of nature. If Quine's criterion of ontological commitment, encapsulated in the famous dictum 'to *be* is to be the value of a variable',[4] is correct, and if expressions of natural law inevitably involve the use (or potential use) of sortal variables, then it seems to follow that the assertion of such laws carries with it commitment to the existence of *sorts* or *kinds*, as distinctive objects existing over and above the individuals which may be said to belong to or instantiate them. (This still leaves open, of course, the question of the 'manner' of their existence, with the traditional 'realist' options on the status of universals – the 'Aristotelian' and the 'Platonic' – pressing their familiar claims and counter-claims.) Thus, even the humble law 'Horses eat grass' will apparently commit anyone asserting it to the existence of the species *horse* and the stuff *grass* above and beyond all the various individual horses and all the various individual blades and clumps of grass. (Of course, 'Horses eat grass' does not itself involve sortal quantification, but it entails both 'Horses eat something' and 'Something eats grass', which do.) Such a conclusion will be repugnant to those with nominalist sympathies. It remains to be seen whether it can be avoided.

There are, I think, three possible strategies whereby one might hope to evade the perhaps unpalatable conclusion of the preceding paragraph. One is to question whether the usual modes of expressing natural laws in ordinary language adequately display their true logical form. Another is to query Quine's criterion of ontological commitment. The third is to argue that sortal quantification does not necessarily extend the *domain* of the variables of quantification beyond that needed for individual quantifiers because although sortal terms *refer*, they do not refer to objects which are not individuals (namely, to *sorts* or *kinds*) but rather refer 'collectively' to the very individuals which are characterizable by them; so that the distinction between the seman-

---

[4] For the source of the dictum, see 'A Logistical Approach to the Ontological Problem', in W.V. Quine, *The Ways of Paradox and Other Essays* (Cambridge, Mass.: Harvard University Press, 1976), p. 199.

tic roles of sortal and individual terms is a distinction between *modes of reference* to the same entities (all of them individuals), not one between *entities referred to*. Of these three strategies, the last seems to me the most promising, though I shall not finally endorse it myself. But first I shall examine the other two strategies, especially the former of them.

The first strategy would assuredly be adopted by those who, following Popper, consider that natural laws are most properly formulated as 'all-statements',[5] translatable into the language of modern predicate logic as universally quantified conditionals whose variables of quantification are *individual* variables (and hence range over some suitable, and potentially infinite, domain of individuals), thus apparently excluding any role for *sortal* variables in the expression of natural laws. For instance, that infamous law 'Ravens are black' will first be reformulated as an 'all-statement', 'All ravens are black', and then translated canonically as '($\forall x$) (If x is a raven, then x is black)', in which 'x' is an individual variable and the colour-adjective is dispositional in force. (The dispositionality has to be emphasized because, of course, the law will not be falsified by the discovery of ravens whose feathers have been dyed green or bleached white.) Such a translation seems, at first blush, not unreasonable. For one thing, it may seem that it is interestingly paralleled by an analogous and highly plausible translation of *occurrent* sentences with sortal terms in subject position, such as 'A horse is eating grass' and 'Salt is dissolving in water', which seemingly go over into *existentially* quantified *conjunctions*, namely, '($\exists x$) (x is a horse and x is eating grass)' and '($\exists x$) (x is salt and x is dissolving in water)', where the variables are again individual variables. Why not correspondingly translate lawlike sentences (i.e. *dispositional* sen-

---

[5] See K.R. Popper, *The Logic of Scientific Discovery* (London: Hutchinson, 1968), p. 63: 'an *all-statement*, i.e. a universal assertion about an unlimited number of individuals'.

tences with sortal terms in subject position) as *universally quantified conditionals* – thus 'A horse eats grass' as '($\forall x$) (If x is a horse, then x eats grass)' and 'Salt dissolves in water' as '($\forall x$) (If x is salt, then x dissolves in water)'?

Unfortunately, this attractively simple proposal runs into a host of difficulties, some of which are well known, others less so. One of the lesser known difficulties is this. Take a lawlike sentence containing more than one sortal term, such as 'Water dissolves salt'. According to the Popperian approach, this may be translated canonically as '($\forall x$) (If x is water, then x dissolves salt)', though it could equally well be translated as '($\forall x$) (If x is salt, then water dissolves x)', so that the fullest translation would be '($\forall x$) ($\forall y$) (If x is water and y is salt, then x dissolves y)', where the last predication is still dispositional in force, meaning 'x is disposed to dissolve y'. Now, clearly, one cannot claim to have captured the logical form of lawlike sentences unless one can show how, in virtue of that form, one lawlike sentence entails another. But Popper cannot explain, consistently with his own constraints on the logical form of a law, why the lawlike sentence 'Water dissolves salt' should entail the lawlike sentence '*Something* dissolves salt'. This is because it is hard to see how *any* remotely adequate canonical translation of the lawlike sentence 'Something dissolves salt' can be found which *both* conforms to the Popperian requirements (that is, which contains only individual variables and no sortal term in subject position, and is governed by a universal quantifier) *and* which is entailed by the Popperian translation of 'Water dissolves salt'. (Of course, if sortal quantification is admitted and Popper's restraints are lifted, then the entailment may simply be taken at its face value as a case of existential generalization.) Clearly, '($\exists x$)($\forall y$)(If y is salt, then x dissolves y)' will not do for Popper, not least because it does not represent a purely universal proposition (doesn't express an 'all-statement'). The only serious possibility which suggests itself is '($\forall x$) (If x is salt, then ($\exists y$)(y dissolves x))', but this too clearly will not do because it could be true even if no lawlike sentence of the form 'φ dissolves salt' were true, where 'φ' is a sortal term: it would be true, for instance, if each individual piece of salt was indeed disposed to be dissolved by *some* individual body of liquid of some sort, but some pieces of salt were only disposed to be dissolved by bodies of liquid of one sort (say water) while other pieces of salt were only disposed to be dissolved by bodies of liquid of a quite different sort (say oil), in which case neither 'Water dissolves salt' not 'Oil dissolves salt' nor any other lawlike sentence of the form 'φ dissolves salt' would be true (and we would in fact appear to have two different *kinds* of salt, one water-soluble and the other oil-soluble).

A much better known objection to the Popperian analysis of laws is that it fails to account adequately for the distinction between nomic or lawlike generalizations and 'accidental' generalizations.[6] I think that this objection is valid, but not for the reason commonly advanced – namely, that laws support counterfactuals. The standard argument is that a Popperian all-statement, such as 'All ravens are black', is translated canonically as a universally quantified *material* conditional, or, in other words, is interpreted as ascribing (dispositional) blackness only to each and every *actual* raven, having nothing to say regarding *possible* ravens: but a natural law, it is said, displays its nomic force precisely in its power to legislate for all possible cases in addition to accurately describing all actual cases.

However, I am doubtful about this argument and its associated 'modal' characterization of nomic force, for two reasons. First of all, it is not clear to me that it is at all desirable to have a theory of natural law according to which a law like 'Ravens are black' supports counterfactuals of the form 'If *a* were a raven, then *a* would be black', where '*a*' is an individual term. For it seems to me that a good many, if not all, such counterfactuals are simply incoherent, for rea-

---

[6] See, e.g., Kneale, *Probability and Induction*, pp. 70ff. It has to be acknowledged that Popper takes careful cognisance of Kneale's views in a new appendix to his own book (*The Logic of Scientific Discovery*, pp. 420ff.).

sons which Kripke has made plain in another connection.[7] For example, is it really clear that the counterfactual 'If this white shoe were a raven, then it would be black' is coherent, let alone true? If Kripke is right, nothing which is not *in fact* a raven (and certainly nothing which is in fact a white shoe) *could* have been a raven, in any metaphysically serious sense of 'could'. (This charge of incoherence only applies to counterfactuals with an antecedent of the form 'If *a* were φ, then . . .', where 'φ' is a natural kind sortal: I do not mean to condemn counterfactuals quite generally. I might also point out that though on some theories of counterfactuals a counterfactual with an impossible antecedent is in fact *trivially* true, this hardly provides any comfort for the view I am criticizing since it renders equally trivial the sense in which laws can be said to support such counterfactuals and the significance of such 'support'.)

Secondly, and more importantly, it is far from clear to me that a law like 'Ravens are black' even purports to describe all *actual* ravens, much less all possible ravens, since we do not take it to be falsified by the existence of abnormal or 'freak' counterexamples, such as albino ravens. Thus my criticism of Popper is not the usual one that he does not throw his net wide enough, but on the contrary that he throws it *too* wide. As I see it, the most that a law like 'Ravens are black' purports to tell us *concerning individuals* is what we should expect any *normal* individual raven to be like, and apart from this it appears to be concerned rather with characterizing the raven *species* or *kind*. Such a law is 'normative' or regulative in force with respect to individuals, and it is precisely in this that its 'nomic' character resides. This, indeed, is why the title 'law' is so appropriate (and no mere relic of theocentrism), for laws, whether of God or man (or, I would add, nature), *are* normative: they set standards. I shall say more of this in a moment. Incidentally, my excuse for concentrating on commonplace and 'unscien-

---

[7] See Saul A. Kripke, *Naming and Necessity* (Oxford: Blackwell, 1980), passim.

tific' examples of lawlike sentences is that in attending to these our intuitive judgements regarding the logical characteristics of laws are likely to be more reliable. My adoption of this course follows a well-established tradition in the philosophy of science, much deplored though it is in some quarters. But this tradition is predicated upon the not unreasonable view that science is but an extension of common sense. That scientific laws are not different in kind from everyday ones seems clear enough from the list of examples given earlier. In particular, the *normative* character of laws in the more advanced sciences is certainly evident, though there is some inclination to speak of such laws as being concerned with 'ideal' rather than merely with 'normal' exemplars (witness the Gas Laws); but this issue is one to which I shall briefly return later.

Before saying more in defence of my own ('normative') account of nomic status, I should briefly mention some further difficulties which attend the more orthodox accounts. First of all, not least amongst the problems of employing modal logic in an analysis of natural law are those connected with the ontological implications of its currently favoured 'possible worlds' semantics: a realism with regard to possible worlds as uncompromising as that of David Lewis would certainly appear, to the nominalist, as the proverbial fire to the frying pan of realism with regard to sorts or kinds,[8] whereas a non-realist account would seem to be in danger of treating as in some way subjective those objects of our knowledge of the physical universe which arguably are, if anything, the most objective, namely the laws of natural science. Besides, a 'possible worlds' account of the truth-conditions of lawlike sentences will require some means of distinguishing those worlds which are *naturally* possible from those which are merely *logically* possible, and it is hard to see how this may be done without circularity (obviously it

---

[8] For Lewis's view, see his *Counterfactuals* (Oxford: Blackwell, 1973), pp. 84ff. and more generally, his *On the Plurality of Worlds* (Oxford: Blackwell, 1986).

will not do merely to define a naturally possible world as one in which all the natural laws of this, the actual, world obtain – plausible though such a definition might be in the context of an independent account of what a natural law is).[9]

In defence of my own account of nomic status I would urge that a recognition of the 'normative' character of natural laws is quite crucial to an understanding of scientific methodology, particularly as regards the empirical confirmation of such laws by experiment and observation.[10] For a feature of this methodology which the 'all-statement' analysis (and *a fortiori* any stronger, modal analysis) has completely failed to explain (in my view) is the willingness of scientists often to accept even a *single* well-conducted experiment or observation as virtually conclusive evidence in support of a law.[11] (Popper at least has the merit of realizing that the 'all-statement' analysis effectively precludes *any* account of the empirical verification of laws even by non-deductive methods: though his consequent recommendation of falsificationism seems like a counsel of despair.) Yet, of course, nothing could be more natural or reasonable than for one to take any arbitrarily chosen normal exemplar of a given sort or kind as its representative: if a normal sample of water is found to dissolve a normal sample of salt, it is eminently rational to conclude, without repeating the experiment, that water dissolves salt, and thus that a certain natural law obtains. (I shall say more in a moment about the

---

[9] For an attempt to tackle this problem within the possible-worlds framework, see Nicholas Rescher, *A Theory of Possibility* (Oxford: Blackwell, 1975), pp. 144ff. I develop an account of my own of the nature of 'natural' possibility in my 'Miracles and Laws of Nature', *Religious Studies* 23 (1987), pp. 263–78.

[10] I discuss some of these matters more fully in my 'What *is* the "Problem of Induction"?', *Philosophy* 62 (1987), pp. 325–40.

[11] My parenthetical remark about this objection applying *a fortiori* to any stronger, modal analysis would, I suspect, be challenged by John Foster – see his 'Induction, Explanation and Natural Necessity', *Proceedings of the Aristotelian Society* N.S. LXXXIII (1982/83), pp. 87ff. However, he himself confesses not to have provided any substantive account of what natural necessity is supposed to *be*, and if, as I believe, it is ultimately to be explicated in terms of laws themselves (see my 'Miracles and Laws of Nature'), the modal analysis must in any case be at the very least implicitly circular.

notion of 'normality' operative here.) Experiments are only repeated when there is some doubt either as to what *sorts* of objects are being tested or as to their *normality* as representatives of sorts to which they are known to belong. And a well-conducted experiment or observation is precisely one in which the experimenter or observer has reason to suppose that he *has* correctly identified what sorts of things he is dealing with and that his specimens or exemplars are indeed 'normal' representatives of those sorts (thus, in a chemical experiment, this will be a matter of correctly identifying the substances under investigation and establishing their 'purity'). Moreover, while one may on occasion, or even fairly often, misidentify an object's sortal character or mistakenly take for a 'normal' specimen of a given sort one which is not, it is surely incoherent to suppose that one might be consistently and systematically mistaken in such matters: it must be reasonable to suppose that our judgements in such matters are *on the whole* correct, and hence that our knowledge of natural law is broadly well founded as a system (though not, of course, infallible at every point). To suppose otherwise would be to suppose that we might consistently and systematically mischaracterize the nature of the objects we confront in our experience of the natural world, which is surely a form of scepticism that is incoherent. (Here we should recall that criteria of identity for individuals are sortal-relative, so that there can be no possibility of our successfully identifying individuals while systematically misidentifying the sorts of individuals that they are, nor of doing without any system of sortal concepts altogether. Furthermore, any workable system of sortal concepts presupposes an ability on the part of its users to distinguish, more often than not, normal exemplars of a given sort from abnormal ones. The 'Kantian' flavour of the arguments I am now deploying will doubtless be manifest.)

It is incumbent upon any satisfactory analysis of natural law to explain how our knowledge of natural laws should be possible upon the basis of experience. For that we actually possess such knowledge seems incontrovertible in view of the progress of the natural sciences, and that it is ultimately empirically founded seems equally clear from the practice of scientists (however much the role of theory in the interpretation of experimental results may very rightly be emphasized). I would claim that this is something which the normative account can explain significantly better than its rivals, while also offering an historically truer picture of scientific method.

While on the topic of confirmation, it is perhaps worth pointing out that Hempel's famous paradox, popularly known as the paradox of the ravens,[12] may be seen as constituting further evidence of the incorrectness of the 'all-statement' analysis of natural laws (whether or not supplemented by a modal interpretation). It will be recalled that the paradox plays upon the fact that the sentences '$(\forall x)$ (If x is a raven, then x is black)' and '$(\forall x)$ (If x is not black, then x is not a raven)' are logically equivalent. To my mind, all that this shows is that the former is not an adequate translation of the law 'Ravens are black'. We should observe that whereas an 'all-statement' like 'All ravens are black' is contraposable as 'All non-black things are non-ravens', there is no corresponding transformation available in the case of a lawlike sentence like 'Ravens are black': that is to say, there is no logically equivalent lawlike sentence in which the terms of the original are negated and transposed. Certainly, 'Non-black things are non-ravens' is *not* a lawlike sentence, because 'non-black things' is not a genuine sortal term: there is no *sort* or *kind* which comprises just those things which are not black.[13] (Even 'black things' is not a genuine sortal term since, as Geach points out,[14] it has no criterion of identity

---

[12] See 'Studies in the Logic of Confirmation', in C.G. Hempel, *Aspects of Scientific Explanation* (New York: Free Press, 1965).

[13] Cf. G. Schlesinger, 'Natural Kinds', R.S. Cohen and M.W. Wartofsky (eds), *Boston Studies in the Philosophy of Science*, vol. III (Dordrecht: D. Reidel, 1967).

[14] See P.T. Geach, *Reference and Generality*, 2nd edn (Ithaca: Cornell University Press, 1968), pp. 38ff. 'Basic' sorts are not now at issue.

associated with it; still less so, thus, could 'non-black things' qualify as a sortal term since, as Geach also points out,[15] even the negation of a sortal term is never itself a sortal term.)

It may be wondered whether the normative account of nomic force just outlined suggests a means of reformulating lawlike sentences containing sortal terms in subject position in terms of sentences making reference only to normal exemplars of the sorts in question, in a way which might satisfy the nominalist. I think not. First of all, the problem of sortal quantification would still remain. Secondly, even if it were the case (which I do not say it is) that the law 'Ravens are black' is true if and only if the universally quantified conditional '$(\forall x)$(If x is a *normal* raven, then x is black)' is true, it is obvious that this equivalence could not be of any use to the nominalist if the notion of 'normality' cannot be defined in a nominalistically satisfactory way. Now my own view is that to say of a given individual that it is a 'normal' raven is just to say that it is a raven which 'conforms to type', that is, which satisfies all the true natural laws pertaining to the raven kind. Thus an albino raven is 'abnormal' precisely because it 'disobeys' the law 'Ravens are black', which is a true law (or so we suppose). So I do not profess to offer an explication of normality which is *independent* of my account of natural law, nor, hence, one which holds out any hope so far of stating the truth-conditions of lawlike sentences without reference to sorts or kinds. (Incidentally, I do not believe that my concept of normality vitiates or undermines my preceding account of scientific methodology: rather, it makes it clear that that account is more 'coherentist' than 'foundationalist' in its tendency, which I take to be no bad thing. As I see it, checking the 'normality' of an experimental specimen is a matter of establishing that it satisfies the *known* or *accepted* laws pertaining to things of its sort: the object of an experiment is then to discover *new* laws by

[15] Ibid., p. 40.

observing the behaviour of this putatively normal specimen in hitherto untried conditions – though in the course of doing so we may eventually come to revise our previous beliefs either about the normality of our specimen or about the truth of the putative laws we previously employed in order to establish its normality.)

The only type of analysis of normality which could conceivably be utilized by the nominalist in this connection would be a *statistical* one, according to which a raven (say) is 'normal' provided that it shares the characteristics of most other members of its species. Such an analysis, however, is plainly unsatisfactory, for a variety of reasons. For one thing, in order to remove apparent reference to a *species* or *kind* to which all these relevant individuals belong, it seems that the nominalist will first have to define the predicate ' — is a raven' in terms of some list or cluster of more or less observable properties (appeal to theoretical properties – e.g. possession of such-and-such a genetic structure – would run the risk of introducing circularity into the account through implicit reliance on the normativity which, I have contended, attaches to all scientific theorizing). Such a project is ill starred, as we know from the work of Kripke and Putnam.[16] But even if it could succeed, it still seems plain that what is normal is not *definable* merely as what is usually the case, even if it is always *reasonable to assume* (in the absence of contrary evidence) that what is normal is usually the case (which is precisely why, on the normative account, laws have predictive utility). A sudden spate of albino ravens would not call into question the normality of black specimens. Only if through an evolutionary process of adaptation to changed circumstances ravens became white would the occasional black 'throw-back' come to be regarded as abnormal. The concept of normality is theory-relative, that is, law-dependent: and for this very reason it is futile to

---

[16] See Kripke, *Naming and Necessity*, and Hilary Putnam, 'The Meaning of "Meaning"', in his *Mind, Language and Reality* (Cambridge: Cambridge University Press, 1975).

attempt to state the truth-conditions of laws in terms of the characteristics of normal specimens, if it is hoped thereby to satisfy nominalist predilections by avoiding reference to all but actual individuals.

Altogether, then, everything that has been said so far tends to reinforce the suspicion that natural laws carry reference to *sorts* or *kinds*, construed as constituting norms or standards to which actual individuals may conform to greater or lesser degrees. Such reference *seems* ineliminable, though even if it is it has still not perhaps been established that this has clear ontological implications. It has perhaps been confirmed (though we have yet to examine the third nominalist strategy mentioned earlier) that we need to 'refer to' and 'quantify over' sorts in order to give an adequate analysis of scientific theory and practice, but whether or not this means that we must regard sorts as being 'real' or part of the 'furniture of the world' in the full-blooded sense that individuals are is still perhaps an open question, depending not least on how much truth there is in Quine's criterion of ontological commitment.

Let us turn, therefore, briefly to the second strategy mentioned earlier as being open to the nominalist: that of querying Quine's ontological criterion. Now, certainly, this frequently *has* been queried, notably by A.N. Prior,[17] particularly in the context of the debate over 'objectual' *versus* 'substitutional' interpretations of quantifiers. And, undoubtedly, a 'substitutional' account of sortal quantification can be advanced: indeed, I implicitly employed just such an account earlier when I explained the use of such quantification in a sentence like 'Something dissolves salt' in terms of the truth of this sentence being conditional upon there being some true sentence differing from it only in that 'something' is replaced by a sortal term – though, of course, to represent this condition as being necessary as well as sufficient we

---

[17] See A.N. Prior, *Objects of Thought* (Oxford: Clarendon Press, 1971), pp. 33ff. Cf. Geach, *Reference and Generality*, 2nd edn, p: 161.

require the notion of a potential stock of sortal terms outrunning the limited actual resources of any natural human language such as English. (It was in fact precisely to avoid begging any ontological questions as to the objective existence of sorts that I earlier exploited such an account of sortal quantification.) All the same, we must break out of the circle of language at some point in explaining how words attach to the world, and it is certainly not clear that a 'substitutional' account of sortal quantification simply *obviates* commitment to the existence of sorts: at best it seems to provide a temporary means of putting off the ontological question, pending the development of some satisfactory theory of the semantics of sortal terms.

The following line of argument does, however, at least seem very plausible. The normal use of *proper names* certainly *does* carry with it ontological commitments, since the standard use of such a name presupposes the existence of the individual which is its bearer or referent.[18] Such ontological implications then naturally carry over to the use of individual *variables*, since these go proxy for proper names; and thus the *ineliminability* from our discourse of individual quantification may indeed be taken as being indicative of our ontological commitment to the real existence of individuals. Similarly, then, whether or not the use of *sortal* variables carries with it ontological implications will depend, in like manner, upon whether or not sortal *terms* are name-like in presupposing the existence of bearers or referents: and so, at the very least, if sufficiently close parallels can be drawn between the semantics of sortal terms and the semantics of proper names, the ineliminability of sortal quantification may then be taken as indicative of an ontological commitment on our part to the existence of such bearers or referents quite as strong as our commitment to the existence of individuals. (I must leave open, however, pending our dis-

---

[18] Cf. Prior, *Objects of Thought*, p. 169 and Geach, *Reference and Generality*, 2nd edn, pp. 162ff.

cussion of the third strategy mentioned earlier, the issue of whether the entities to which sortal quantification would thus commit us are objects other than the very individuals to which individual quantification itself commits us.)

Now, that sortal terms (especially simple natural kind terms) are indeed name-like in important respects has been argued recently by a number of philosophers: notably by Geach on the one hand, who has drawn attention particularly to the syntactical similarities,[19] and by Kripke and Putnam on the other, who have emphasized the semantic similarities.[20] On the latter score, a point I take to be of immense importance is that simple natural kind terms are no more *definable* in terms of lists or clusters of describable characteristics or physical properties than proper names are equivalent to lists or clusters of identifying descriptions. Just as 'Aristotle' cannot be taken to *mean* anything like 'the most famous pupil of Plato, tutor of Alexander the Great, born in Stagira in 384 BC, author of the *Metaphysics*, etc., . . .', neither can 'gold' be taken (*pace* Locke) to *mean* anything like 'ductile, malleable metal, with a melting point of 1062°C and density of 19.3 gm/cc, soluble in aqua regia, . . .'. That gold is, for example, soluble in aqua regia can in no sense be taken to be a 'defining characteristic' of gold, simply because the term 'gold' is actually *in*definable. 'Gold is soluble in aqua regia' is in fact a purely *a posteriori* statement of *natural law*; and the same applies with regard to all the other physical characteristics of gold just cited. (It is of course perfectly feasible to maintain this position while acknowledging that investigation of a specimen's physical properties *guides* us in classifying it as being an item of this or that sort, say gold – just as information about an individual guides us in identifying it as the bearer of a given proper name, even though the name is not equivalent to a descrip-

---

[19] See Geach, *Reference and Generality*, 2nd edn, especially the closing remark on p. 191; see also the 3rd edn (Ithaca: Cornell University Press, 1980), p. 216.
[20] See Kripke, *Naming and Necessity*, and Putnam, 'The Meaning of "Meaning"'.

tion with that informational content.) But if the meaning of the term 'gold' is not a function of the meanings of any set of purely descriptive expressions, i.e. if the predicate '— is gold' is not 'shorthand' for a predicate expressing a complex physical property, then there seems little alternative but to suppose that it has meaning just in the way that a proper name does: simply by standing for or referring to some existent *thing* or *things* – I should say, simply by referring to a certain *kind of stuff*.

My concurrence with the views of Kripke and Putnam does not, I might remark, extend to an acceptance of the suggestion that '— is gold' means, or at least is in some sense 'ostensively definable' in terms of, anything like '— is the same kind of stuff as *this*', where 'this' refers to some favoured or paradigm individual exemplar or sample.[21] There are, I believe, grave difficulties with this line of thought. First, this could not suffice as a general account of the semantics of sortal terms simply because, as I have emphasized in previous chapters, successful reference to individuals itself already presupposes an ability to individuate them as individuals of this or that *sort*, so that the semantics of sortal terms cannot be, as implied, logically posterior to that of individual terms; rather, there must be an even-handed mutual dependence between the two. Secondly, our possession of the notion of two or more individuals being individual exemplars of *the same kind of stuff* (i.e. being 'consubstantial') stands in need of some sort of explanation, and the only plausible one I can envisage will turn on our familiarity with *instances* of this relationship; we possess the notion, that is, precisely because we can at least *sometimes* judge simply that *this* is (a piece of) φ as is also *that*. So our *general* capacity to judge that an individual instantiates some particular sort or kind is presupposed by, and so cannot be explained in terms of, our capacity to judge that

---

[21] See, e.g., Putnam, 'The Meaning of "Meaning"', p. 225, and Kripke, *Naming and Necessity*, pp. 135–6.

two or more individuals are individuals of the *same* sort or kind. This indeed should be evident inasmuch as the sentence-form '*x* is the same kind of stuff as *y*' is plausibly analysable just as meaning 'For some kind of stuff φ, *x* is φ and *y* is φ', and hence cannot be usefully invoked in explicating what I call instantiation sentences, i.e. sentences of the form '*x* is φ' – a form which, indeed, I hold to be basic and irreducible. In short, the notion of an individual's being (instantiating) a certain kind of substance is *logically prior* to the notion of two or more different individuals being 'consubstantial'.

Suppose it is conceded now, as I think it must be, that the ineliminability of sortal quantification *does*, as Quine's criterion would have us believe, commit us ontologically to the existence of a domain of entities over which the variables of such quantification range.[22] There still remains the *third* strategy I described earlier as being open to the nominalist who denies the objective existence of sorts or kinds. According to this suggestion, sortal variables need only be supposed to range over *individuals*, not over entities of a quite different order. What lies behind this is the idea that though sortal terms, like individual terms, have meaning by virtue simply of standing for or referring to certain objects, their 'bearers' or 'referents', the semantic difference between them resides not in the *nature* of their referents but solely in the 'mode' of reference they possess. Thus, on this view, whereas the individual term 'Caesar' refers to just one particular man, the sortal term 'man' (or 'men') refers not to the sort *mankind*, conceived as having an objective existence distinct from that of any or all particular men, but rather simply refers 'collectively' to all such particular men: in short, 'man' refers to *men in general* (as we say) rather than

---

[22] Quine himself, it is worth remarking, seems to think that reliance on sorts or kinds can be dispensed with in 'mature' or 'advanced' sciences: see W.V. Quine, 'Natural Kinds', in his *Ontological Relativity and Other Essays* (New York: Columbia University Press, 1969), p. 138. I see no reason for such optimism, which fails to perceive how deep seated the individual/sort distinction is.

(as a proper name may) to any *man in particular*. (On this view, one *can* go on talking about 'sorts', but only on the understanding that this is just a way of talking about their individual members 'collectively'.) The old-fashioned grammatical description *common name* for terms like 'man' may seem to accord with this proposal, the suggestion being that 'man' differs from 'Caesar' substantially only in being a name for *more than one* individual, i.e. not only for Caesar but also for Brutus, Cassius, etc.

The basic difficulty with this account of the semantics of sortal terms may perhaps be most graphically brought out by recalling that most proper names in common use are of course *not* tied to a single individual: there are any number of different Joneses and Smiths and even quite a few different Caesars. That is to say, proper names *themselves* seem to have the very semantic property which, on the account just advanced, is alleged to be distinctive of sortal terms as opposed to proper names. To this it may be objected that when a speaker uses a token of a given proper name, say 'John Smith', on a particular occasion, he or she will be using it to refer only to some *one* John Smith, not 'collectively' to all the various John Smiths that there are. This is of course normally true, but it raises the following further point. *As the previous sentence itself displays*, we *can* and *do* speak of John Smiths plurally or collectively, in what appears to be, according to the nominalist account under consideration, the very way in which we allegedly speak of 'men' and 'horses' and so forth – yet, of course, the John Smiths do *not* comprise a sort or kind, classifiable together as they are only in virtue of their common possession of the name 'John Smith'. Plainly we *do* assert generalizations such as 'John Smiths are plentiful in this part of town', which superficially may seem akin to ones like 'Elephants are plentiful in Africa': but it is manifestly incorrect to suppose that the grammatical subjects of these two assertions submit to the same sort of semantic treatment. Of course, what one *may* be tempted to say in response to this objection is that 'man' functions as a genuine sortal term in a way that 'John Smith' cannot because, though both *may* be understood as referring 'collectively' to a plurality of individuals, the individuals so referred to by 'man' are classifiable together *not* purely in virtue of their common possession of the name 'man' but rather in virtue of their being individuals of a single *sort* or *kind* – man*kind*: but, transparently, this is not a response available to the nominalist, however plausible it may be in itself. Nor, clearly, will it do for the nominalist to say instead of this that the individuals referred to by 'man' are classifiable together in virtue of their common possession of certain *describable characteristics* – for we have already seen that natural kind terms like 'man' are *not* definable in the sort of way that this proposal would imply.

A further problem for the nominalist strategy now under consideration – that of attributing to sortal terms only a distinctive *mode of reference* to individuals – is that, as I have repeatedly emphasized in this study, reference to *individuals* (whether it be 'singular' reference or the species of 'collective' reference now being canvassed) only makes sense relative to a background of classification into sorts or kinds, since individuals are only individuable at all *qua* individuals of some *sort* or other. Hence, sense cannot be made of the notion of affirming of an individual that it belongs to a certain sort φ – e.g. that it is a man – if the only account available of the meaning of the sortal term 'φ' is that it refers collectively to a certain plurality of individuals: for this already presupposes as given what is now at issue, namely, some account of the notion of each of these individuals being individuable as an individual *of some sort*. (That what may be called 'plural' – as opposed to 'singular' – reference is a genuine feature of natural language cannot I think be in doubt, neglected though it has been by modern logicians. [23] It is clearly at work in *plural* definite descrip-

---

[23] But see George Boolos, 'To Be is to Be a Value of a Variable (or to Be Some Values of Some Variables)', *Journal of Philosophy* 81 (1984), pp. 430–49.

tions and demonstrative noun-phrases, like 'the horses in Farmer Brown's field' and 'those men'. What I am now contending is that the distinction between *individual* and *sortal* reference and variables of quantification is not to be confused with that between *singular* and *plural* reference and variables of quantification, which in fact cut quite across each other.)

I should, incidentally, make it quite clear that my opposition to the nominalist strategy now being discussed by no means obliges me to *deny* that a sortal term like 'man' refers 'collectively' or 'plurally', in the way suggested, to individual men 'in general'; for I can allow that it may do so precisely in virtue of referring (singularly) to a sort or kind of which they are all individual instances. It is indeed highly plausible, of course, to say that when one affirms some nomic generalization such as 'Men are bipeds' one *is* in some sense speaking 'about' *individual men* and not just 'about' the sort mankind, as it were *in abstracto*. However, that is really beside the point, first because the semantic notion of 'reference' with which we are now operating is not to be confused with the pragmatic notion of a speaker's using an expression to speak 'about' (and in this sense 'refer to') an object or objects; but secondly and more obviously because the observation is satisfactorily accounted for by the fact that the nomic generalization in question may be expanded, *without alteration either of sense or of logical form*, as 'Individual men are bipeds'. The real issue is whether an adequate account of the meaning of the sortal term 'man' (or indeed 'individual man', with its redundant qualification) can be given solely in terms of its semantic relations to certain *individuals* or *particulars*, or whether in the course of such an account the existence of a distinctive *sort* or *kind* must be adduced to which these individuals belong. I consider that the latter is the case. And that is why I consider that the apparent ineliminability from our discourse of sortal quantification does indeed commit us ontologically to the objective reality of sorts or kinds. As to the *style* of realism regarding sorts or kinds that I favour, I should say that I lean very much towards the 'Aristotelian' as opposed to the 'Platonic' option, seeing the existence of sorts as *distinct* but not *separable* from that of their individual instances – which is one reason why I am loth to countenance the existence of sorts that are not individually instantiated. Beyond this I am not at present prepared to speculate. But I would stress that my 'Aristotelianism' does not extend to conceding any sort of *ontological priority* to individuals or particulars, whereby they are in any sense 'more' real than sorts or kinds: rather I see the notions of *individual* and *kind* as standing in a quite symmetrical relationship of mutual conceptual dependence – individuals being no less essentially individuals *of some kind* than kinds are essentially *kinds of individual*.

9

Laws, Dispositions and Sortal Logic

The view to which the arguments of the previous chapter lead is this: that dispositional predications with sortal terms in subject position (that is, nomic generalizations) constitute a fundamental and semantically irreducible category of elementary sentence, just as occurrent predications with individual terms in subject position do (I shall suggest later that dispositional predications with individual terms in subject position and occurrent predications with sortal terms in subject position are *not* irreducible). This being so, however, the categories and symbolism of orthodox formal logic are quite obviously inadequate for some of our most important scientific and philosophical purposes, and need to be revised accordingly. I shall now briefly indicate the sort of revisions I have in mind.

I shall begin by describing a *formalized sortal language*, which I shall call S. The *vocabulary* of S is as follows:

individual constants:	$a, b, c, \ldots$	⎫
individual variables:	$x, y, z, \ldots$	⎪
sortal constants:	$\alpha, \beta, \gamma, \ldots$	⎬ objectual
sortal variables:	$\phi, \chi, \psi, \ldots$	⎭ symbols
n-ary predicate letters:	$F^n, G^n, H^n, \ldots$	$(n \geqslant 1)$

identity sign:	=
instantiation sign:	/
truth functional operators:	–, &, v, →, ↔
quantifiers:	∃, ∀
brackets:	(,)

Syntax: atomic formulae of S consist of either (1) an n-ary predicate letter *either* preceded *or* followed by a string of n objectual symbols or (2) the identity sign or the instantiation sign flanked by a pair of objectual symbols. Complex formulae are constructed from atomic ones and logical constants in the usual manner (the logical constants being all those symbols of the language apart from objectual symbols and n-ary predicate letters).

Semantics: by the 'informal semantics' for a formalized language I mean its intended interpretation in terms of natural language (in contrast with the 'formal semantics', i.e. so-called model theory, with which I shall not be concerned here). Inevitably, informal semantics are to a degree an imprecise device for attaching meaning to symbols, simply because the semantic and syntactic distinctions of natural language are themselves imprecise.[1] However, briefly what we may say with regard to the informal semantics for S is this. Individual constants of S translate proper names in natural language, and sortal constants translate (semantically) simple sortal terms (though more cautiously we should perhaps say that they only translate simple *natural kind* terms). n-ary predicate letters translate n-adic predicates, where by a *predicate* I do not now mean just any expression completable by one or more noun-phrases to form a sentence, but rather only one of that proper subset of

---

[1] Nonetheless, it is ultimately only via the informal semantics that a formalized language can be said to have any substantive philosophical interest – firstly because natural language is the primary vehicle of human thought and secondly because the construction of a formal semantics, while indispensable for certain metalogical purposes, is an exercise which need pay scant regard to any practical application of the formalized language in question.

such expressions to which the dispositional/occurrent distinction applies.[2] When an *n*-ary predicate letter is *preceded* by a string of *n* objectual symbols, *dispositional* predication is intended; when it is *followed* by such a string, *occurrent* predication is intended. The identity sign translates the 'is' of identity, while the instantiation sign translates the 'is' of instantiation. (Observe here that the syntax of *S* permits the instantiation sign to be flanked on *both* sides by individual symbols, which may seem odd: but we may simply stipulate that any such instantiation formula is equivalent to the corresponding identity formula, so that we may indifferently translate 'Cicero is Tully' by the formula '$a = b$' or by the formula 'a/b'.) The truth-functional operators of *S* are translated in the usual ways by 'not', 'and', 'or', 'if . . ., then — ' and 'if and only if' (with the usual precautions and provisos). Quantifiers are used with individual variables to provide a means of translating individual quantifier expressions such as 'some (particular) horse' and with sortal variables to provide a means of translating sortal quantifier expressions such as 'some (sort of) animal'. For instance, 'Some horse is eating grass' might be represented as '$(\exists x)(x/\alpha \,\&\, F^1 x)$', where '$\alpha$' translates 'a horse' and 'F^1' translates ' — is eating grass' (taking its argument on the right to indicate occurrent predication). By contrast, 'Some animal eats grass' might be represented as '$(\exists \phi)(\phi/\beta \,\&\, \phi F^1)$', where '$\beta$' translates 'an animal' and 'F^1' translates ' — eats grass' (taking its argument on the left to indicate dis-

---

[2] Thus '— is a horse' and 'Someone is a brother of — and nephew of . . .' will not qualify as predicates in this restricted sense, while '— is red', '— eats grass' and '— is dissolving . . .' will. More generally, expressions that qualify will typically be verb-phrases whose main verb is either the 'is' of attribution or else a verb (transitive or intransitive) indicative of a state or an activity (so that a *predicate* in this narrow sense may perhaps be defined as an expression used to predicate a property or a relation either occurrently or dispositionally of an object or objects). It must be appreciated, then, that the expressive power of *S* under its intended interpretation is considerably less than that of a natural language like English. This should not be seen as a defect in *S*, however, since the point of constructing it is to provide a means of representing formally only a selected set of the inference-patterns discernible in our use of natural language.

positional predication). (Of course, we can if need be break these sentences down still further, isolating the sortal term 'grass' and revealing the dyadic predicates ' — is eating . . .' and ' — eats . . .'.) And thus, for example, we are equally able to represent as the result of existential generalization the entailment of 'Some horse is eating grass' by 'Dobbin is a horse and Dobbin is eating grass' and that of 'Some animal eats grass' by 'A horse is an animal and a horse eats grass'. (It is perhaps worth noting here that although S has in some respects more expressive power than orthodox formalized first-order languages, S is itself still a 'first-order' language in the sense that it involves no quantification over *predicates*, and is moreover a purely *extensional* language.)

It will be observed that in S atomic monadic predicative formulae fall into four categories, depending on whether the predication is dispositional or occurrent and on whether the objectual symbol is an individual or a sortal one. I have already indicated that of the four corresponding basic types of sentence in natural language I take two to be indisputably primitive and irreducible: dispositional predications with sortal terms in subject position, and occurrent predications with individual terms in subject position. That *occurrent* predications with *sortal* terms in subject position are very arguably not irreducible was recognized in the previous chapter, where it was observed that a sentence such as 'A horse is eating grass' is plausibly analysable in terms of an existentially quantified conjunction, '($\exists$ x) (x is a horse and x is eating grass)'. Notice that one of the conjuncts here, 'x is a horse', expresses an instantiation while the other, 'x is eating grass', is an occurrent predication with an individual variable in subject position. Formally, we may represent the principle behind such a reduction by the following biconditional (or, more precisely, by its universal closure), which may be regarded as *a theorem of sortal logic*:[3]

---

[3] Here it may be wondered how one should represent the English sentence 'A horse is *not* eating grass' in the symbolism of our formalized language S. The

S1 $F^1\phi \leftrightarrow (\exists x)(x/\phi \ \& \ F^1 x)$

(It may perhaps be inquired whether, in a sentence like '*A horse is eating grass*', it is in fact legitimate to regard the indefinite article as merely being a logically redundant part of a (simple) sortal term which is the subject of the sentence. My answer, applying the test adverted to in the previous chapter, is that this *is* legitimate if the sentence is given an interpretation on which it differs merely stylistically from one employing the plural form, i.e. from '*Horses are eating

answer is that it depends on how that sentence, which is ambiguous, is parsed – and, in particular, whether the 'not' figuring in it is taken to express *sentence* negation or *predicate* negation, i.e. whether the sentence is taken to mean 'It is not the case that a horse is eating grass' or to mean 'A horse is-not-eating-grass'. In the former case, the sentence may be represented by the formula '$-F^1\alpha$', where 'F^1' translates '— is eating grass' and 'α' translates 'a horse'. But in the latter case the best we can do given the syntactical limitations of S is to represent the sentence by the *atomic* formula '$G^1\alpha$', where 'G^1' translates the complex English predicate '— is-not-eating-grass'. This is because S itself contains no resources for constructing complex predicates by means of operations on simple ones. In chapter 10 this limitation will be lifted, so that it will be possible to represent our English sentence on its *second* reading by the formula '$(-F^1)\alpha$', where 'F^1' again translates '— is eating grass'. And then, of course, it will be vital to distinguish between the truth-conditions of the two formulae '$-(F^1\alpha)$' and '$(-F^1)\alpha$', since we take the former to be equivalent to '$-(\exists x)(x/\alpha \ \& \ F^1 x)$' and the latter to be equivalent to '$(\exists x)(x/\alpha \ \& \ (-F^1)x)$'. Thus sentence negation and predicate negation are obviously non-equivalent where occurrent predications of *sorts* are concerned – though not, it should be said, where occurrent predications of *individuals* are concerned (so that, for instance, '$-(F^1 a)$' and '$(-F^1)a$' *are* equivalent, since 'a' is an individual constant). These matters will receive fuller treatment in chapter 10. For the moment it is only necessary, in order to avoid possible confusion, to point out that since sentence negation and predicate negation are *not* equivalent where occurrent predications of sorts are concerned, and since '$-F^1\phi$' may only be taken to represent *sentence* negation in our formalized language S, it would be quite improper to substitute '$-F^1$' for 'F^1' in theorem S1 and expect still to be left with a valid formula. (Such illicit moves are formally disqualified in the axiomatized system of sortal logic presented in the appendix to this chapter.) At the same time, it should be appreciated that the limitation in S, whereby predicate negation (along with predicate conjunction, disjunction and so forth) is not expressible in it, is irrelevant to my purposes in the present chapter and will only become relevant with the concerns of chapter 10, where the limitation will be lifted. (Such syntactic limitations in formalized languages are, of course, a common feature of them, arising from their limited and selective ambitions to represent formally inference-patterns discernible in natural language: think, for instance, of the language of the propositional calculus, which has no means to represent syntactic complexity within an atomic sentence.)

grass'. Now, certainly, there *are* interpretations of these two sentences on which they actually differ in *sense*, and on these interpretations the singular and plural forms are performing substantive quantificational roles conveying distinctions of *number*: on these interpretations, '*a* horse' effectively means '*just one* horse' while 'horse*s*' means '*more than one* horse'. However, there is, I submit, also a reading of these English sentences on which they do not thus differ in sense – a reading on which what they express could equally, if less idiomatically, be expressed by something along the lines of the sentence 'Grass is being horse-eaten', in which no distinctions of number are conveyed in connection with the sortal term 'horse'. It is on this interpretation that the indefinite article in 'A horse is eating grass' may be seen as logically redundant and hence 'a horse' as constituting a simple sortal term; and it is on this interpretation that the reduction proposed above is conceived as obtaining – for, of course, on the standard reading of the existential quantifier '∃' it too conveys no distinctions of number, '$(\exists x)(\ldots x \ldots)$' meaning merely 'There is *at least one* (individual) x such that $\ldots x \ldots$'. It is perhaps worth remarking that where only *mass* terms are involved no such ambiguities can arise and the reduction proposed is quite uncontentious: consider, for example, a sentence like 'Water is dissolving salt', used perhaps to describe what is going on in some receptacle – plainly the implication is that some *particular* quantity of water is dissolving some *particular* quantity of salt.)

Now, it would be pleasing if, paralleling S1, we could find an analogous reduction of *dispositional* predications with *individual* terms in subject position, such as 'Dobbin eats grass'. And I think we can. It is not altogether implausible to suggest that this sentence too is reducible to an existentially quantified conjunction, but one involving *sortal* quantification, namely, '$(\exists \phi)$(Dobbin is ϕ and ϕ eats grass)'. Here the first conjunct, 'Dobbin is ϕ', again expresses an instantiation while the second, 'ϕ eats grass', is a dispositional predication with a sortal variable in subject position (that is, has lawlike form). In short, the following seems plausible as a theorem of sortal logic paralleling S1:

S2 $xF^1 \leftrightarrow (\exists \phi)(x/\phi \;\&\; \phi F^1)$

Why do I consider this plausible? Because it seems quite reasonable to suppose that when a disposition is predicated of an individual, it is thereby implied that that individual satisfies some (possibly not as yet fully specifiable) natural law. Thus when I point to a grain of white, crystalline substance and say that it is *water-soluble*, is it not plausible to suppose that I imply thereby that this piece of matter is an exemplar of some *sort* of substance φ such that 'Water dissolves φ' is a true nomic generalization?[4] That it is seems to be indicated by the fact that very often my grounds for ascribing such a disposition to an individual are precisely that I *do* have such further beliefs concerning it. Thus one very good reason for supposing that this grain of white, crystalline substance is water-soluble would be that I believe it to be *salt* and know that 'Water dissolves salt' is a true nomic generalization. Similarly, a good reason for supposing that Dobbin eats grass is that Dobbin is a *horse* and 'Horses eat grass' is a true nomic generalization.

If the reductions represented by S1 and S2 are valid (and I shall have more to say on the issue in a moment), then ultimately we need recognize in the 'deep structure' of natural language only two types of elementary predicative sentence: dispositional predications involving only sortal terms, and occurrent predications involving only individ-

---

[4] This is quite close to a view that W.V. Quine has at one point expressed about dispositions: see 'Natural Kinds', in his *Ontological Relativity and Other Essays* (New York: Columbia University Press, 1969), p. 130, where he writes: 'Intuitively, what qualifies a thing as [water-]soluble though it never gets into water is that it is of the same kind as the things that actually did or will dissolve.' But there are also important differences between Quine's views and mine on this matter, not least as regards the scientific respectability of disposition-statements, which he rather calls into question.

ual terms. This naturally suggests that the occurrent/dispositional distinction itself, fundamental though it is, is in fact grounded ultimately simply in the very distinction between individuals and sorts. That is to say, dispositional predication, on this view, just *is*, ultimately, predication with regard to sorts, and occurrent predication just *is*, ultimately, predication with regard to individuals. Thus we could extend our formalized sortal language S by introducing symbolism for what might be called 'basic' predication, as follows. An *atomic basic predicative formula* consists of an *n*-ary predicate letter followed by a string of *n* objectual symbols, either *all* individual symbols or *all* sortal symbols, enclosed in a pair of square brackets. Then we may add the following definitional equivalences:

$F^n [x_1 x_2 \ldots x_n] =_{df} F^n x_1 x_2 \ldots x_n$

$F^n [\phi_1 \phi_2 \ldots \phi_n] =_{df} \phi_1 \phi_2 \ldots \phi_n F^n$

Thus we are left with one unequivocal mode of predication, 'basic' predication, and all formulae involving dispositional or occurrent predication may be reduced, by means of S1 and S2 and these definitional equivalences, to formulae involving only 'basic' predication. (To be precise, we shall of course require the *n*-ary versions of S1 and S2 for a quite general execution of this procedure; these will however be found to be embodied in the axiomatized system of sortal logic presented in the appendix to the present chapter.)

What we may *seem* to have achieved now is nothing less than a *reductive analysis* of dispositionality, a possibility concerning which I was sceptical in the previous chapter. But observe that we have not really achieved this other than perhaps in a purely technical sense. Our only substantive achievement still consists in the effective eliminability of dispositional predication *with respect to individuals* (and, paralleling this, that of occurrent predication with respect to sorts). Above all we have certainly *not* achieved a reduction of the dispositional to the occurrent (the 'potential' to the 'actual', in Aristotelian terms), nor of course *vice versa*: the mutual irreducibility of these notions is still something I want vigorously to defend. By contrast, the more familiar and currently more popular *conditional* analyses of dispositionality *do* seemingly attempt to reduce the dispositional to the occurrent. Thus one common view is that a disposition-statement like 'This grain of salt is water-soluble' is analysable in terms of some such counterfactual or subjunctive conditional as 'If this grain of salt were in water, it would be dissolving'. Now I do not necessarily want to dispute (here, at least) that the disposition-statement in question entails (or at least strongly supports) some such conditional,[5] but it does seem futile to suppose that a quite general reduction of dispositional sentences could succeed along these lines. For it seems likely that the truth-conditions of counterfactuals cannot be explicated without at least tacit reference to natural laws (though perhaps to unspecified, or not fully specified, laws): thus if they are explicated in terms of naturally possible worlds, as is currently fashionable, then since the notions of natural necessity and possibility carry at least tacit reference to laws, laws must certainly be appealed to at some stage. But we have already seen that laws are themselves expressed by dispositional sentences, and by ones which are certainly not reducible to conditional sentences involving only occurrent predication: hence a counterfactual analysis of dispositionality holds out no hope at all

---

[5] In fact, however, I would argue that the relationship between disposition-statements and conditionals is much more complex than has usually been recognized and is not such as to permit even a partial analysis of the former in terms of the latter. The main reason for this is that the *manifestation* of any disposition (such as water-solubility) – which is what one expects to find mentioned in the consequent of any conditional offered in analysis of it – can be *prevented* by indefinitely many (and quite possibly still unknown) *interfering factors*: for instance, by the saturation of the solvent in the case of water-solubility. Hence it proves impossible to state any stable conditional with a definite antecedent which can legitimately be said to be *entailed* by any given disposition-statement, and recourse must be had to the catch-all of a '*ceteris paribus* clause' in the antecedent – a manoeuvre which is effectively tantamount to a confession of defeat for the conditional analysis. Compare W.V. Quine, *The Roots of Reference* (La Salle: Open Court, 1974), pp. 12ff.

for a thoroughgoing reduction. Moreover, if laws have to be appealed in explicating counterfactuals, there is little point in appealing to the latter even in the analysis of dispositional sentences with *individual* terms in subject position, since we might as well appeal directly to the laws themselves – and this is precisely what, by principle S2 above, my own account of dispositionality does. (I should stress that I am by no means denying the propriety of counterfactuals in general, only their usefulness is explicating the meaning of dispositional sentences.)

I now have to introduce a complication into the account developed during the last few paragraphs. This is that principle S2, as it stands, is *not* in fact valid, and requires emendation. It is not valid precisely because laws are 'normative', as explained in the previous chapter. The law 'Ravens are black' is true even though some individual ravens – 'freak' or 'abnormal' ravens such as albinos – are *not* black by disposition. Suppose that Tom's pet raven Nipper is such a freak. Then the following two sentences are apparently true: 'Nipper is a raven' and 'Ravens are black'. But, by existential generalization, these together imply '$(\exists \phi)$ (Nipper is ϕ and ϕ is black)' and this, according to S2, implies 'Nipper is (dispositionally) black'. But the latter is *ex hypothesi* false. So S2 is not valid.

This looks serious and, though I believe it will eventually be possible to remedy the problem, at present we lack certain vital logical resources for doing so – in particular, resources for analysing complex sortal terms. Let me explain. Suppose that Nipper is an albino, and so white by disposition. Is it not still plausible to suppose that there is some (possibly *complex*) sortal term 'α' such that 'Nipper is α' is true and 'α is white' is a true nomic generalization or law? Surely it is: indeed, 'albino raven' will itself perhaps do for 'α', but presumably so too (and rather more informatively) would some more complex sortal term involving microbiological genetic descriptions (perhaps as yet unknown, or not fully known, to microbiologists). For surely we assume that the odd appearance of Nipper is ultimately *explicable*, and this is just to say that it is law governed. So it might seem that S2 *is* valid when read from left to right and is only invalid in the reverse direction – and hence that all that is required is some further clause on the right-hand side. However, matters are unfortunately not quite as straightforward as this because the formalized sortal language S in which S2 is couched can only cope with (semantically) *simple* sortal terms, and the foregoing argument depends for its plausibility on allowing that the envisaged sortal term 'α' may very possibly be (semantically) *complex* (as indeed 'an albino raven' is). A complete resolution of this difficulty must accordingly at least await the analysis of complex sortal terms that I shall attempt later, and for the time being the problem must be set on one side.

Meanwhile, however, it is interesting and important to note that S2 *is* I think valid for a certain restricted category of sortal terms – which I propose to call 'perfect' sortals – namely, the *theoretical* sortal terms of the more advanced sciences. These denote sorts which admit of *no* 'abnormal' or 'freak' individual exemplars. For instance, take the nomic generalization 'Protons carry unit positive charge'. Now 'protons' (or 'a proton') is, or so it would seem, a perfect sortal: anything which is a proton *must*, it would appear, by theory satisfy all the true natural laws pertaining to the proton kind and so must, amongst other things, carry unit positive charge. But this is just to say that there can be no 'abnormal' protons since (as I explained in the previous chapter) a *normal* exemplar of any sort ϕ is simply one which satisfies all the true natural laws pertaining to ϕ. However, it is I think no mere coincidence that perfect sortals are *theoretical* terms. Such tidiness is not to be found amongst the objects of everyday experience (like ravens). Indeed, it would appear that the price that advanced scientific theorizing pays in return for the extrusion of abnormal individuals from its purview is that the entities whose existence it postulates take on a semi-ideal status – they are just too uniformly perfect to be fully real. Or, to put the point less picturesquely, the exceptionless laws of the advanced sciences relate only indirectly to the real world, via simplified 'models' of it. Seen in this light, the idealizing tendency of scientific theory-construction is just a response to the perfectionist urge to refuse to allow abnormality to enter the most fundamental description of nature, but still involves an implicit recognition of the normative character of nomic generalizations. Advanced theoretical laws, no less than common-or-garden 'empirical' laws, dictate only to the normal exemplars of their respective kinds; it is just that the theorist will not countenance the existence of *any but* normal exemplars, and consequently introduces an element of fiction into his picture of reality. (I might point out here that what I have just been saying, in terms of the normative account of laws, about the distinction between 'theoretical' and 'empirical' laws and its relation to the idealizing tendency of advanced scientific theory, could perhaps also be made in a manner more familiar to orthodox philosophers of science in terms of the presence or absence of '*ceteris paribus* clauses' in the expression of laws. The normative account has no need to invoke such clauses, since from its perspective they are merely devices to defeat the falsification of a putatively nomic 'all-statement' by abnormal counterexamples.)

Sortal logic can, I believe, throw considerable light on the rationale of scientific method, particularly as regards the empirical confirmation of natural laws by experiment and observation. (This was something I touched on in the previous chapter, but there I lacked the logical apparatus to represent formally any principles of scientific inference.) One point especially worth emphasizing is that the 'normative' account of laws can explain why it is that scientists can sometimes take just a *single* well-conducted experiment to provide virtually conclusive evidence in support of a law (something which more orthodox 'inductivist' accounts of scientific method leave, in my opinion, quite inexplicable).

A 'well-conducted' experiment, it should be said, is one in which the experimenter at least has reason to suppose that he has correctly indentified what *sorts* of objects his experimental specimens are and that they are *normal* exemplars of those sorts. Given such knowledge he may apparently fairly safely infer that any disposition displayed by these specimens reflects a law governing the sorts to which they belong. Thus, if a normal sample of water is found to dissolve a normal sample of salt, it is eminently reasonable to conclude that 'Water dissolves salt' is a true nomic generalization. However, while reasonable, this inference is not in fact *deductively valid*, since it is possible that there should be more one *kind* of salt, say $salt_1$ and $salt_2$, such that water dissolves $salt_1$ but not $salt_2$. (And similarly there may be more than one kind of water.) What *does* seem deductively valid, though, is an inference from the fact that a normal sample of water is found to dissolve a normal sample of salt to the conclusion that the following *disjunction* of nomic generalizations is true: '*Either* water dissolves salt *or* some kind of water dissolves salt *or* water dissolves some kind of salt *or* some kind of water dissolves some kind of salt'. It is, however, reasonable to assume, in the absence of evidence to the contrary, that water and salt have no distinctive sub-kinds: such sub-kinds would only have to be postulated if various putatively normal samples of salt and water were found to behave in distinctive ways. So, in the absence of such contrary evidence, the truth of the law 'Water dissolves salt' (i.e. the disjunct of widest scope) may reasonably be assumed on the basis of experimental data of the type described. (Here it may be asked precisely how we are to ascertain empirically that an individual possesses a given disposition, which is the type of experimental 'datum' with which we are now concerned. The answer is not quite as straightforward as might be assumed, since it would appear that 'is Fing' doesn't always entail 'can F', where the 'can' is the 'can' of dispositionality. Nonetheless, it seems clear that a very strong evidential relation does usually obtain here, even if it falls short of entailment. That x is actually *being dissolved* by *y*, for instance, leaves little scope for denying that *y can dissolve x*, in the appropriate sense of 'can'. It must be conceded, however, that with other properties or relations things are not always so clear cut. These are complications which, frankly, I shall not address in the present study.)

It is not difficult to see why the inference just mentioned should appear deductively valid, for it *is* so, at least under the simplifying assumption that principle S2 is valid. When sortal logic is made subject to this simplification, I call it *restricted* sortal logic; such a system, while inadequate to accommodate the imperfect sortals of everyday language, is nonetheless useful as a first approximation to a fully adequate system of sortal logic, and it is with that object chiefly in mind that I employ it. For present purposes, however, the important point to realize is that if a result can be proved in restricted sortal logic, then even with reference to *imperfect* sortals it may be expected to hold in respect of *normal* exemplars of the sorts in question – and we are of course precisely supposing our samples of water and salt to *be* normal in the case under consideration.[6]

The proof we seek may be presented as follows. Suppose, as hypothesis, that *a* is a (normal) sample of water and *b* is a (normal) sample of salt, and that *a* is found to dissolve *b*, that is, that the dispositional sentence '*a* dissolves *b*' is true. Now, by applying S2 (or more precisely its binary counterpart) we may deduce from this true dispositional sentence

---

[6] I do not mean to imply that this expectation is guaranteed against disappointment by virtue of my very definition of 'normality'. For while that definition guarantees that S2 holds in the *right-to-left* direction for normal exemplars of their kinds, it does not provide a corresponding guarantee for the *left-to-right* direction. Nor – as I explained a little earlier in this chapter – is the left-to-right reading of S2 guaranteed simply by the presumption that the characteristics of all individuals are explicable and hence law governed: for an appeal to this presumption requires the invocation of complex sortal terms, which are not catered for by the formalized sortal language *S* in which S2 is expressed. None the less, I submit that the expectation in question is for the most part a reasonable one. And, in any case, the limitations of restricted sortal logic and of our formalized sortal language *S* will be transcended in the next chapter, when we shall see how to replace S2 by a more realistic (though also more complicated) principle, but one which can equally be invoked to sustain a form of the thesis now being argued for in the text.

the truth of an existentially quantified conjunction of the following form: '(∃φ) (∃χ) (*a* is φ and *b* is χ and φ dissolves χ)'. So, by existential instantiation, we are already assured that *some* lawlike sentence of the form 'α dissolves β' is true, where α and β are sorts instantiated by *a* and *b* respectively. But we have the additional information that '*a* is water' and '*b* is salt' are true instantiation sentences. So we know that *a* instantiates both the water kind and the α kind, while *b* instantiates both the salt kind and the β kind. However, it would appear to be a valid principle of sortal logic that if an individual instantiates both of two kinds, then either these kinds are identical or one is a sub-kind of the other or else the individual in question instantiates some third kind which is a sub-kind of both the first two. Formally, then, we appear to have as a theorem of sortal logic the following principle:

S3 x/ϕ & $x/\chi \rightarrow \phi = \chi$ ∨ ϕ/χ ∨ χ/ϕ ∨ (∃ψ) (x/ψ & ψ/ϕ & ψ/χ)

(It will be recalled in fact that we earlier had recourse to this very principle in chapter 4, though in a very different context.) Thus, in the example under discussion, sixteen possible cases arise (i.e. taking each of the four possible relationships between α and water and, independently, each of the four possible relationships between β and salt), upon examination of which we find that in each case one or other of the disjuncts in the disjunction of nomic generalizations stated earlier must be true. I omit the proof because it is elementary, though I should mention that it involves appeal to one further important principle of sortal logic, which may be stated formally (for the dyadic case) in the form:[7]

---

[7] It is this principle which sanctions the inference, for instance, from 'Mammals breathe air' and 'Dolphins are mammals' to 'Dolphins breathe air'. By way of presenting an apparent counterexample, it might be objected that 'Mammals reproduce their kind' and 'Mules are mammals' are both seemingly true, but 'Mules reproduce their kind' plainly false. To this the reply may be made that the falsehood of the conclusion precisely demonstrates the *falsehood* of the first premise, which should be replaced by something like 'Non-hybrid mammals reproduce their kind' (involving, of course, a complex sortal term). Furthermore,

S4 $\phi/\chi \,\&\, \chi\psi F^2 \to \phi\psi F^2$

So, by disjoining all the sixteen possible cases, we are able to deduce, as promised, the stated disjunction of nomic generalizations from the dispositional sentence '*a* dissolves *b*' in conjunction with the instantiation sentences '*a* is water' and '*b* is salt'. And more generally, we may say that the following conditional (or more strictly its universal closure) is a theorem of (restricted) sortal logic:

S5 $xyF^2 \,\&\, x/\phi \,\&\, y/\chi \to \phi\chi F^2 \vee (\exists \psi)(\psi/\phi \,\&\, \psi\chi F^2) \vee (\exists \xi)(\xi/\chi \,\&\, \phi\xi F^2) \vee (\exists \psi)(\exists \xi)(\psi/\phi \,\&\, \xi/\chi \,\&\, \psi\xi F^2)$

Of course, the preceding result rested on a presupposition that our experimental exemplars (of water and salt, in the case illustrated) were *normal*. And here it might be protested that given our definition of 'normality' we can simply never determine whether an individual x is a normal specimen of kind ϕ, since to establish conclusively that x is normal we must establish that it satisfies all the true natural laws governing ϕ, whereas our only empirical grounds for believing such laws to be true involve an appeal to the behaviour of putatively normal specimens of ϕ. However, as I suggested in the previous chapter, what this really implies is just that we must adopt a *coherentist* view of scientific knowledge, rather than a naive *foundationalist* one. There is no *beginning* to the process of acquiring scientific knowledge: the growth of scientific knowledge always presupposes an existing framework of accepted nomic truths. So we cannot intelligibly conceive of an epoch when *no* nomic generalizations were accepted as true by the human community (unless perhaps we retreat to a period prior to the

---

however, it is in fact questionable whether 'mule' should be regarded as a semantically simple sortal term, as the semantics of *S* require: for arguably 'mule' just *means* 'sterile offspring of a male donkey and a female horse'. I take no determined stand on this particular issue, though it is worth remarking that a zoologist would *not* regard mules as constituting a distinct *species* in their own right.

inception of language altogether). Coherent thought about the natural world necessarily presupposes, for reasons I have stressed before, *some* framework of law-governed sortal concepts, and cannot be restricted (say) merely to occurrent predications concerning individuals. (The reason, once again, is that the very criteria of individuation and identity of *individuals* presuppose some such framework – individuals only being conceivable as individuals of some recognizable *sort* or *kind*; while sorts or kinds – at least *natural* sorts or kinds – are themselves distinguishable in large measure precisely on the basis of differences in the laws governing them.) The growth of natural knowledge then consists in a process of revision and refinement of the framework from within (calling to mind Neurath's famous metaphor of the ship which we rebuild as we float in it). Thus for a great many sortal concepts at any given time we shall inevitably have an accepted body of law to which we may appeal for the purposes of testing the normality of experimental specimens exemplifying the sorts in question: *new* laws governing these sorts may then be discovered by subjecting putatively normal specimens to hitherto untried experiments – though in the process of doing this we may of course have to revise the existing system of concepts and laws. (Testing the normality of an experimental specimen as an exemplar of a given sort is, thus, essentially a matter of determining whether it satisfies certain well-established laws pertaining to that sort: for instance, in the case of a sample of water, its normality – or, if you like, its 'purity' – is to be ascertained by seeing whether it is tasteless and colourless, whether it boils at 100°C, whether it expands on freezing, and so forth. Obviously, no such test – even if it involves advanced techniques of chemical analysis – can be completely decisive in the sense that its verdict is immune to subsequent reversal: new evidence can always in principle lead one to classify as 'abnormal' a specimen hitherto regarded as 'normal', or even, more radically, to reclassify it as belonging to another sort or species altogether.)

Appendix: An Axiomatic System of Sortal Logic

The axiomatic system of sortal logic presented below is a system of 'restricted' sortal logic in the sense explained in the present chapter. It is however stronger in one or two minor respects than is required for the purposes of this chapter, as will be pointed out later.

The *symbols* and *rules for well-formed formulae* of the system are simply provided by the vocabulary and syntax of the formalized language S described at the beginning of the chapter. The *axioms* and *rules of inference* of the system may be specified as follows. First of all we shall appropriate any suitable set of axioms for standard predicate logic with identity which utilizes *modus ponens* and definitional interchange as the only rules of inference,[8] admitting however suitable modifications to allow for the presence in S of dual-sorted variables and constants and dual-mode predication. (What these modifications amount to are the requirements (1) that the axioms governing quantifiers and identity be specified separately but in parallel fashion for individual and for sortal variables and constants, and (2) that formulae differing only in respect of the mode of predication of some predicate letter be thus far handled as though they involved different predicate letters uniformly predicated.) Secondly, we shall adopt in addition the following axiom-schemata:

I Axiom-schemata of instantiation

where o_1, o_2 and o_3 are objectual symbols

A1 o_1/o_1

A2 $(o_1/o_2 \ \& \ o_2/o_3) \rightarrow o_1/o_3$

---

[8] See, e.g., Benson Mates, *Elementary Logic*, 2nd edn (New York: Oxford University Press, 1972), pp. 165f.

A3 $(o_1/o_2 \,\&\, o_1/o_3) \rightarrow (o_2/o_3 \vee o_3/o_2)$

II Axiom-schemata of occurrent and dispositional predication

where $o_1, o_2, \ldots, o_n$ are objectual symbols and P^n is a predicate letter

A4 $P^n o_1 o_2 \ldots o_n \rightarrow o_1 o_2 \ldots o_n P^n$
where $o_1, o_2, \ldots, o_n$ are all *individual* symbols

A5 $P^n o_1 o_2 \ldots o_i \ldots o_n \longleftrightarrow (\exists v)(P^n o_1 o_2 \ldots v \ldots o_n \,\&\, v/o_i)$
where o_i is a *sortal* symbol and v is an *individual* variable not occurring amongst $o_1, o_2, \ldots, o_n$

A6 $o_1 o_2 \ldots o_i \ldots o_n P^n \longleftrightarrow (\exists v)(o_1 o_2 \ldots v \ldots o_n P^n \,\&\, o_i/v)$
where o_i is an *individual* symbol and v is a *sortal* variable not occurring amongst $o_1, o_2, \ldots, o_n$

A7 $(o_1 o_2 \ldots o_i \ldots o_n P^n \,\&\, o_j/o_i) \rightarrow o_1 o_2 \ldots o_j \ldots o_n P^n$
where o_i and o_j are both *sortal* symbols (with $j \geq 1$)

A8 $(P^n o_1 o_2 \ldots o_i \ldots o_n \,\&\, o_j/o_i) \rightarrow P^n o_1 o_2 \ldots o_j \ldots o_n$
where o_i and o_j are both *individual* symbols (with $j \geq 1$)

The axioms of instantiation and of occurrent and dispositional predication will consist of the universal closures of all formulae exemplifying the foregoing schemata.[9]

---

[9] It should be emphasized that we must not suppose that what would standardly be called a 'substitution-instance' of an axiom of the system is necessarily itself a theorem of the system. For instance, it will not do to argue for the theoremhood of '$(\forall\phi)(-F^1\phi \leftrightarrow (\exists x)(-F^1 x \,\&\, x/\phi))$' on the grounds that it is a 'substitution-instance' of the axiom '$(\forall\phi)(F^1\phi \leftrightarrow (\exists x)(F^1 x \,\&\, x/\phi))$', arising from the latter by the substitution of the stencil '$-F^1$ ①' for the stencil 'F^1 ①'. (For the standard notions of a 'substitution-instance' and a 'stencil', see Benson Mates, *Elementary Logic*, pp. 178f. Mates's metatheorem 309, ibid., stating that a substitution-instance of a theorem is itself a theorem, does not hold for sortal logic.) The reason for this restriction is that sortal logic, unlike orthodox first-order predicate logic, does not in general equate *predicate* negation (conjunction, disjunction, etc.) with *sentence* negation (etc.). See also note 3 above.

Consistency

That the foregoing system is consistent is easy enough to demonstrate. We have merely to re-interpret formulae of the system in such a way that (1) the distinction between individual and sortal symbols is discounted, (2) the instantiation sign is equated with the identity sign, and (3) the distinction between occurrent and dispositional predication is discounted, thus equating an atomic formula consisting of a predicate letter *preceded* by a string of objectual symbols with the formula consisting of the same predicate letter *followed* by that string of symbols. Under this interpretation, it is easily seen that axiom-schemata A1 – A8 all reduce to theorem-schemata of standard predicate logic with identity, while the rules of inference of the system remain of course those of the previously adopted axiomatization of standard predicate logic with identity. Hence, granted the consistency of standard predicate logic with identity, sortal logic as axiomatized above must be consistent.

Some remarks on the axioms

It may be noted that axiom-schema A5 supplies us with the generalized version of the principle S1 stated earlier in the present chapter, while A6 supplies us with the generalized version of S2 and A7 with the generalized version of S4. A8 becomes of course redundant once it is stipulated that a formula in which the instantiation sign is flanked on both sides by individual symbols is equivalent to an identity. A3 is clearly stronger than is required for the truth of principle S3 stated earlier in this chapter, and A4 ignores our previous *caveat* about the entailment of 'can F' by 'is Fing'.

The definition of identity

It should be observed that if the definition of identity as mutual instantiation (mooted earlier in chapter 3) is adopted, namely:

$o_1 = o_2 =_{df} o_1/o_2 \ \& \ o_2/o_1$

where o_1 and o_2 are objectual symbols, then the laws of identity may be recovered from the remainder of the system (where by the 'laws of identity' I mean the principles specifying that identity is an equivalence relation together with the principle of the substitutivity of identity).

10

Complex Sortal Terms and the Differentiation of Sorts

I pass on now to a problem which I have so far had to postpone: that of the analysis of (semantically) complex sortal terms (or, more accurately, that of the analysis of sentences containing such terms, since it will transpire that such terms do not really constitute genuine logico-semantic units in their own right). Complex sortal terms, as we have seen, are formed (syntactically) from simple ones by the adjunction of adjectives or adjectival phrase as in, e.g., 'wild horses', 'boiling water', 'an animal which lactates' and 'a tree which sheds its leaves in winter'. A little regimentation will provide all such terms with a common form, namely, 'α which is F', where 'α' is a simple sortal term and 'F' is a predicate. Thus 'a wild horse' may be rewritten as 'a horse which is wild' and ' boiling water' as 'water which is boiling'. (This, however, properly only applies to syntactically complex sortal terms which are also semantically complex: 'heavy water' is *not* synonymous with 'water which is heavy', for instance. And this indeed supplies us with a test for semantic complexity, albeit one only directly applicable to syntactically complex sortal terms. In the case of a syntactically simple sortal term which is suspected of being semantically complex, like 'ice', one must first establish its synonymy with a syntactically complex sortal term, like 'frozen water', to which the test may then be applied – in this case with a positive result, since 'frozen water' *is* synonymous with 'water which is frozen'.) Applying however the distinction between dispositional and occurrent predication, we can nonetheless see that even if we rewrite all complex sortal terms in the form 'α which is F', they will still fall into two grammatically distinct classes, depending on whether the predicate 'F' is used dispositionally or occurently. And we shall in fact discover that this grammatical distinction reflects logical ones of considerable importance. Thus, for example, two sentences which differ only in that one contains the complex sortal term 'an animal which *lactates*' (dispositional) where the other contains the complex sortal term 'an animal which *is lactating*' (occurrent) will in general turn out to have quite different underlying logical forms.

In the formalized sortal language S described in the previous chapter, the distinction between dispositional and occurrent predication is marked by writing objectual constants and variables (whether individual or sortal) to the *left* of predicate letters to signify dispositional predication and to their *right* to signify occurrent predication. So we are now in a position to extend our formal system so as to permit the symbolization of our two classes of complex sortal terms. Thus a complex sortal term involving *dispositional* predication, like 'an animal which lactates', may be symbolized as, let us say, '$\alpha < \alpha L^1 >$', while one involving *occurrent* predication, like 'an animal which is lactating', may correspondingly be symbolized as '$\alpha < L^1 \alpha >$' – where 'α' translates the simple sortal term 'an animal' and 'L^1' translates the monadic predicate(s) '—lactates/is lactating'. Such complex sortal symbols may now be permitted to occupy all the positions in atomic formulae open to the simple sortal symbols (sortal constants) of S. The problem of analysis which lies before us now is that of providing transformation rules which will enable us, if possible, to *eliminate* complex sortal symbols from all such positions by replacing the formulae in which they occur by equivalent formulae utilizing only the original vocabulary and syntax of S. The problem may usefully be compared to Russell's problem of eliminating definite description symbols of the form '$(\imath x)Fx$'.[1] For we analogously shall want to say that complex sortal symbols are 'incomplete symbols': that they do not constitute genuine semantic units and that they cannot be properly interpreted apart from the complete sentential formulae of which they form a part. However, we shall also see that in fact the original vocabulary and syntax of S are *not* fully adequate to complete the task of elimination, but require extension in important new ways.

For present purposes I am going to concentrate on two sorts of sentences featuring complex sortal terms: dispositional predications with complex sortal terms in subject position, and instantiation sentences featuring proper names and complex sortal terms. Examples of the former type would be 'An animal which lactates is warm-blooded' and 'Water which is boiling gives off steam'. Examples of the latter type would be 'Daisy is an animal which chews the cud' and 'Dobbin is a horse which is eating grass'. I shall begin with the latter type of sentence, whose analysis is relatively straightforward.

Sentences of this latter type have the form '$a/\alpha<\alpha F^1>$' or '$a/\alpha<F^1\alpha>$' in our new notation. (To simplify matters I shall for the time being restrict myself to monadic predicates.) And it should be clear enough that with sentences of this type we have a case in which our two classes of complex sortal terms call for quite different logical treatments. In fact, the following two definitional equivalences immediately suggest themselves:

1 $a/\alpha<\alpha F^1> =_{df} (\exists\phi)(\phi/\alpha \,\&\, a/\phi \,\&\, \phi F^1)$

2 $a/\alpha<F^1\alpha> =_{df} a/\alpha \,\&\, F^1 a$

---

[1] See A.N. Whitehead and B. Russell, *Principia Mathematica*, 2nd edn (Cambridge: Cambridge University Press, 1927), vol. I, pp. 66ff.

(Observe here that the righthand side of (2) is equivalent to '$(\exists x)(x/\alpha \ \& \ a/x \ \& \ Fx)$', so that there is a greater parallelism between (1) and (2) than at first meets the eye.) For example: in accordance with (1), 'Daisy is an animal which chews the cud' may be taken to mean 'There is some sort of animal, ϕ, such that Daisy is ϕ and ϕ chews the cud' – which will be true if, say, Daisy is a cow (since cows are animals and cows chew the cud). And recall here that this may be true even if, through some aberration of anatomy or upbringing, Daisy herself does *not* chew the cud, i.e. is not a normal cow. By contrast, in accordance with (2), 'Dobbin is a horse which is eating grass' may be taken to mean, quite simply, 'Dobbin is a horse and Dobbin is eating grass'. The essential point which emerges, then, is that in the analysis of the *first* class of sentence a (dispositional) predication is made of a *species* or *sort* to which the given individual belongs, whereas in the analysis of the *second* class of sentence an (occurrent) predication is made of that individual itself. (I do not dispute, incidentally, that 'Daisy is an animal which chews the cud', *could* be read as equivalent to 'Daisy is an animal and Daisy chews the cud', though this would not be its more natural reading. But my present task is to assign an *unambiguous* meaning to formulae of the form '$a/\alpha<\alpha F^1>$', which will enable me to use such formulae to represent sentences in natural language of a certain grammatical form: and hence I adopt what is the theoretically more interesting – as well as the more natural – reading of the sentences in question.)

It may be observed that in the case of sentences of the form '$a/\alpha<\alpha F^1>$' we may replace the individual term 'a' by a *sortal* term 'β' and the resulting sentence will admit of an analysis closely paralleling that given in (1), namely:

3 $\beta/\alpha<\alpha F^1> =_{df} (\exists \phi)(\phi/\alpha \ \& \ \beta/\phi \ \& \ \phi F^1)$

For example, 'A cow is an animal which chews the cud' is very naturally interpreted as meaning 'There is some sort of animal, ϕ, such that a cow is ϕ and ϕ chews the cud'. To this it might be objected that in fact the sentence in question is even more naturally interpreted quite simply as meaning 'A cow is an animal and a cow chews the cud'. But this objection is misconceived since very arguably the two interpretations are actually equivalent. All we need to assume to this end is that 'β/ϕ & ϕF^1' entails 'βF^1' (which is implied by principle S4 of the previous chapter) and that the instantiation relation is reflexive and transitive. For given this it may be proved that the righthand side of (3) is equivalent to 'β/α & βF^1'. Notice, however, that we do *not* correspondingly have any very natural use for a form of sentence obtained by replacing the individual term 'a' in a sentence of the form '$a/\alpha{<}F^1\alpha{>}$' by a sortal term 'β'. Thus, for instance, 'A cow is an animal which *is chewing* the cud' makes very doubtful sense, in contrast both to '*Daisy* is an animal which is chewing the cud' and to 'A cow is an animal which *chews* the cud'.

I turn now to the case of *predicative* formulae containing complex sortal symbols and more specifically those involving *dispositional* predication, which are particularly important because they are required for the representation of many nomological generalizations. These again fall into two classes depending on whether the complex sortal symbols involved themselves involve either dispositional or occurrent predication. I shall deal first with the easier class, which is the former. These, then, are formulae of the form '$\alpha{<}\alpha F^1{>}G^1$' (I again restrict myself for the time being to monadic predicates). Such a formula could be used to represent, for example, the nomological generalization 'An animal which chews the cud lactates'. And here I propose the following definitional equivalence:

4   $\alpha{<}\alpha F^1{>}G^1 =_{df} (\forall\phi)((\phi/\alpha \ \& \ \phi F^1) \rightarrow \phi G^1)$

By this account, 'An animal which chews the cud lactates' may be taken to mean 'For any sort of animal, ϕ, if ϕ chews the cud, then ϕ lactates' – from which one might infer, for instance, 'If a cow chews the cud, then a cow lactates'. One very important implication of this analysis is that in a sentence like 'An animal which chews the cud lactates' the complex sortal term which is the *grammatical* subject does not play the role of a *logical* subject. From '$\alpha < \alpha F^1 > G^{1}$' one cannot validly infer '$(\exists \phi) \phi G^{1}$', if (4) is correct. Thus 'an animal which chews the cud' is not in such a context to be seen as denoting any *sort* or *kind* of thing, such as the zoological suborder of *ruminants*. Analogously, 'an animal which lactates' should not be regarded as denoting the sort or kind *mammal*; which of course casts serious doubt on the ancient notion of defining species *per genus et differentiam* (at least if such definition is regarded as establishing synonymy).[2] However, this is a notion that I am opposed to in any case, on other grounds (namely, because I do not believe that natural kind terms are *definable* at all, and hold that generalizations like 'Mammals lactate' or 'Ruminants chew the cud' are not analytic truths but rather *a posteriori* statements of natural law).

The second class of dispositional predicative formulae I have to deal with are those involving complex sortal symbols which themselves involve *occurrent* predication, i.e. formulae of the form '$\alpha < F^1 \alpha > G^{1}$', which might be used to represent a nomological generalization such as 'Water which is boiling (boiling water) gives off steam'. (Clearly, this is to be distinguished from '*Water which boils* (boilable water) gives off steam', where the complex sortal term involves dispositional predication; and indeed the undeniable odd-

---

[2] Cf. P.T. Geach on 'rhombus' and 'parallelogram that has equal sides': *Reference and Generality*, 3rd edn (Ithaca: Cornell University Press, 1980), pp. 147f. Geach indeed maintains quite generally that complex sortal terms are 'a sort of logical mirage' (ibid., p. 145), and I agree with him, at least in spirit. I disagree, thus, with the contrary view of Anil Gupta; see his *The Logic of Common Nouns* (New Haven: Yale University Press, 1980), pp. 10ff. Geach's arguments for his position have, it must be said, received incisive criticism at the hands of Gareth Evans: see his 'Pronouns, Quantifiers and Relative Clauses (II)', in his *Collected Papers* (Oxford: Clarendon Press, 1985). However, whatever may be the impact of Evans's criticisms on Geach's own arguments, they do not touch on the considerations which lead me into sympathy with Geach.

ness of the latter sentence can readily be explained by our preceding analysis as stemming from the fact that we assume that *every* sort of water boils.) Other appropriate examples would be, say, 'An animal which is lactating is placid' and 'A dog which sees a cat barks'. (Plainly, 'sees' in the latter sentence demands an occurrent reading if the sentence as a whole is plausibly to receive its most natural interpretation.) Now, of course, according to a Popperian 'all-statement' analysis of laws, a formula of the form now under consideration would naturally be taken to be equivalent to one of the form '$(\forall x)((x/\alpha \ \& \ F^1x) \rightarrow G^1x)$', which even presents a pleasing symmetry with our proposed equivalence (4) above. Thus 'Water which is boiling gives off steam' would be taken to mean 'For any individual (body of) water, x, if x is boiling, then x is giving off steam'. However, this is not a suggestion that I can accept, for reasons which I have already made plain. Laws, by my account, do not primarily concern individuals but rather the sorts or species to which they belong. Thus the law 'Water which is boiling gives off steam' is, I would urge, a proposition primarily concerning the sort or kind *water* and only derivatively its individual exemplars or instances. At the same time, it must also be sufficiently clear that in this nomological generalization the complex sortal term 'water which is boiling' cannot be taken to denote a distinctive *sort* or *kind* of water (in the way, say, that 'heavy water' does). My suggestion, then, is that the logical subject of the sentence is the *simple* sortal term 'water' and that the adjectival clause 'which is boiling' is more properly to be seen as contributing to the *predicate*. This could be made more manifest by paraphrasing the whole sentence in the form: 'Water *gives off steam if it is boiling*'. Similarly our other two examples could be paraphrased respectively by the sentences 'An animal *is placid if it is lactating*' and 'A dog *barks if it sees a cat*'.

At a formal level, what we would now appear to require are means of building up *complex predicates*, by allowing the sentential connectives of S to double as *predicate connec-*

tives. Thus, taking the two predicate letters 'F^1' and 'G^1' and the conditional connective '$\rightarrow$', we may form the complex predicate '$(F^1 \rightarrow G^1)$', which, we may suppose, may be predicated either occurrently or dispositionally of an object (whether an individual or a sort). This understood, I propose the following further definitional equivalence to deal with the class of formulae currently under consideration:[3]

5   $\alpha <F^1 \alpha> G^1 =_{df} \alpha(F^1 \rightarrow G^1)$

What now requires special emphasis is that a formula of the form appearing on the right-hand side of (5) is not equivalent to any formula constructed from atomic formulae involving only *noncomplex* predicates. Thus, in particular, '$\alpha(F^1 \rightarrow G^1)$' is *not* equivalent to '$\alpha F^1 \rightarrow \alpha G^1$'. 'Water gives off steam if it is boiling' is not equivalent to 'If water boils, then water gives off steam'. Again, 'A dog barks if it sees a cat' is not equivalent to 'If a dog sees a cat, then a dog barks'. These non-equivalences may be made still more manifest by considering sentences in which *individual* terms are made the subjects of the same complex dispositional predicates – for example, 'Fido barks if he sees a cat', which by my account is of the form '$a(F^1 \rightarrow G^1)$'. This, I say, is *not* equivalent to 'If Fido sees a cat, Fido barks' – not, at least, where the latter sentence is seen as genuinely being of the form '$aF^1 \rightarrow aG^1$', i.e. as being constructed by conditionalization from the sentences 'Fido sees a cat' and 'Fido barks'. (In fact it would appear that many such 'conditional' sen-

---

[3] At the first blush there may seem to be little parallel between definitional equivalences (4) and (5), but in fact they may be rewritten in forms which bring out both a striking resemblance and an important difference, namely, as follows:

4* $\alpha <\alpha F^1> G^1 =_{df} (\forall \phi)(\phi/\alpha \rightarrow (\phi F^1 \rightarrow \phi G^1))$

5* $\alpha <F^1 \alpha> G^1 =_{df} (\forall \phi)(\phi/\alpha \rightarrow \phi (F^1 \rightarrow G^1))$

What these reformulations make clear is that the logical differences between our two *definienda* turn wholly on the distinction between complex sentences and complex predicates.

tences in natural language should in reality be seen as constructed by conditionalization on *predicates* and hence not as being of the form 'If p, then q', where 'p' and 'q' are sentences.[4]) Nor will it do to suggest that '$a(F^1 \to G^1)$' is equivalent to '$F^1a \to G^1a$', in which *occurrent* predication features exclusively. 'Fido barks if he sees a cat' is *not* equivalent to 'If Fido sees (= is seeing) a cat, then Fido is barking'. The second sentence, in conjunction with 'Fido sees (= is seeing) a cat', entails 'Fido is barking'. Not so the first, which only predicates of Fido a (conditional) *disposition* to bark – a disposition to bark-if-he-sees-a-cat. Fido's failure to bark upon seeing a cat would not defeat an ascription of this disposition to him, provided an appropriate explanation of the failure was forthcoming (e.g. Fido might be muzzled on the occasion of failure). For the same reason we may also dismiss the proposal that 'Fido barks if he sees a cat' is analysable as meaning something like 'For all times t, if Fido sees a cat at t, then Fido barks at t', where 'sees' and 'barks' are *tenseless*.[5]

So far I have restricted my examples to ones involving only *monadic* predicates, but further complications arise when we take into consideration cases involving polyadicity. For instance, I need to be able to extend my treatment to a sentence like 'A dog which sees a cat chases it',[6] which I

---

[4] Cf. V.H. Dudman, 'Parsing "If"-Sentences', *Analysis* 44 (1984), pp. 145–53.

[5] Such a proposal is implicit in, e.g., Ivor Alexander, '"If" and Quantification', *Analysis* 45 (1985), pp. 186–90.

[6] The example may call to mind Geach's well-known problem sentence 'Any man who owns a donkey beats it' (see his *Reference and Generality*, 3rd edn, pp. 143ff.). Geach holds, of course, that 'man who owns a donkey' in this sentence should not be regarded as a genuine semantic unit synonymous with 'donkey-owner', which Evans ('Pronouns, Quantifiers and Relative Clauses (II)') has disputed. My sympathies lie with Geach, though I would emphasize that his sentence crucially differs from the one I am now concerned with, in that his features an *individual quantifier expression* whereas mine involves (or so I would hold) no quantification over individuals at all. I would only add – without going into details – that in my opinion what plausibility Evans's view has as against Geach's rests on an assumption that 'man' designates (or has as its semantic value) the set of all individual men, of which 'man who owns a donkey' designates a subset: an assumption which, as I hope I have shown, finds no place in an adequate semantics of sortal terms – though it is one whose inadequacy does not manifest itself directly

would wish to paraphrase in the form 'A dog chases a cat if it sees it'. The original sentence could, I suggest, be represented symbolically by a formula of the form '$\alpha < F^2 \alpha \beta > \beta G^2$'. And, again, my approach is to regard such a sentence as dispositionally predicating of dogs and cats a certain complex relation. The relation in question is one representable as constructed by conditionalization from the simple dyadic predicates '— sees . . .' and '— chases . . .', and so we might think to represent the paraphrase by the formula '$\alpha \beta (F^2 \rightarrow G^2)$'. The trouble with this, however, is that it provides us with no means of distinguishing between the sentences 'A dog chases a cat if it (the dog) sees it (the cat)' and 'A dog chases a cat if it (the cat) sees it (the dog)'. The answer (or, at least, *an* answer) is to append appropriate subscripts to the predicate letters contained in the complex predicate, so that the two sentences are represented respectively by formulae of the forms '$\alpha \beta (F^2_{\alpha\beta} \rightarrow G^2_{\alpha\beta})$' and '$\alpha \beta (F^2_{\beta\alpha} \rightarrow G^2_{\alpha\beta})$'. (Such subscripts were obviously otiose in the monadic cases, but could be added for the sake of uniformity of notation.) Thus the latter two formulae would constitute, respectively, our *definiens* for '$\alpha < F^2 \alpha \beta > \beta G^2$' and our *definiens* for '$\alpha < F^2 \beta \alpha > \beta G^2$', these *definienda* representing, respectively, such sentences as 'A dog which sees a cat chases it' and 'A dog which a cat sees chases it'.

Of course, a question which I have so far skirted is that of how we can satisfactorily account for the proposed dual role of the logical connectives, whereby they double as both sentential and predicate operators. I strongly suspect that we shall have to rest content here with an irreducible systematic ambiguity. We can of course build on the idea that the connectives are interdefinable in the *same* standard ways in *each* of their roles, seeing the isomorphism between the interrelationships of a connective with others in one of its roles with those of 'the same' connective in its other role as

---

in the case of Geach's sentence precisely because that sentence involves only quantification over individuals.

substantially underpinning our talk of these connectives as indeed being 'the same' (which is why the ambiguity may be described as *systematic*). Thus just as the complex sentence 'p → q' is definitionally equivalent to '– (p & –q)', so the complex predicate '$F \to G$' is definitionally equivalent to '– $(F \& -G)$': a fact which is borne out by examples. For instance, 'Fido barks if he sees a cat' *is* plausibly equivalent to 'Fido doesn't see a cat and not bark'. We are at liberty, then, to take predicate negation and conjunction as our primitives, just as we are at liberty to take sentential negation and conjunction in this way.

The reason, it would seem, why the irreducible duality in role of the connectives has hitherto not been much appreciated is just that logicians have ignored *sorts* as proper subjects of predication and have moreover not been even-handed in their attitudes towards dispositional and occurrent predication, according the latter primary status: for if our attention is restricted to *occurrent* predications of *individuals* we may indeed see apparent equivalances between complex sentences and sentences containing complex predicates. Thus 'It is not the case that this coin is landing heads' *is* apparently equivalent to 'This coin is-not-landing-heads', as is 'Smith is eating and Smith is reading' to 'Smith is-eating-and-reading'. But once *dispositional* predications are taken into account, such equivalences begin to look like special cases. Thus it is fairly clear that 'It is not the case that this coin lands heads' is *not* equivalent to 'This coin doesn't-land-heads' (since the former but not the latter is consistent with the coin being an unbiased one); and equally that 'Smith eats and Smith reads' is *not* equivalent to 'Smith eats-and-reads'. Now no doubt the common response here would be to take the latter non-equivalences as *prima facie* evidence that dispositional predication involves hidden operators or quantifiers in the 'deep structure' of the sentences featuring it: and of course where dispositional predications of *individuals* are concerned (as in these examples) I can agree, since I see these as implicitly involving sortal quantification. (Similarly, analogous non-equivalences in the case of *occurrent* predications of *sorts* are by my account explicable in terms of differences of scope arising from the implicit involvement of *individual* quantifiers.) But such an approach cannot, if earlier arguments of mine are correct, be applied to dispositional predication quite generally. For non-equivalences of the kind we are interested in at present are unquestionably discernible in *nomological generalizations*, which I have argued comprise a fundamental and irreducible logico-semantic category. Thus 'Horses don't eat meat' is clearly stronger than 'It is not the case that horses eat meat' – and by my account 'Horses eat meat' is indisputably an *atomic* sentence, which hence contains no 'hidden' operator or quantifier. Altogether, then, it seems evident that an adequate formalized sortal language will *have* to contain both sentential connectives and predicate connectives, so that my introduction of the latter for the purposes of analysing complex sortal symbols cannot be seen as a merely *ad hoc* manoeuvre.

I am now in a position to return briefly to some unfinished business. We saw in the previous chapter that principle S2,

$xF^1 \leftrightarrow (\exists\phi)(x/\phi\ \&\ \phi F^1)$

is not valid unless the range of individual variables is restricted (at least) to individuals that are *normal* exemplars of their sorts or kinds. Nonetheless we saw that even where x is an abnormal individual of its kind(s), it was still reasonable to suppose that where 'xF^1' is true, so too will be certain propositions *ostensibly* of the forms 'x/α' and 'αF^1', at least if we allow here that 'α' may very possibly be a *complex* sortal term (though this is strictly contrary, indeed, to the semantical rules of our formalized language S as originally formulated). But this does not imply that some proposition of the form '$(\exists\phi)(x/\phi\ \&\ \phi F^1)$' is true, because (as we have now seen) complex sortal terms do not designate *sorts or kinds* in the way that simple sortal terms do, so that where 'α' is a complex sortal term the rule of existential generalization cannot be invoked to enable us to pass from '... α ...' to '($\exists\phi$)(... ϕ ...)' – not, at least, on an 'objectual' reading of the quantifiers such as I have been assuming. Even so, we now know enough about the semantics of complex sortal terms to be able to see that where 'xF^1' is true, at least a proposition of the form '($\exists\phi$)(x/ϕ & G^1x & $\phi(G^1 \to F^1)$)' will almost certainly be true, precisely *because* there will be some possibly complex sortal term 'α' such that 'x/α & αF^1' is true: for 'α' if complex will have, it would almost certainly appear, the form '$\beta<G^1\beta>$', and we have by implication seen above that '$x/\beta<G^1\beta>$ & $\beta<G^1\beta>F^1$' entails 'x/β & G^1x & $\beta(G^1 \to F^1)$', where 'β' is a *simple* sortal term with respect to which the rule of existential generalization may be invoked. This we may illustrate by means of our former example of the albino raven Nipper, which is white by disposition. As I suggested previously, we have every reason for confidence that there is some complex sortal term, of the form 'raven which is G' where 'G' expresses perhaps some arcane genetic condition, such that 'Nipper is a raven which is G' is a true instantiation sentence and 'Ravens which are G are white' is a true nomological generalization – and moreover one which may be recast in the form 'Ravens are white if they are G'. Hence we may confidently affirm that some proposition of the form 'For some sort, ϕ, Nipper is a ϕ and Nipper is G, and ϕs are white if they are G' is true. Formally, we seem entitled to endorse the following general principle:

S6 $\quad xF^1 \to (\exists X^1)(\exists\phi)(x/\phi$ & X^1x & $\phi(X^1 \to F^1))$

where 'X^1' is a variable ranging over (monadic) predicates (so that we have now been forced to transcend the confines of first-order logic). But of course S6 is not a *bi*conditional, as S2 was, and the question arises as to whether it is also valid in the right-to-left direction. The answer would appear to be 'No', as may again be seen from our raven example.

For even given that a certain individual raven is G and that ravens which are G are white, it does *not* inevitably follow that that individual is white by disposition – again because of the possibility of abnormality. A raven might possess the genetic mechanism which in albino ravens is responsible for their whiteness, and yet *not* be white by disposition because of some abnormality in the functioning of that very genetic mechanism in this particular case. I shall not attempt to say explicitly what refinements to S6 are required to overcome this difficulty: rather, I shall tackle the problem in a different way, by reverting to the use of complex sortal terms (safe in the knowledge, now, that these are *in principle* eliminable).

Suppose, to avoid confusion, we add to our formalized language S a stock of a new style of sortal constants and variables – $\bar{\alpha}, \bar{\beta}, \bar{\gamma}, \ldots$ and $\bar{\phi}, \bar{\chi}, \bar{\psi}, \ldots$ respectively – on the understanding that the constants may be used to represent *either* simple *or* complex sortal terms in natural language, while the quantifiers in use with the variables are given a 'substitutional' interpretation (so that, for example, '$(\exists \bar{\phi})(\ldots \bar{\phi} \ldots)$' may be taken to be true just in case some sentence of the form '$\ldots \bar{\tau} \ldots$' is true, where '$\bar{\tau}$' either belongs to our stock of sortal constants or could be added to it). The reasons which led us to endorse S6 now lead us to endorse the following principle (which just reads like S2 in the left-to-right direction, apart from the presence of the new-style variable):

S7 $\quad xF^1 \to (\exists \bar{\phi})(x/\bar{\phi} \ \& \ \bar{\phi} F^1)$

Thus where 'xF^1' is intepreted as 'Nipper is white', what verifies the right-hand side of S7 is, we may suppose, the truth of a conjunction of the form 'Nipper is a raven with genetic feature G and ravens with genetic feature G are white'. That is to say, S7 is, given our analysis of complex sortal terms, just a convenient shorthand for S6. This understood, what I *suggest* is required in order to transform S7 into a valid *bi*conditional is that its right-hand side be strengthened so as to give us:

S8 $xF^1 \leftrightarrow (\exists\bar{\phi})(x/\bar{\phi}\ \&\ \bar{\phi}F^1\ \&\ (\forall\bar{\chi})((\bar{\chi}/\bar{\phi}\ \&\ x/\bar{\chi}) \rightarrow \bar{\chi}F^1))$

What the new clause on the right-hand side implies, in the context of our raven illustration, is that there is no (possibly complex) sortal term '$\bar{\tau}$' such that '$\bar{\tau}$ is a raven with genetic feature G' and 'Nipper is $\bar{\tau}$' are both true, while '$\bar{\tau}$ is white' is false. What motivates this idea is the thought, explained earlier, that what might account for Nipper's failure to be white despite his being a raven with genetic feature G would be the fact that in Nipper the genetic mechanism in question was in some way *defective* – so that '$\bar{\tau}$' in this case might be something of the form 'a raven with genetic feature G defective in respect H'. To the extent that this is the *only* sort of consideration which precludes our replacing the conditional connective in S7 by a biconditional connective, it would appear that S8 is indeed the biconditional we seek. And here I shall leave the issue, emphasizing in conclusion only that however the problem is to be solved of finding a substitute for S2 which does not restrict us to the domain of normal individuals, the solution will inevitably require us to transcend the limitations of a system of first-order sortal logic in which the quantifiers are given an 'objectual' reading. The complexities of concrete physical reality outrun by far the descriptive resources of our original formalized sortal language *S*.

One last important question which we have not yet adequately addressed is this: how are we to *ascertain* that a given sortal term in natural language is semantically *simple* rather than *complex*? It is no use, I believe, just appealing to 'linguistic intuition', whatever that might exactly be. (This is the drawback of the test for semantic complexity adverted to in the opening paragraph of this chapter.) On this basis, no doubt, some would urge, for instance, that 'ice' *is* synonymous with 'frozen water' and is for this reason semantically complex, while others would equally strongly deny this. In any case, I am not really interested in the question of whether a given sortal term in natural language *is regarded by speakers of that language* as semantically simple or complex (a matter on which their 'linguistic intuitions' might indeed have some bearing), but rather in the question of whether such a term *ought* to be interpreted as semantically simple or complex – and for me this is a matter of whether or not there *exists in fact* a distinct *sort* or *kind* of things or stuff which that term may appropriately be regarded as designating. Thus I would claim that 'ice' should *not* be regarded as designating a distinct kind of stuff, whereas 'heavy water' *should*. And what motivates such claims is not linguistic intuition but *scientific knowledge*. Thus, in scientific ignorance one might have *thought* that 'tadpole' denoted a distinct *kind* of creature: it is science, not linguistic intuition, that tells us that tadpoles just *are* young frogs, and equally that ice just *is* frozen water. It is to the philosophy of science, then, that we must look for an account of the principles upon which we are to acknowledge the existence of and distinctions between the various different *sorts* or *kinds* of things that there are.

By appeal to what criteria, then, *does* science (in the broadest sense of the term) distinguish sorts or kinds? Why, for instance, are tadpoles and caterpillars *not* thought to constitute distinct kinds of creatures, nor ice a distinct kind of stuff? Part of the answer, no doubt, lies in the fact that science (or at least *modern* science) embodies a general antipathy towards the notion of *transsubstantiation* – to the idea, that is, that one sort of substance may be transformed into another. Ice regularly changes into (liquid) water and tadpoles into (adult) frogs, which creates a *prima facie* presumption in each case in favour of these being things of the *same kind*, differing merely in *phase*. Here one might be inclined to object that a quantity of heavy water will, presumably, eventually turn into ordinary water through the radioactive decay of its deuterium atoms, yet we are not on that account persuaded to regard 'heavy water' as (in Wiggins's terminology) a *phased sortal*. Nor will it do simply to reply by pointing out that the change from ice to liquid water is naturally *reversible*, whereas that between heavy water and ordinary water is not: for natural irreversibility is not held to count against the change from tadpole to adult frog being merely one of phase.

One may be strongly tempted to resort at this point to a theory of *essence*. Thus it may be urged that it is of the 'essence' of ordinary water to be constituted by hydrogen and oxygen in the ratio of two to one, and of the 'essence' of frogs to possess a certain genetic blueprint; and this, it may be supposed, is why heavy water is not just a *phase* of ordinary water like ice, whereas a tadpole is just a phase of a frog. Unfortunately, however, saying this has more the air of re-labelling the problem than of genuinely resolving it. For, of course, it immediately prompts the further question of what warrants the selection of this or that feature as the 'essence' of a given sort or kind. Far from identity of genetic blueprint explaining the consubstantiation of tadpoles and frogs, it would appear that it is only because they are antecedently regarded as consubstantial that their identity of genetic blueprint can be regarded as 'essential'. Were we to find that tadpoles underwent extensive genetic changes upon turning into frogs, this would not I think persuade us that tadpoles and frogs were *not* after all the same kind of creature, but only that having a certain genetic structure was not in fact 'essential' to a creature's being one of this kind. I am *not* saying that all talk of 'scientific essences' in the manner of Kripke and Putnam is perfectly idle – merely that I doubt that it can have any very fundamental role to play in an account of the ways in which we identify and distinguish between substances (sorts or kinds); in which respect I am to some extent in agreement with Locke, who likewise thought that we cannot be supposed to rank things into sorts or kinds primarily on the basis of their 'real essences'. (Where I am at odds with Locke is in believing, unlike him, that our distinctions between substances are not purely the workmanship of the understanding, but often reflect real boundaries in nature.) Having said this, I can still concede that reference to a thing's scientific (or 'real') essence may have a role to play in explaining *why* a thing of its kind undergoes a change from one phase to another (e.g. it is to the frog's genetic blueprint that we look for an explanation of its development from the larval to the adult phase). All that I am denying is that reference to such an 'essence' can explain our original decision to interpret a given transformation as being one between phases of the same substance, since it is only subject to such a decision that the feature in question can be accounted an 'essence' in the first place. The criteria of sortal distinctness we seek must, I believe, be ones which principally find their application at the macroscopic, observable level, at least in the case of familiar, non-theoretical objects like whole organisms and quantities of gross material stuff (water, gold and the like).

Earlier I remarked that it would not do simply to try to explain our regarding the change from ice to liquid water as a change of phase in terms of its natural reversibility, since we deem this irrelevant to the case of tadpoles and adult frogs. However, the lesson, I believe, is *not* to dismiss the point about reversibility as a red herring, but rather to see that criteria of sortal distinctness are *category-relative*. That is to say, the sorts of consideration that bear upon questions of 'consubstantiation' in the case, say, of *kinds of material stuff* (like water and gold) may be quite different from those that are relevant in the case of *kinds of living creature* (something which should hardly surprise us given the very different criteria of identity governing *individuals* of these different kinds). That reversibility of phase changes *is* generally demanded in the case of kinds in the former category seems to me to be quite well attested: this partly explains, for instance, why we regard the change of paper into ash through combustion as a genuine change of substance. Again, another example of a criterion of sortal distinctness which is quite evidently category-relative is the interbreedability principle for conspecific animals. Now, in view of this category-relativity of many of the criteria of sortal distinctness, it would I think be pointless for me to attempt a complete inventory of such criteria. But what is in any case more important is that we should appreciate the status of such criteria as grounded for the most part in considerations of empirical scientific fact rather than in *a priori* reasoning or linguistic convention.

To say this is not to deny, what also seems evident upon examination, that at least some such criteria are also intimately linked to some of the general methodological and quasi-metaphysical principles that regulate scientific investigation and theory-construction. One such principle already mentioned is the presumption against transsubstantiation, which is effectively a principle of ontological parsimony: we are not to multiply substances beyond necessity, that is, we should prefer, other things being equal, to explain a physical transformation as being one of phase rather than one of substance. But, of course, other things are *not* always equal, which is why we must reject the rationalist vision of material substance as essentially *one*, with the transformation of paper into ash, say, being conceived of merely as the change of 'prime matter' from one of its phases to another. The point is that considerations of ontological parsimony have always to be weighed against (amongst other things) considerations of nomological explicability. Different substances (sorts or kinds) are governed by different laws – that indeed is in itself one of the principles of sortal distinctness, albeit one that is not effectively applicable in isolation from other considerations (after all, solely on the basis of the laws governing their appearance and behaviour, one might have thought tadpoles and frogs to be as different as dolphins and horses).[7] But there are laws, for instance, of biology which

---

[7] Observe that prior to the identification of tadpoles as the larval stage of frogs, one might have been ready to endorse both of the following simple and apparently

are not apparently reducible to laws of chemistry or physics, so that we are obliged to recognize biological sorts or kinds over and above chemical and physical ones. The answer, then, which begins to emerge to the question 'What *sorts* of things are there?' is one that is broadly realist without being naively so. Science *can* help us to 'carve nature at the joints', in the sense that it can motivate the recognition of sortal distinctions that are plainly not just the offspring of linguistic or cultural convention nor the mere tools of pragmatic convenience – though we should not lose sight of the fact that science itself is guided by architectonic and methodological principles whose application often involves a trade-off between conflicting values and priorities, sometimes issuing in no clearly preferred solution to a boundary dispute between species.

---

quite unrelated nomological generalizations: 'Tadpoles have tails' and 'Frogs lack tails'. The identification yields gains in ontological economy and nomological systematicity, by enabling us to replace these laws by two with the same logical subject – 'Frogs which are in their larval stage have tails' and 'Adult frogs lack tails' – but only at the cost of an increase in nomological complexity.

Index

Absoluteness Thesis (A)   64–5
action   109–10, 112–18, 122
aggregates   89–90, 92, 94, 98–100, 106
Alexander, I.   193n.
'all-statements'   145
Alston, W.   105n.
Aquinas   9n., 41n.
Aristotle   11, 13, 141
artefacts (*see also* kinds, artefactual)   90, 119
atoms   98–9, 106, 128–9
axiom-schemata (of sortal logic)   182
Ayer, A. J.   138n.

Barnes, J.   77n.
Bennett, J.   105n.
biological functions   101–2
bodies (in Locke's sense)   98, 106
bodies of persons   2, 97, 108–9, 118–21
Boolos, G.   161n.
Bower, T.   25n.
Boyle, R.   129
Brody, B. A.   24n.
Butler, J.   22n., 127

calculus of individuals   85, 93–4
Cartesian dualism   2, 120
Cartesian egos   38, 82, 111
Cartwright, H. M.   38
ceteris paribus clauses   172n., 175
co-consciousness   124–8
collections of material particles   97, 100, 108
collectives   89–90, 94
commissurotomy   126–7
common names   160
composite objects   84, 89
composition   87
conscious states   130–1
consciousness   122–32
constitution (*see also* 'is' of constitution)   13, 77–8, 97, 108–9
  necessities of   106–8, 119
  statements   4, 81–2
  transitivity of   119–20
consubstantiation   158–9, 201
continuants   15, 82–3, 113
conterfactual conditionals   147–8, 172–3
counting   10–11, 25, 94, 104–5, 114n., 115, 116
count nouns   11, 25, 30, 31,

INDEX

32–3, 44, 52–3, 55–6
criteria of identity (*see also* identity; 'is' of identity) 1–2, 9–10
  and circularity 99–100, 101, 134
  as evidential principles 15–16, 136–7
  and form 104
  informativeness of 16, 20–1, 128–9
  learning of 25–6
  and philosophical analysis 26–7
  and proper names 28–9, 58–9, 73–4
  same for co-instantiated sorts 2, 18, 56–7, 97, 104, 109, 112
  as semantic rules 1, 15–16, 24–5
criterion of identity
  for events 113n.
  general form of 13
  for living organisms 100–4, 107–8, 109, 112
  for lumps/parcels of matter 98–100, 104, 109, 112
  for men 60–1, 102
  for ordered sets 17
  for persons 109–10, 112, 121–37
  for sets 16–17

Davidson, D. 113n., 117n.
definite descriptions 30, 140
  plural 161–2
  Russell's theory of 35n., 187
definition *per genus et differentiam* 190
Descartes, R. 111
disposition statements, conditional analyses of 140–1, 172–3
dispositional/occurrent distinction 140–1, 171–3
dispositional predication (*see* predication, dispositional)
dispositionality, 'can' of 176–7, 183

dispositions of individuals 170
Doepke, F. C. 82n.
Dudman, V. H. 193n.
Dummett, M. 9n., 12n., 60n.

Eccles, J. C. 126n.
essence 14, 107
  real/scientific 201–2
essential properties 107, 111
Evans, G. 190n., 193n.
events 83n.
  criterion of identity for 113n.
  mental 113–14
existence 4
  and identity 57
  intermittent 49, 50, 60–1, 67, 129
  relativist conception of 57, 71, 72
  univocality of 4

form 101, 104
Foster, J. 150n.
Frege, G. 9n.

Geach, P. T. 2, 9, 10, 19, 28, 32, 36, 42n., 43–66, 67–77, 152–3, 155n., 156n., 157, 190n., 193n.
Geachian heralds 49, 60–1, 67
God 106
Goodman, N. 93n.
Griffin, N. 19n.
Gupta, A. 16n., 190n.

Hanson, N. R. 33n.
heaps 88–90
Hempel, C. G. 152
Heraclitus's problem 77–80
Hirsch, E. 25n., 100n.
holism of the mental 117, 132
homeostasis 102, 104
Hornsby, J. vi
human beings (*see also* men) 57–8, 108
Hume, D. 128n., 132

identity (*see also* criteria of

INDEX

identity; 'is' of identity) 1–2
absolutist conception of 19, 43, 63, 66, 67–9, 77–8, 86, 98
  definition of 20, 22–4, 39–40, 183–4
  and existence 57
  of indiscernibles 23, 24–5
  relativist conception of 19, 36, 67–8, 75–6, 84, 86, 90–3, 98, 104–5
  sign 23, 165
  univocality of 22
indefinite article 31–2, 139, 168–9
individual quantifier expressions 166
individual terms 28, 63, 140
  and criteria of identity 28–9
individual variables 34–5, 39, 156, 164, 166
individuals (*see also* particulars) 4–5, 11
  abstract/concrete 1, 16, 38, 57, 67, 89
  'consubstantial' 158–9
  definition of 38–42
  as lowest species 41
  scattered 37, 88–90
individuation 1, 3, 5, 11–13, 25, 29, 61–2, 65–6, 94, 113, 115, 161, 180
  of mental states 131–2
infimae species 40–2
instantiation (*see also* 'is' of instantiation)
  axiom-schemata of 182
  relation 38–40
  sentences 28, 32, 36–7, 48, 52, 53, 74
  sign 38, 165
integrates 89–90, 91, 94
'is' of attribution 3–4, 28, 33–5
'is' of constitution (*see also* constitution) 3–4, 36–7, 53, 60, 67, 68
  definition of 79, 81–3
  distinct from 'is' of identity 71–2

'is' of existence 4
'is' of identity (*see also* identity) 3–4, 39
  distinct from 'is' of attribution 34–5
'is' of instantiation (*see also* instantiation) 3–4, 28, 32, 59, 61, 78, 86
  distinct from 'is' of attribution 34–6
'is', varieties of 3–4

Karmo, T. 76n.
kinds (*see also* sorts) 1, 4–5
  artefactual 5–6
  hybrid 54
  natural 5–6, 157–9, 190, 200–4
Kirk, R. 114n.
Kneale, W. 138n., 147n.
Kripke, S. A. 6, 29, 119n., 148, 154, 157–8, 201
Kuratowski, K. 17, 18n.

laws (*see also* nomological generalizations) 2–3
  and counterfactual conditionals 147–8
  empirical and theoretical 175
  knowledge of 151–2, 179–80
  natural 5–6, 35, 138–9, 142–3
  normative account of 148–9
  Popperian account of 145–8, 150, 191
Leibniz, G. W. 41n.
Leibniz's law 62, 65, 66, 67, 78
Leonard, H. S. 93n.
Lewis, D. 134n., 149
life 102–3
life-histories 83n.
living organisms 97, 100–8
  and persons 108–21
Locke, J. 5, 10, 12, 13, 97–106, 108–9, 118n., 201–2
  on personal identity 121–5
logical connectives, dual roles of 194–6
logically dependent objects 95–6
lumps/parcels of matter 88–90, 98–109

INDEX

McGinnn, C. 113n., 134n.
Madell, G. 137n.
mass nouns 11, 30, 44
  and colour terms 35n.
  as sortal terms 32–3, 37–8, 52
Mates, B. 181n., 182n.
matter (*see also* lumps/parcels of matter)
  atomic theory of 98–9
  'prime' 203
Mellor, D. H. 83n.
memory 127, 130–1
men (*see also* human beings) 60–1, 83n., 102–3, 118, 162
men and heralds argument 44–50, 60–1
mental states 130–3
mereological sums (*see also* sums) 37
mereology (*see* calculus of individuals)
merging 106
metamorphosis 14, 103–4, 108, 120, 200–4
metaphysics (and empirical science) 6–8, 203–4
mind-brain identity theory 113–14, 132–3
minds 111, 126
mixtures 100
multiple personality 115

Nagel, T. 115n.
names 'for' and names 'of' 75–7
natural laws (*see* laws)
necessity (and possibility) 6–8
  a posteriori 107–8
  a priori 103, 106, 107–8, 110
  metaphysical 148
  natural 103, 149–50
nominalism 138, 153–5, 159–62
nomological (nomic) generalizations (*see also* laws) 35, 138–9, 164
  and complex sortal terms 189–92
Noonan, H. W. 19n., 84, 95

normal specimens 148–9, 151, 174–5
  tests for 180
normality 153–5

occurrent predication (*see* predication, occurrent)
ontological commitment 49, 67
  Quine's criterion of 143–4, 155–9
'ontologically complete' objects 91–3
ordered pairs, Kuratowski's definition of 18n.
organisms (*see* living organisms)

paradox of the ravens 152–3
paradox of the 1,001 cats 68–73
Parfit, D. 127, 131n.
part-whole relations 93–4
particulars (*see also* individuals)
  'bare' 3, 4–5, 11–13, 39, 65
  'basic' 15, 129n.
parts 84–5, 99
  addition and subtraction of 85, 95–6
  adhesion of 88–9
  individuation of 94
  spatial 80, 82–3
  temporal 15, 79–83, 129, 134–5
Peacocke, C. 114n.
Penelhum, T. 110n.
perception 109–10, 112–18, 122
Perry, J. 131n.
persistence conditions 14, 57, 71
  of aggregates 88–90
personal embodiment 118–21
personal names 118–19
persons 2, 97, 108–21
  as a 'basic' sort 21, 110n., 121, 129–37
  criterion of identity for 109–10, 112, 121–8
  disembodied 110, 112n., 119–20
  essential historicity of 135

not essentially material 110–12
  recognition of 117–18
phase changes 200–3
phased sortals 54, 58, 201
Plato 77n.
plural suffix 31–2, 139, 168–9
Popper, K. R. 126n., 145–8, 150
possibility (*see* necessity)
possible worlds 149–50
predicate/sentence connectives
  191–6
predicate/sentence negation
  168n., 182n., 195–6
predicates 34
  complex 191–6
  in narrow sense 165–6
  polyadic 193–4
predication
  'basic' 171
  dispositional/occurrent 139–43,
    166, 171, 195–6
Prior, A. N. 155, 156n.
processes 82
proper names
  and criteria of identity 28–9,
    58–9, 73–4
  descriptive theory of 29, 34–5
  and identifying descriptions
    29, 157
  mythological 41–2
  and ontological commitment
    156
  and plural reference
    160–1
protons 99, 129, 174
psychology
  autonomy of 121
  and philosophy 27
Putnam, H. 154, 157–8, 201

quantification
  existential 169
  individual 34–5, 156–7, 166
  objectual 155
  sortal 34–6, 143–4, 155–7, 159,
    166–7
  substitutional 155–6, 198

quantities 38
Quine, W. V. 15, 34–5, 37n.,
  78–83, 143–4, 155, 159,
  170n., 172n.

realism
  about individuals 5, 12
  about sorts/kinds 5, 12, 144,
    149, 162–3, 204
Reducibility Thesis (R) 64–6
reference
  collective/plural 144–5, 159–62
  to individuals 12, 29, 158
  to sorts/kinds 158, 162
Reid, T. 127
relativity of identity thesis 43,
  62, 64, 68
Rescher, N. 150n.
robots 111, 117
Russell, B. 35n., 187

S (formalized sortal language)
  164–7
  addition of complex sortal
    symbols to 186–7
scattering (*see also* individuals,
  scattered) 88–90
'schematic' objects 91–3
Schlesinger, G. 152n.
scientific knowledge, growth of
  179–80
scientific method 150–4, 175–80
scientific-theory construction
  174–5
  and metaphysics 7–8, 203–4
Searle, J. R. 29
self-consciousness 109–10,
  112–18
semantics
  formal and informal 165
  of natural language 2, 7
sets 16–21, 89
Sharvy, R. 100n.
Shoemaker, S. 134n.
Siamese twins 104, 127, 131
Simons, P. 82n., 94n.
sortal concepts 1–2

not purely observational 87
Sortal Expandability Thesis (S) 61–2, 63–6
Sortal Individuation Thesis (I) 65–6
sortal logic
  axiomatic system of 181–4
  principle S1 of 167–8, 183
  principle S2 of 170, 173–4, 183, 196
  principle S3 of 54, 178, 183
  principle S4 of 179, 183
  principle S5 of 179
  principle S6 of 197
  principle S7 of 198
  principle S8 of 199
  and scientific method 175–80
sortal quantifier expressions 143, 166–7
sortal terms 2, 10–11, 24–5
  complex/simple 30–1, 41, 58, 115, 118, 139, 185–200
  'dummy' 25, 94
  as grammatical subjects 34–6, 139, 141–3
  mythological 41
  'perfect' 174–5
  phased 54, 58, 201
sortal variables 34–6, 39, 63, 143–4, 156, 164, 166
sorts (*see also* kinds) 1, 3, 9, 11, 13, 24–5
  'basic' 20–1, 25, 28, 129
  co-instantiable 2, 18, 54–5, 56–7, 68, 70, 178
  definition of 38–42
  differentiation of 200–4
  realism about 5, 12, 144, 149, 162–3, 204

spatiotemporal coincidence 80–1, 87, 92, 95, 104–6
spatiotemporal continuity 129
species-genus relation 18, 37, 54, 56
Sperry, R. 126
'split-brain' patients 115, 126–7
stages (*see* parts, temporal)
Stevenson, L. 72n.
Strawson, P. F. 9n., 15, 20n., 112n., 129n., 131n.
substances 11, 105–6
  spiritual 123, 130
substitution-instances 182n.
sums 37, 84–96, 99
supervenience 82
systematic ambiguity 36, 194–5

Tarski, A. 93n.
'things' 10–11, 25
Tiles, J. E. 114n.
time 134n., 137n.
transsubstantiation 200, 203

universals 2, 4, 13, 144

'water' (as a count noun) 52–3, 55–6
water and rivers argument 44, 50–3, 59–60
Whitehead, A. N. 187n.
wholes (*see also* part-whole relations) 84
Wiener, N. 17
Wiggins, D. 14n., 43n., 53, 54, 60, 61, 63, 72, 77–8, 93n., 103, 111, 116n., 127
Wilkes, K. V. 115n.
Williams, B. 115n.

Zemach, E. M. 91–3, 95